UNDEFEATED

UNDEFEATED

From Basketball to Battle: West Point's Perfect Season 1944

JIM NOLES

CASEMATE

Philadelphia & Oxford

Published in the United States of America and Great Britain in 2018 by
CASEMATE PUBLISHERS
1950 Lawrence Road, Havertown, PA 19083, USA
and
The Old Music Hall, 106–108 Cowley Road, Oxford OX4 1JE, UK

Hardback Edition: ISBN 978-1-61200-511-9
Digital Edition: ISBN 978-1-61200-512-6 (epub)

A CIP record for this book is available from the Library of Congress and the British Library

Printed and bound in the United States of America

Typeset in India by Versatile PreMedia Services. www.versatilepremedia.com

For a complete list of Casemate titles, please contact:

CASEMATE PUBLISHERS (US)
Telephone (610) 853-9131
Fax (610) 853-9146
Email: casemate@casematepublishers.com
www.casematepublishers.com

CASEMATE PUBLISHERS (UK)
Telephone (01865) 241249
Fax (01865) 794449
Email: casemate-uk@casematepublishers.co.uk
www.casematepublishers.co.uk

Contents

For my Beast squad mates Kristin Baker, Dave Ciesinski, Jeff Clark,
Kim Darby, Kelly Demers, Bob Guerriero, Steve Meyer, Adam Muller, and
Howie Webb, my Beast squad leaders Cliff Daus and Jacqueline Peterson,
and everyone in Company G

Acknowledgments and Appreciation

Thank you to my friend and former editor Bob Pigeon, whose enthusiastic, steadfast, and unselfish support for this book took me from vaporous proposal to a willing publisher.

And, speaking of editors and publishers, thank you to Ruth Sheppard of Casemate Publishers, my editor "across the pond"—patient, good-humored, supportive, and thoroughly professional. Thanks also to David Farnsworth, who got this ball rolling at Casemate, to eagle-eyed copyeditor Don McKeon, cartographer Declan Ingram, Isobel Nettleton, Sam Caggiula, Carlie Rivera, and the rest of the Casemate crew.

Thank you to my partners at Barze Taylor Noles Lowther, LLC, who tolerated the distraction of my completion of this book with characteristic good humor and grace.

Thank you to Marilee Meyer and the rest of the incredibly helpful staff at the West Point Association of Graduates.

Kudos and thanks to Wes Tyler, creator and administrator of www.413thfightergroup.com, and Steve Dixon, president-elect of the 70th Infantry Division Association and webmaster of www.trailblazer-sww2.org. And thank you for the fine work of the men and women of the 65th Infantry Division Association as well, at www.65thdiv.com.

Thank you to my good-natured, keen-eyed cadre of volunteer copyeditors, reviewers, and cheerleaders—folks such as Hunter Barnhill, Mark Cauley, Dave Ciesinski, Adam Cohen, Tony Cox, Luke Day, Paul Howell, Mike Kramer, Jack Kubiszyn, Matt Mitchell, Scott Maytan, Richard Muller, and Howie Webb. If I forgot anyone, the next beer is on me—you know where to find me!

Thank you to John Hennessey, Class of 1970, son of Jack Hennessey, who was, along with his family, incredibly helpful in this process. And thank you to all of the other people I have met during this process who are, in some way, associated with the Class of 1944 and other classes of that era. I know that I am forgetting someone, but their numbers include Don Carter, Chick Cleveland, John Cleveland, Michael Davis, Ginny Day, Louisa Enright, Dylan Faas, Ted Geltz, Daniel Grieve, Susan Heath, Susan Risher. Ann Swank, and Woody Vaughan.

Thank you to the host of kind and helpful archivists, historians, curators, administrators, and athletics affairs and public affairs staff I've encountered along the way. Their numbers include Gordon Blaker (Fort Sill Museum); Kat Castner and Brian Gunning (Army West Point Athletics); Suzanne Christoff, Casey Madrick, and Alicia Mauldin-Ware (United States Military Academy); Steve Domboski (St. John's University); Marlana Cook and Michael McAfee (West Point Museum); Lynn Gamma and Dan Haulman (Air Force Historical Research Agency); Col. Steven dePyssler, Craig Ferguson, and Father Leo Gluckert (Mount Carmel High School); Amy Hedrick (University of North Texas); Patrice Kane (Fordham University); Ann Kenne (St. Thomas University); Matt Lehman (DeLaSalle High School); Troy McDonald (LaCrosse Central High School); Dusty Mercier (Mississippi Armed Forces Museum), Sue Ottignon (Villanova University); Dave Schoen (Niagara University); Nathan Rosser (Georgia Institute of Technology); Michelle Smith (Colgate University); Heidi Stover (Smithsonian Institution); and Jocelyn Wilk (Columbia University).

Thank you to Baldassare Castiglione, author of *The Book of the Courtier*, and George Garrett, author of *Death of the Fox*. I'm just kidding, of course. (My fellow students from Plebe English will understand this reference.)

No thanks to the Physics Department, spring semester, 1988. (My fellow students from West Point's illustrious Summer Training Academic Program will understand this reference.)

And of course, thank you to my wife, Elizabeth, and my sons, James and John. No book is ever completed without time taken away from them. This one was no exception, and, once again, their patience and support was a steady constant in my life and in this particular effort.

Prologue

Can there be any college campus in the world grimmer than West Point in January?

At other times, in other seasons, the campus of the United States Military Academy, perched atop a bluff overlooking New York's Hudson River, can be beautiful—even breathtaking.

In late May, the vivid green grass of the Plain accents the fairy-tale tableau of cadets, resplendent in black ostrich-plumed shako hats, full-dress gray blouses, and starched white trousers, marching in perfect step with glittering bayonets affixed to their rifles as the academy's band belts out "The Thunderer," "The Stars and Stripes Forever," or "Americans We."

In the fall, as the warm summer nights give way to frosty mornings and Army's football team takes to its storied field at Michie Stadium, the trees covering the rocky slopes above the campus flaunt red, yellow, and orange leaves so brilliant that it almost hurts to look at them in the bright sunlight.

Even in early winter, the first snowfall adds a cottony, cushiony touch to the hard granite barracks and bestows thick white epaulets on the statues of long-dead graduates.

But in January, when the warmth of Christmas has already faded and holiday cheer has been supplanted by the relentless grind of examinations, weekly room inspections, and the rote routine of three meals a day in the cavernous confines of the academy's mess hall, life at West Point is grim indeed. The buildings are gray, the Hudson River is gray, the sky is gray, the surrounding mountains are gray, the cadets' uniforms are gray, and the cadets' very demeanor is gray.

This is the time of the year the cadets dolefully call "the Gloom Period." Called to attention in predawn darkness, they march to breakfast; at the end of the day, they march to dinner cloaked in the winter night. In the meantime, they hurry back and forth between classes drawn from the brutal required core curriculum: calculus, chemistry, physics, a slew of engineering courses, foreign language, English, and history, to name only a few. And with every step outside, they are assailed by a razor-sharp north wind, screeching remorselessly down the Hudson River, so cold that it frosts their eyeglasses and freezes their very nose hairs.

Even at home in their barracks rooms, the cadets lead a life regimented to such a painful point that manuals dictate even the shelf on which a cadet's toothbrush is to be placed and the direction in which its bristles are to be aligned. Folding and placement of underwear in a drawer is a science; alignment of shoes underneath a bed is a matter of mathematical precision. Inspecting officers expect to find floors swept, trash cans clean, sinks dry, and rifles spotless. A well-made bed, with its scratchy gray woolen blanket stretched as taut as a drumhead, is so prized that cadets will sleep atop it to save valuable time in the morning rather than "break sheets" and sleep beneath their covers.

It is both the magic and the curse of West Point that a cadet from 1819 or 1919 or 2019 would nod in knowing agreement with the preceding paragraphs. Even as today, the winter darkness would have descended before the cadets' mandatory dinner formation. Even as today, their long overcoats, woven of heavy gray wool and sporting archaic shoulder capes, would have failed to ward off the cold's cruel clutches.

The evening of Wednesday, January 12, 1944, would have been no different, and, at such times, the cadets took advantage of whatever distractions available. And on that particular night, the most promising distraction available—other than a stealthy excursion to an off-limits tavern in the nearby village of Highland Falls for an illicit draft of beer—would have been found in the Academy Field House. There, in the shadows of Trophy Point, where West Pointers proudly displayed the captured ordnance of past wars, West Point's basketball team was preparing to take the court for the inaugural game of its 1944 season.

*****

With Wednesday night's dinner—a mandatory affair attended by each of the school's approximately 2,400 cadets en masse—warming their stomachs, basketball fans across the academy signed out in their barracks' orderly rooms under the envious eye of each company's duty-bound cadet in charge of quarters. Then, duly excused from their otherwise mandatory presence in the barracks for their evening studies, those cadets began the three-quarter-mile hike to the field house. With a north wind blowing off the Hudson River into their whiskerless faces and moon-lit snow clouds scudding across the imposing monolith of Storm King Mountain to their front, the young men walked briskly through the evening darkness. Despite the cold, they relished the prospect of an hour or so free from the watchful eyes of the demerit-dispensing Tactical Department, the baleful attention of upperclassmen, and the burden of their books.

Congealing in small, silent groups of twos and threes, the cadets skirted the western edge of the Plain, where so many of their hours had been spent in parades and company drills, and subconsciously quickened their pace as they passed the superintendent's quarters. Then, when reaching the edge of the plateau upon which the main academy grounds sat, they picked their way, whether by sidewalk or wooded path, down to the academy's imposing brick field house. Pulling their leather-billed service caps from their heads, the cadets happily entered the warm bricked confines of the field house and, shoulder to shoulder, found seats for the impending contest against Swarthmore College.

As the color returned to their cheeks and the warmth returned to their toes, the assembled collection of future second lieutenants turned their attention to their comrades on the basketball court. In the field house's locker room, those particular cadets had already traded their stiff-collared dress gray uniform blouses and scratchy wool trousers for tank-top jerseys, athletic shorts, black canvas-and-rubber court shoes, and, in several cases, knee pads. The team's previous season had been a brutally disappointing one—the Cadets had, in the winter of 1942-1943, barely amassed an embarrassing 5–10 record—but it had ended on a high note with an upset victory against archrival the United States Naval Academy on the Midshipmen's home court in Annapolis. Would the momentum of last March's final victory carry over to the new season? Or were the Cadets on the verge of another mediocre campaign? Within an hour, they would have their answer.

*****

With the field house's clock ticking down toward game time, Army's team captains led the squad through its pregame paces. Edward "Big Ed" Charles Christl Jr., the team's center, stood at 6'4" and wore a jersey with the numeral "9" emblazoned on it. He was a quiet, amiable Minnesotan, with his scalp carved into a dense flattop. The tallest man in his class, Christl had huge hands that were almost capable of spanning the top of a cadet's service cap. Christl was a "firstie" (or, more properly, a first classman—a senior in the eyes of those few civilians in the field house), destined to graduate in five short months.

Robert "Bob" William Faas, a fellow firstie and the team's cocaptain, joined Christl on the floor. With his dark eyes, elven face, and ready smile, Faas had brought a reputation as a ladies man with him to West Point from his hometown of La Crosse, Wisconsin. Standing at 5'10" and wearing the number "5," Faas was short for a forward, but his speed, agility, and shooting skills made him a keen competitor with a dangerous versatility.

Christl and Faas were not the only two firsties warming up on the Academy Field House's hardcourt that January evening. Three years earlier, the army had selected their classmate Theodore H. "Spike" Geltz, of Pittsburgh, Pennsylvania, from the enlisted ranks to attend West Point. Alan E. Weston, a Missouri native, ranked fourth in the Class of 1944 and, in addition to playing basketball, commanded one of the academy's cadet battalions. Another firstie, Edwin O'Donnell, of Norwalk, Ohio, was, like Weston, ranked high enough in the class to one day claim, in the academy's merit-based selection of branches, a coveted spot with the Corps of Engineers upon his impending graduation. Finally, Charles D. Daniel, a high school football legend from Tupelo, Mississippi, had played football at Vanderbilt University before arriving at West Point for "R-Day" – the day new cadets reported for duty at the Academy — on July 1, 1941, where he ultimately found a place on the academy's basketball roster.

But in this collection of talent, it was John Joseph Timothy Hennessey—"Jack" to his friends in the Class of 1944—who completed the trio of firsties selected to be in the squad's starters. An Irishman from South Chicago, Hennessey had serious eyes that were as steely as the neighborhood mill in which he had labored during his summers in high school. But those same eyes belied a streak of good-natured humor that had won him friends across the Corps of Cadets. Hennessey, at 6'2", played guard.

Despite their rank as first class cadets, and their pending graduation in June, Hennessey and his classmates were, at the time, only in their third year at West Point. Normally, the academy's course of study encompassed four years, and they would have been second class cadets (juniors, on a civilian campus), destined to graduate in June of 1945. The exigencies of World War II, however, had demanded that the cadets' tenures at West Point be shortened to three years. Accordingly, Hennessey's classmates in the Class of 1945 had skipped their second class year and, pinning on the chevrons of first classmen, become the Class of 1944. Below them, in the cadet hierarchy, what might have been the Class of 1946 in peacetime had, upon its arrival at West Point in the summer of 1942, been designated the Class of 1945. In turn, the Class of 1947's freshmen had become the Class of 1946.

Two members of the Class of 1945 rounded out the team's starters. They took the form of a pair of remarkably talented athletes, Dale Hall and Edgar Douglas "Doug" Kenna II. Hall, from Kansas, had already sculpted a reputation on Army's football team the past autumn, while Kenna, a Mississippian, had been sidelined from the gridiron with a knee injury. But Kenna's knee had since healed, and both he and Hall were destined to be key players on the academy's basketball team.

Hall and Kenna's classmate Bill Ekberg was, like Ed Christl, another giant from Minnesota. And, like Christl, he also played center. Standing at 6'6", Ekberg may have been the only man in the Corps of Cadets taller than Christl. Michigan native William Gilbert, another third classman, had honed his basketball skills at Fort Sheridan, Illinois, on the post's basketball team—and, in an unusual feat, had even earned a commission as a second lieutenant as an army weather officer before securing an appointment to West Point. Harle "Red" Damon, of Council Bluffs, Iowa, rounded out the cohort of yearlings (second-year cadets); he had spent two years at Iowa State before joining the Corps of Cadets.

Equal on the basketball court (if nowhere else on the academy's grounds) were the team's plebes—its fourth class cadets. Members of the Class of 1946, they had entered West Point the previous summer, in 1943. Their ranks included Oklahoma's Bobby Dobbs, who had arrived at West Point seven months after playing for Tulsa University in 1943's Sugar Bowl. Richard Walterhouse, another plebe player in the Class of 1946, had played football at the University of Michigan before transferring to West Point. Their classmate John W. Nance had come to West Point after a two-year sojourn at the University of Arkansas. Peter Molnar, of Sharon, Pennsylvania, completed the team's contingent of plebes.

Working together, the team—upperclassmen and plebes—continued their pregame warmup drills. Layups followed layups, with the Cadets dishing the ball off to one another and fielding the rebounds. An informal round of shooting from around the key came next, with the net swishing reassuringly with most of the Cadets' shots. Then, as game time approached, they trotted over to their coach for a final word of direction. On the other side of the court, the Garnet of Swarthmore College did likewise. Tip-off for the first game of the Cadets' 1944 season was a matter of moments away.

*****

Of course, in the second week of January, in the year 1944, there were far bigger contests—with far larger stakes involved—afield. By then, the United States' involvement in World War II was slogging into its third year. In the skies over Europe, the United States Eighth Air Force battled abysmal weather, heavy flak, and fierce German fighters as it pursued its costly bombing campaign against the Nazis. Based in southern Italy, the United States Fifteenth Air Force faced its own challenges, including marathon missions and the perils of piercing the Alps, as it brought the bomber war to southern Germany and its allies in Central Europe. On the European mainland, the Americans and their allies were bogged down south of Rome, stymied by the stubborn defenders of the Gustav Line, while in England infantry divisions such as the fabled Big Red One could only train in preparation for a cross-Channel assault still months away. In the Pacific, commanders Chester Nimitz and Douglas MacArthur confronted the daunting tasks of capturing Japanese-held territory in New Guinea and the Marshalls.

Perhaps the tide had turned since 1941's cataract of defeat, but the war was far from won—or even over. Before it would be done, first class cadets such as Christl, Hennessey, and Faas would all find themselves joining the combat already faced by teammates from earlier classes. "Big Ed" Christl would become a field artillery officer, crouching in foxholes with frontline infantrymen to call in artillery strikes on their German enemy. Jack Hennessey, the scrappy Irishman from Chicago, would lead infantrymen into the final apocalyptic battles against the Third Reich. And, on the other side of the world, in combat with the Japanese, Bob Faas would fly the final air missions of the war. Of these three men from the Class of 1944, only two would live to see the end of the war their nation had called them to fight. But, happily, those days were still in the future. First, there was one last season of basketball to play.

PART I

Basketball

"Upon the fields of friendly strife are sown the seeds that, upon other fields, on other days, will bear the fruits of victory."

—GEN. DOUGLAS MACARTHUR

CHAPTER I

A Coach and His Sport

As West Point and America's other universities and colleges began their 1944 basketball campaigns, the sport of basketball was entering its fifth decade of existence. And, like too many fifty-something-year-olds, college basketball was, in 1944, facing somewhat of a midlife crisis. Then again, perhaps it was more evolution than crisis. But, at any rate, change was afoot on the college courts in those days, and, like many times of change, it is best understood by identifying and appreciating the baseline against which such changes were measured.

For basketball, that baseline was drawn, literally and figuratively, in 1891. Unlike the other great American athletic pastimes of the age—football and baseball, in particular—basketball could trace its roots directly to a specific founding father. He was Dr. James Naismith, a Canadian-born physical education teacher whose professional calling had brought him to Springfield, Massachusetts, in 1891. It would be there and then that Naismith would invent basketball.

At Springfield's International Young Men's Christian Association (YMCA) Training School, the thirty-year-old Naismith faced the unenviable task of keeping restless students active and exercised during the indoor tedium that accompanied the cold New England winter. Naismith responded by crafting, out of whole cloth, a new indoor sport for his students. Putting pen to paper, he inked thirteen rules to govern an as-of-yet unnamed game. At its most basic, Naismith's game called for a contest between two teams—no set number of players was established—battling on an indoor court over the course of two fifteen-minute halves. Each team sought to score goals by tossing a soccer ball into a peach basket fastened above the players' heads to the wall on the opponent's side of the court. To advance the ball up and down the court, the players had to pass the ball to one another; no running with the ball, or dribbling the ball for that matter, was allowed.

The national network of YMCAs provided fertile ground for the spread of the game that would become known as "basket ball" [sic]. By 1895, the first intercollegiate game was played between Hamline University of St. Paul, Minnesota, and the Minneapolis State College of Agriculture—although, with nine players on each team, it was a crowded affair that culminated in an unimpressive 9–3 score, with the win going to the Aggies. Thereafter, basketball soon settled, thankfully, on five-man teams. The sport's evolution into the spectacle familiar to the modern fan, however, required an iterative journey through the nation's YMCAs, high schools, colleges, military bases, and even nascent professional leagues over the next few decades.

"For its first thirty years, basketball was a rough, slow, and deliberate game, played mostly by working-class kids with little formal education," wrote Douglas Stark in his book *Wartime Basketball*. "Scores were low, and teams with leads late in the game would stall the ball. The only requirement was to possess the ball after each center jump. This feat placed a premium on having one tall center whose only objective was to win the center jump after each basket and obtain the ball for his team."[1]

As Stark alludes, a key aspect of the game's early form was the postscore jump ball. After each basket scored, the opposing teams would reconvene at center court for a jump ball. The start-and-stop nature of a game laboring under this rule is difficult for a fan of the fast-paced modern game to imagine. Perhaps not surprisingly, basketball's rules changed in 1937 to eliminate the incessant center-court jump balls. It was the same year that Howard Hughes set a new record for the fastest flight from Los Angeles to New York City, the Golden Gate Bridge opened for traffic, and Frank Whittle successfully ground-tested the first jet engine. The world, it seemed, wanted to get places faster, and basketball proved no exception.

At the same time, the players themselves were bringing exciting innovations to their game. Historians differ as to whether it was Emory and Henry College's Glenn Roberts, Missouri University's John Cooper, Wyoming University's Ken Sailors, or some other hoopster, but, whoever he was, he introduced the jump shot to basketball in the 1930s. Meanwhile, to a sport premised on staid two-handed sharpshooters, Stanford University's Angelo "Hank" Luisetti introduced the remarkable concept of a one-handed shot.

If these innovations were viruses, then they found a ready vector in the popular and profitable college doubleheaders hosted by New York's Madison Square Garden in the latter half of the 1930s. National enthusiasm for the collegiate sport reached such a point that, in 1938, New York's Metropolitan Basketball Writers Association conceived the National Invitational Tournament (NIT), which saw Temple University beat the University of Colorado to claim the NIT's first championship. A year later, in 1939, the National Collegiate Athletic Association (NCAA) joined the fray with its own championship tournament. The University of Oregon bested Ohio State in that inaugural affair.

For its part, the United States Military Academy at West Point first fielded an intercollegiate basketball team in 1903, when a second classman—a junior named Joseph Stilwell—organized a team and defeated the Yonkers YMCA. Three years later, Stilwell returned to the academy as a professor in the Department of Modern Languages and, from 1907 to 1911, compiled an impressive 41–9 record as West Point's basketball coach.[2]

After a few seasonal stumbles in the wake of Coach Stilwell's departure, West Point's basketball program built an impressive record through the 1920s and 1930s. Its high point came with an unblemished 1922–23 season under the legendary Harry Fisher—a feat that, for two decades, had not been repeated. Nevertheless, until 1941, fans of the academy's basketball team could take pride in a stretch of 22 years that had never seen a losing season.

In 1941, however, the streak suddenly snapped. The Cadets, under second-year coach Valentine "Dutch" Lentz, could only count on two returning starters. The first two games of the season—which witnessed Army go into overtime against first Harvard and then Princeton—showcased the Cadets' competitive spirit but, at the same time, exposed the squad's lack of experienced depth. With a season-ending loss to Navy, West Point recorded a humbling 5–11 record. Fate was kinder to Lentz and his Cadets in 1942. Led by their hard-charging team captain Ernest "Dirty Ernie" White, the Cadets secured a 10–6 record and, equally important, a narrow 35–34 win over Navy to finish the season.

But in 1943, Coach Lentz managed only an ignominious 5–10 season. In fairness to Lentz, few coaches have ever labored under such challenging circumstances. First, in the fall of 1943, he had been called back to active duty and now, in addition to his coaching duties, was assigned as the supply officer to the West Point Station Hospital while awaiting assignment overseas. Second, a number of his would-be starters from his '43 squad had opted to train as "air cadets" at nearby Stewart Army Air Field and, understandably, had decided to focus on flight school rather than basketball at this critical juncture in their nascent military careers. Finally, Lentz's class of seniors—his firsties—had been ordered to graduate a semester early, on January 19, 1943, due to the manpower demands of the war. This meant that Lentz lost his team captain, the talented George Rebh, only two games into the season.

If Coach Lentz questioned or complained about the circumstances fate had foisted upon him, history does not record it. After all, a cadet at West Point was—and still is—taught that there are only three proper responses to a question—"Yes, sir," "No, sir," and "No excuse, sir." In the late winter of 1943, as Lentz's depleted team endured one loss after another, that third response was likely often on the coach's lips. And so, when the springtime brought with it orders for Lentz to leave West Point and join the army's 3rd Infantry Division encamped in North Africa, one could forgive the battered coach if he accepted the new assignment with a certain degree of relief.

*****

Fortunately for West Point, in the wake of Lentz's departure, the academy's leadership found a ready replacement for the departed officer—and it came in the less-than-soldierly form of the bespectacled, slightly chunky gentleman now standing courtside for the impending tilt with Swarthmore College. Poised to helm his first game for Army, the 49-year-old Edward

A. Kelleher looked more like a genial small-town banker than a collegiate coach. But any cadet in the stands with a more than a passing knowledge of college hoops must have taken heart at seeing Kelleher standing by Army's bench.

Kelleher was born in 1893, the same year collegiate basketball teams began appearing in newspapers, and it takes little prosaic license to say that the New York City native's growth matched that of the sport he came to love. He began his collegiate basketball career at Niagara University, where he captained the school's intercollegiate squad from 1910 to 1914. Kelleher then entered dental school, only to set aside his studies to volunteer for the military when the United States entered World War I in the spring of 1917. Kelleher spent a total of 22 months in the army, including service as an ambulance driver in France.

Perhaps Kelleher's wartime service in the mud and blood on the western front, matched shortly thereafter by what would have been a front-row seat to the horrors of 1918's deadly influenza pandemic, convinced the former basketball star that life was too short not to pursue his earlier passion on the hardcourt. Perhaps, more mundanely, the appeal of a career as a dentist had already faded in the former dental student's mind's eye. Whatever the reason, after Kelleher's military service drew to a close, he returned to basketball and, in 1921, landed a job in Brooklyn as the basketball coach for St. John's University.

Although the St. John's Redmen managed only a 10–11 record in the 1921–22 season, Kelleher's stint with the squad propelled him from Brooklyn to the Bronx where, at Fordham's historic Rose Hill campus, he took the reins of Fordham's cagers. The former dental student and wartime ambulance driver was destined to spend the next 11 seasons with the Rams, whom he soon built into a formidable basketball force. In his heyday, Kelleher's teams, christened the "Wonder Fives," only lost nine games from 1924 to 1929. A four-season interlude interrupted Kelleher's run at Fordham in the mid-1930s, but, upon his return to Rose Hill in 1938, he amassed a 61–38 record over the course of the next five seasons.

Looking back on Kelleher's time at Fordham, the university's athletic director, Jack Coffey, remembered a "quiet, gentle sports-loving man completely loyal to his job." Some even went so far as to describe the coach as "a devotee of the [Knute] Rockne system of team play, perhaps even before Rockne himself used it."[3] And like Rockne, Kelleher—despite his affable personality and calm demeanor—was a stern taskmaster. A regular aspect of his modus operandi was to match his starting squad against his freshman team. He would spot the freshmen 40 points and continue the scrimmage until the starters took the lead. "We had some long practices," Kelleher protégé Johnny Bach remembered laconically.[4]

Kelleher's work with the Rams peaked with the 1943 season, when Fordham handed the Cadets an embarrassing 68–42 defeat en route to Fordham's first NIT appearance. Capping an otherwise triumphant 16–6 season, the Rams lost in the NIT's semifinals to the tournament's ultimate champion, St. John's University. In the wake of his team's historic tournament appearance, the National Association of Basketball Coaches elected Kelleher to serve an unprecedented second term as president. For the moment, the coach's future seemed brighter than ever at Rose Hill.

But then fate intervened. In 1943, with the maw of America's growing war machine consuming more and more young men, Fordham University shuttered its intercollegiate athletic programs—including basketball. Only the university's rifle team survived the cut, and Coach Kelleher found himself without a job. "When the axe fell on Fordham athletics a few weeks back, Rose Hill lost a pretty likeable guy in the person of Ed Kelleher," the *Fordham Ram* moaned.[5]

Meanwhile, an hour's train ride up along the Hudson River, the United States Military Academy needed a head basketball coach in the wake of Dutch Lentz's departure, and, in West Point's eyes, the World War I veteran was just the man for the job. And, from Kelleher's perspective, the opening had offered a unique opportunity. Always an assiduous student of the game, Kelleher had in recent years broken ranks with many of his brethren along the Atlantic seaboard and become a disciple of the West Coast's fast-breaking, high-scoring offensive game schemes. He knew full well that, at West Point, he would be inheriting a team that had struggled to an embarrassing 5–10 record the previous season. But at the same time, he would have access to the kind of national-caliber athletes capable of the run-and-gun offense he had envisioned. And so, as the curtain fell on intercollegiate sports at Fordham, Kelleher inked Army's contract in the early fall of 1943 and, in November, headed north to his new job.

Fortunately, at West Point, as Kelleher began to take stock of his new team, he found a scrimmage squad against which to test them—and it was a squad that would be the envy of any college coach. The West Point garrison, a military formation separate from the Corps of Cadets, boasted a basketball team of enlisted men that would play in service games against other units and rival services. Its ranks included Harry Boykoff, a former St. John's player who had earned most valuable player honors in 1943's NIT, his St. John's teammates Dutch Garfinkel and Bob Tough, who would both one day play in the infant National Basketball Association (NBA), former University of Kentucky team captain Bernie Opp, and Seton Hall star Kevin "Chuck" Connors—who, in the years to follow, would not only play in the National Football League and major league baseball but also be known to a later generation of Americans as the star of the Western television series *The Rifleman*.

In a series of scrimmages, Kelleher deployed his Cadets against the 6'9" Boykoff and company, and, for the first several games, the enlisted men schooled the future officers. But, under Kelleher's careful tutelage and relentless conditioning, his Cadets began to gel as a team. Slowly but surely they developed a self-confident poise that, coupled with their ever-sharpening shooting skills, enabled them to ultimately turn the tide against their cross-post rivals. "I'll bet there isn't a team in the country that can match their physical conditioning … and their man-to-man defense is rugged. Zowie! 'Rugged' is the word for it," Connors warned.[6]

*****

Scrimmages, of course, were one thing, even against a collection of former collegiate basketball stars such as Boykoff, Connors, and their comrades. An actual game, on the other hand, was quite another. And so now, four months after his departure from Fordham, Coach Kelleher watched the Cadets warm up with the narrowed, tense eyes of a coach who was about to see his team play its first game under his watch. Within a matter of minutes, he would find out if the seeds of his basketball philosophy would bear fruit in the academy's spartan confines.

CHAPTER 2

Ed Christl

At first blush, as West Point squared off against Swarthmore College, the two academic institutions represented on the hardcourt that frigid Wednesday evening seemed polar opposites. The United States Military Academy traced its roots to 1802, when Thomas Jefferson signed the Military Peace Establishment Act into law, which empowered him "to organize and establish a corps of engineers" that "shall be stationed at West Point in the state of New York, and shall constitute a military academy."[1]

For the next two decades, Jefferson's academy constituted the only engineering school in the United States and, in the years to follow, would grow to become a byword for military professionalism around the world, along with such institutions as Great Britain's Sandhurst and France's Saint-Cyr. By the conclusion of the Mexican War, the academy's graduates' performance in that conflict inspired Gen. Winfield Scott to offer an observation still memorized by West Point plebes today. "I give it as my fixed opinion," Scott declared, "that but for our graduated cadets, the war between the United States and Mexico might, and probably would have, lasted some four or five years, with, in its first half, more defeats than victories falling to our share; whereas, in less than two campaigns, we conquered a great country and a peace, without the loss of a single battle or skirmish."[2]

Less than a decade later, America's Civil War visited a fratricidal conflict on West Point and its graduates, with classmates and old friends, clad in blue or gray, arrayed against one another in theaters of war across the

United States. By the end of the war, Robert E. Lee (Class of 1829, who also led West Point as the school's superintendent from 1852 to 1855) had surrendered his Army of Northern Virginia to Ulysses Grant (Class of 1843) at Appomattox Court House, Joseph E. Johnston's (Class of 1829) Army of Tennessee had capitulated to William Sherman (Class of 1840), and the Confederacy's hopes for independence, led by President Jefferson Davis (Class of 1828), were dashed decisively.

Despite the savagery of the Civil War, or maybe even because of it, West Point and its graduates played a leading role in the national reconciliation that followed. Indeed, by the time of the Spanish-American War, Joseph "Fighting Joe" Wheeler (Class of 1859), a former Confederate general and commander of cavalry, was back in his blue uniform as a major general, commanding US cavalry in Cuba. He would become one of a handful of Confederate officers to be buried at Arlington National Cemetery. And when the United States joined the fighting in World War I, it was John "Black Jack" Pershing (Class of 1886) who led the American Expeditionary Force to France.

In 1944, as America entered its second year of combat in World War II, most of the generals who had become household names in the United States—Dwight Eisenhower (Class of 1915), George Patton (Class of 1909), Henry H. "Hap" Arnold (Class of 1907), Omar Bradley (Class of 1915), and Douglas MacArthur (Class of 1903), to name a few—had all had their second lieutenant's bars pinned on at West Point. Similar bronze bars awaited the cadets on Kellcher's basketball squad once they graduated and went to war. Like their illustrious predecessors, they had struck a bargain with both the War Department and the American people: four years (if not shortened by a war) of a free education at West Point in exchange for whatever service commitment (typically five years of active duty) that the army might require.

Viewed in such terms, Swarthmore College offered a stark contrast to West Point. The vision of the liberal Hicksite branch of the Society of Friends (Quakers), Swarthmore's inaugural class entered the campus near Philadelphia in 1869, with the school's first graduates—one man and five women—receiving degrees in 1873. That cohort of women included

Helen Magill, destined to become the first woman in the United States to earn a PhD. West Point, on the other hand, would not graduate its first female cadet until more than a century later.

Meanwhile, at Swarthmore, Quaker sensibilities and values remained integral parts of the college's character—so much so that when the school opted to form a Student Army Training Corps during World War I, it was berated by the journal *The Friends Intelligencer*, which declared the college had "compromised with evil" and had been "put to the test and found wanting." Then, in 1930, the school's president, Frank Aydelotte, enthusiastically embraced the idea of Swarthmore becoming the repository of the so-called Peace Collection of archival materials and papers. "World Peace may not be attained in this generation or the next," Aydelotte wrote to the collection's first curator, "but eventually, the nations will find a way to solving their troubles besides fighting it out."[3]

That day might yet come, but, with Japan's attack on Pearl Harbor and America's entry into World War II, it was clear to even Swarthmore that such a time had not yet arrived. If Swarthmore needed any further convincing, it came in July of 1943, as the first of some nine hundred of the US Navy's aviation cadets in its V-5 program and officer candidates in its V-12 program took up residence on the campus. The Navy needed officers, but it also needed those same officers to have mastered a certain degree of college-level courses. At colleges and universities around the nation, the V-5 and V-12 programs provided those courses for would-be naval officers who lacked a college degree. In time, in what would have seemed an ironic turn of events for Swarthmore's founders, Navy personnel would constitute nearly half of Swarthmore's student body and outnumber their civilian male counterparts by a ratio of two to one.

Faced with such a turn of events, Swarthmore's young basketball coach, Bill Stetson, cobbled together a collection of cagers—a "short-statured, stout-hearted" team, in the words of the *Philadelphia Inquirer*—as best he could to try to match the team's 11–8 record from the previous season. For the '44 season, only one member of the Garnet squad was not a V-12 cadet, but at least Stetson could count on players such as Ray Winch, a former Rutgers University standout now a V-12 midshipman at Swarthmore. Winch was joined by players such as Jake Earley, Bobby Adams, and Bill Emmett, who had played ball at Lehigh College, Grove City College, and Lafayette University, respectively, before enlisting in the V-12 program and reporting to Swarthmore. And so, despite its opponent's pacific Quaker roots, West Point's first foray into the 1944 basketball season was very much an army-navy affair.

*****

Although history does not record the two players who paired off in West Point's field house for the opening jump, the moment would have most likely seen Ed Christl, Army's center, dispatched to midcourt for the home team. "Quiet, good-natured Big Ed is the tallest and one of the best-liked men in our class," that year's yearbook, the *Howitzer*, declared. "In becoming such an excellent cadet, and then officer, and in being chosen co-captain of the basketball team, he fulfills his two main ambitions at West Point."[4]

A month shy of his 23rd birthday, Christl had been born in Milwaukee, Wisconsin, but grew up in Minneapolis, Minnesota. West Point's records reflect his home address as 5341 Colfax Avenue South. It was a white, wood-framed, two-story home on a pleasant tree-lined street, with sidewalks that stretched with linear certitude north and south, east and west. Christl's father, Edward Sr., was the manager of the Froedtert Grain & Malting Company's Minneapolis operations, and Christl attended school first at the Annunciation School and then at DeLaSalle High School, both Catholic parochial schools. Christl played tennis and basketball at DeLaSalle and, after graduating in 1938, enrolled at St. Thomas Military Academy, attended summer camp at Northwestern Military and Naval Preparatory School, and ultimately enrolled at the University of St. Thomas in nearby St. Paul.

But even as Christl attended classes at the latter, he harbored dreams of attending West Point—and, no doubt to the chagrin of the university's basketball coach, even declined to join the squad lest he compromise any years of college eligibility that he might enjoy at West Point. Christl studied at St. Thomas in the fall of 1938 and then later during the 1940–41 school year. While at St. Thomas in the fall of 1940, Christl befriended John Flynn, a future West Pointer who would eventually be awarded three Purple Hearts in Korea, as he played amateur ball in Minneapolis' Catholic and Amateur Athletic Union leagues to keep his basketball skills sharp. "Ed had a very high moral character," Flynn recalled. "He was respected and admired by all. He was a quiet, but effective, person. He performed well at everything he did."[5]

In January of 1941, Christl's dreams of becoming a West Point cadet were fulfilled when Congressman Oscar Youngdahl nominated him to the academy. Christl subsequently passed the academy's entrance examination and reported for the dreaded "Beast Barracks"—the month of basic training for the new cadets—on R-Day, July 1, 1941.

Some five decades later, Christl's classmates would put pen to paper and capture their memory of that first morning at West Point in a class history titled *Whom Shall We Send?* It is difficult to best the scribe of that class as he recounted his and his classmates' experience upon arriving at the train station below the academy's main grounds, being shepherded into a nervous crowd by unsolicitous cadet officers, and marching uphill for their particular rendezvous with destiny:

> Above, beside and beneath them as they climbed with the warm sun on their backs was the grey granite of the Hudson trench. Then ahead they saw it, piled and mortared into walls they would come to know all too well: their new highland home. Through an archway they reached a level street and some two hundred yards beyond were directed into a building for a cursory physical check and assignment to New Cadet companies. They were marched by their sergeants through a high, wide archway into a large plaza; somebody called it the "sally port of Central Area." They were then at West Point.[6]

Now Christl and his fellow new cadets found themselves in a maelstrom of noisy, sweaty activity and action. Constantly supervised by omnipresent upperclassmen, they made trip after trip—always at double time—to the "C-Store" (the Cadet Store, which served as the quartermaster for the cadets) to draw issues of mattresses, underclothing, socks, shirts, trousers, belts, gym shorts, shoes, and ties. Other trips garnered their military gear—an M1903 Springfield rifle, a cartridge belt, a first-aid packet, a shelter half, tent pegs and poles, and a World War I doughboy-style helmet. Somewhere along the way, they also picked up a copy of *Bugle Notes*—a small but densely packed book that contained myriad items of "plebe knowledge" to be memorized and recited upon demand.

For their part, the upperclassmen did not seem interested in exercising their own powers of memory. Rather than bothering to learn Christl's and his fellow new cadets' names, they simply referred to the new arrivals as "Dumbjohn" or, more formally, "Mr. Dumbjohn."

"We learned quickly that we were but plebes at the very bottom of the scale and that it was healthy to keep our necks in and our mouths shut," the class's yearbook reminisced of those days. "We began to learn the elements of close order drill, manual of arms, rifle marksmanship, and standing guard interspersed with periods of physical exercise and athletics. It was a continual rush with little time to sit back and figure it all out."[7]

Meanwhile, in the broader world beyond the confines of West Point, international events marched on. During the summer of Christl's arrival at West Point, the United States was still technically at peace—although the larger world was anything but. A week earlier, Nazi Germany disastrously broadened its war by turning against its former ally and invading the Soviet Union. A week later, US troops landed in Iceland, replacing the British in order to maintain a presence there that would, hopefully, continue to deny the strategic island to Hitler.

Despite such developments elsewhere, Christl's attention was, no doubt, focused on the task at hand—surviving Beast Barracks. Happily, the initiation drew to a close on July 26, 1941, as Christl and 544 of his classmates officially became Fourth Classman – or, in the vernacular of West Point, "plebes." It was an important step toward ultimately joining what the academy's alumni reverently called "the Long Gray Line."

Tall as he was, Christl was assigned to Company M—one of the "flanker" companies of the Corps of Cadets. At the time, West Point routinely assigned cadets to companies based on their height, with the tallest cadets in companies A and M, which stood on the flanks of the Corps when it was arrayed on the Plain (the academy's parade field) – thus the nickname "flankers." From the flanks, the companies' heights decreased subtly toward the shorter, center companies. With the companies arranged by height, the Corps presented an orderly arrangement that tourists and officers found most pleasing. It was just one more example of West Point's regimented – literally and figuratively – approach to life.

Christl and his fellow plebes joined the rest of the Corps to bivouac at nearby Camp Clinton for summer camp. In the orderly tent city that constituted Camp Clinton, the new plebes lived in walled tents with wooden floors, each tent housing four plebes. Two wash stands stood outside in front of each tent. Inside the tent, on its center pool, hung a mirror. Glued to the mirror's back was a tent-arrangement diagram. Pursuant that diagram, folding cots stood along the walls, while a quartet of new footlockers formed a double row in the center of each tent (and also served as seats and tables). Uniforms hung on a rack at the tent's rear.

Camp Clinton would be Christl's home for the next three weeks, while President Franklin Roosevelt and Prime Minister Winston Churchill would secretly meet in Newfoundland to ink the Atlantic Charter and the US Congress would approve—by a single vote—an extension of the terms of service for America's first class of draftees. The United States was not at war quite yet, but the writing certainly seemed to be on the proverbial wall.

Fortunately, at the time, Maj. Gen. Robert L. Eichelberger (Class of 1909) led West Point as its superintendent. He had taken the reins of the academy the previous fall and had already set to work bringing the school into the 20th century. For the time being, traditional vestiges of the academy's past such as horseback riding would remain, but in other areas Eichelberger worked hard to modernize the institution. He added course hours in military instruction and physical training, cut back on the Napoleonic close-order drill that delighted the weekend tourists, brought in regular army soldiers to help train the cadets on the techniques and tradecraft of modern warfare, and acquired an air base in nearby Newburgh for future flight training.

Eichelberger's focus on military training was reflected in a set of late-August maneuvers that marked the end of Christl's first summer. Bedecked in campaign hats and carrying full field packs with their steel helmets and entrenching tools, the plebes marched out of West Point, their dusty column snaking through the nearby towns of Cornwall,

Middletown, and Goshen. They also carried their rifles with them, complete with cartridges of blank ammunition. Some of the upper-classman were still astride their cavalry mounts, but others, in a nod toward modern mechanized warfare, rode in trucks that towed 37-mm antitank guns. At times, "enemy" aircraft swooped in to "strafe" the columns, sparking a fusillade of blanks being fired in return. At first, the plebes enjoyed the excitement—until they realized, belatedly, how badly firing blanks fouled their rifle bores. Even worse were the times when the aircraft would spray the cadets with smoke, simulating a poison-gas attack and forcing the cadets to don their gas masks in the hot August sun.

Divided into two opposing forces—one wearing gray coveralls and leggings, the other distinguished by gray trousers and gray wool shirts—the cadets fought against one another in a set of war games that included clashes in the forested highlands and combat river crossings in small assault rafts. The maneuvers culminated in an all-night battle, followed by a welcome day off before the march back to West Point and the start of the 1941–42 academic year.

As the cadets were confronted with the challenges of academics and the baleful oversight of the upperclassmen and blessed with the occasional distractions of the football season, the military lessons of the preceding summer faded into the background. But then, on Sunday, December 7, 1941, breaking news over the radio suddenly reminded Christl and his classmates of why West Point existed in the first place.

That afternoon, Christl's classmate, Don Carter, was catching a movie in an impromptu theater set up in the academy's gymnasium after the day's mandatory chapel service and lunch. As he stepped back outside to return to his barracks at the end of the movie, he and his fellow moviegoers could instantly sense something was amiss.

"What's going on?" a cadet asked another.

"The Japanese attacked Pearl Harbor!" came the answer.

"Where the hell's that?" the first cadet replied.[8]

Other cadets remember hearing of Pearl Harbor when WOR interrupted its radio broadcast of the Brooklyn Dodgers–New York Giants football game to break the news.[9] Another heard the news over the radio while sitting with his date on Flirtation Walk overlooking the Hudson River.[10]

Yet another group of cadets was engaged in a Sunday afternoon "clothing formation"—a form of hazing in which upperclassmen ran the plebes through an increasingly frantic series of uniform changes, showers, and then more uniform changes. The center of this particular activity was the barracks' latrine and shower room—known in cadet slang as "the sinks"—and, in the midst of all of the chaos, the company's tactical officer emerged. Each company had a "tac"—who was an active-duty officer—assigned to it as a combination of disciplinarian and mentor

Entering the sinks, the tac climbed atop a bench and addressed the sweaty gathering.

"Men, the Japanese bombed Pearl Harbor in Hawaii this morning, hitting several U.S. Navy ships," he told his cadets. "I have no further information except that this appears to be an act of war. If war should be declared, I expect significant changes to occur here at the Academy."

Then he left the cadets—upperclassmen and plebes alike—in stunned silence.[11]

Whatever the source, in the wake of the news of the Japanese attack, excitement and unease swept the Corps. Some cadets, with fathers serving in Hawaii, the Philippines, or in the Pacific Fleet, worried quietly about the safety of their families. Others, more boisterously, began an impromptu football chant of "Beat Japan! Beat Japan! Beat Japan!" before being quieted by an upperclassman.[12]

By the next morning, the headlines of the *New York Times* reported "Tokyo Bombers Strike Hard at Our Main Bases on Oahu," and rumors of early graduations—or possible resignations to take up arms in active-duty units—were making the rounds in the barracks and classrooms. In response, Col. Frederick Irving, the commandant of cadets, addressed the cadets at their lunchtime meal in the mess hall. Irving, as commandant, was the academy's second-highest ranking officer after the superintendent and was responsible for the cadets' military training and discipline. He had graduated from West Point in 1917 and had been wounded in the Saint-Mihiel offensive a year later during World War I; in many ways, he could relate to the emotions boiling in the mess hall that December morning.

"Gentlemen, I know many of you are anxious to get into action as quickly as possible," he assured the Corps of Cadets. "Many of you have friends and relatives in uniform and may be thinking of resigning. The Superintendent has asked me to inform you that no resignations will be accepted."

"Your duty is to complete your education as cadets and to qualify yourselves in the best way possible for whatever may lie ahead," the commandant continued. "I can assure you that every officer on the staff and faculty wants to return to line duty as much as you do. It is our duty to help you learn everything possible before you graduate."[13]

That evening, the entire Corps of Cadets convened to listen to President Roosevelt's war message to Congress piped over the mess hall's public address system.

"Yesterday, December 7, 1941, a date which will live in infamy, the United States of America was suddenly and deliberately attacked by naval and air forces of the Empire of Japan," the president intoned over the radio, his familiar nasal cadence voicing solemn indignation. He concluded with a final call to action: "I ask that the Congress that since the unprovoked and dastardly attack by Japan on December 7, a state of war has existed between the United States and the Japanese empire."[14]

As soon as their commander in chief's last word died away, Christl and the rest of the Corps of Cadets jumped to their feet, carrying each other away in a primeval storm of applause. The cadets clapped and clapped until their palms were blackened and bruised, the noise echoing thunderously off the mess hall's stone walls and hard floors. President Roosevelt had cried havoc and let slip the dogs of war.

In those days, plebes did not merit Christmas leave, and so, even with his nation at war and his worried parents at home in Wisconsin, Christl spent a lonely holiday at West Point, hitting the books and honing his basketball skills. When he wasn't studying for a test ("written partial reviews," or WPRs, as West Point called them) or polishing his shoes or brass, he played third string for Dutch Lentz on the academy's basketball squad and served as an acolyte in the Catholic chapel.

Christl's long year of plebe purgatory ended with the Class of 1942's graduation parade on May 27, 1942, the day before graduation of the first classmen. In a marked change from the usual parade formations, the Corps's first classmen formed in the rear of each company, without rifles, and the companies marched out of the barracks area and came on line on the Plain. The cadets presented arms for the bugle call "Retreat." After "Retreat" had sounded, the cadets received the command "Graduating class, front and center!" Then the first classmen—all 374 of them—filed out from the rear of each company to form a line and moved forward to form a single rank facing the Corps. Their line extended almost the length of the Plain.

Then, upon the shouted command to pass in review, the companies began wheeling right and then, wheeling left, began passing the long rank of first classmen. As Company A, the first company, came abreast of the first man, the firsties removed their hats. The rest of the Corps then marched past the entire rank of first classmen at "eyes right" and, wheeling left once again, marched back toward the barracks and Central Area, the large paved courtyard situated between the cadets' barracks.

Once back in Central Area, Company M came to a halt. The company commander shouted, "About face!," and Christl pivoted to see an upperclassman reaching for his hand with a smile.

"Glad to know you," the upperclassman said with the traditional greeting of recognition.

"Glad to know you, sir," Christl responded. And with that, Christl and his classmates were "recognized." Their plebe year was over.[15]

The next day, May 28, 1942, the Class of 1942 graduated, joyously hurling their white hats into the air at the command "Class, dismissed!" Sadly, within a little over three years, seventy of them would be dead— nearly one out of every five. The ranks of the fallen would range from John Baker, killed when his B-17 Flying Fortress was shot down over Cherbourg, France, to James Woolfolk, who lost his life flying a training mission in Texas.

Although Christl welcomed the end of his plebe year and the recognition of the upperclassmen, the summer of 1942 otherwise offered little respite. Military training immediately commenced, with the cadets being issued khaki uniforms for the first time in the academy's history. "We moved immediately to summer camp [at Camp Clinton]," the *Howitzer* recalled, "and set to work. Machineguns, grenades, assault course, field artillery, M1 [rifle] qualifications—it was all stuffed into six short weeks."[16] During this time, Christl qualified as a rifle expert and a machine-gun marksman and, with the rest of the Corps, paraded in New York City's massive "New York at War" parade on June 13, 1942.

After concluding the six-week encampment at Camp Clinton, Christl and his classmates then entrained for Pine Camp, New York (today's Fort Drum), where they received an orientation to armored warfare with the 4th Armored Division and put their gloved hands and booted feet at driving tanks and half-tracks. Upon their return to West Point, the cadets occupied the new "firing center" at Lake Popolopen (today's Camp Buckner) on the distant reaches of the academy's reservation, for two weeks and practiced firing each of the many weapons in the army's arsenal—including 105-mm howitzers, mortars, and machine guns—and drove light tanks. The summer training concluded with a truck convoy back to Pine Camp for a final week of maneuvers, joined there by the rest of the Corps of Cadets.

"Across the sandy plains and wooded slopes of this military reservation, 2,000 cadets of the United States Military Academy were in action today," reported the *Poughkeepsie Eagle-News*, "giving lie to that old chestnut about generals dying in bed. Not one future general has seen a bed in more than 48 hours and not a buck private in the Army is receiving tougher treatment than these cadets participating in the most intensive maneuvers in the 140-year history of the academy."

"The cadets moved out of bivouac early Monday and took up positions as opposing Red and Blue armies," the newspaper gushed. "They were infantry men, artillery, engineers, signal men, anti-tank and anti-aircraft units, equipped with helmets, full packs, and the most modern weapons."

"Since then, all have marched at least 20 miles, crawled through undergrowth, tried to catch an hour's nap rolled in blankets in fence corners where mosquitoes swarmed, and waited patiently for chow wagons that sometimes couldn't find them."[17]

With the Pine Camp maneuvers concluded satisfactorily (other than one of Christl's classmates making the expensive mistake of driving an M3 tank off into a swamp), Christl and his classmates trucked back to West Point on August 16, 1942, for the start of their second year. Back at the academy, however, Christl and his classmates received the decidedly unwelcome news that, due to the pending expansion of the Corps from 1,960 to 2,496 cadets and the arrival of some 950 new cadets for 1942's Beast Barracks, their old companies had been effectively scrambled as the Corps was realigned into two regiments. Now Christl found himself in H Company of the 2nd Regiment, known as H-2.

"It is a hard thing to break up a company," the class's yearbook lamented, "even harder the splitting of roommates who had weathered plebe year together, but with pride we claim that wherever went a member of the old company, there went a little of the flanker tradition, the easy familiarity and comradeship of a company which never failed to take life as a pleasant thing and to temper cadet routine with a touch of humor all its own."[18]

Another change also greeted Christl back in garrison. As part of the ongoing modernization of training at the academy, the cadets turned in their old M1903 Springfield rifles and were issued new M1 Garands. The cadets learned to field-strip the rifles blindfolded and then qualified on them at the National Guard range at nearby Camp Smith—and, for the first time since the Civil War, stood guard duty at the academy with loaded rifles.

But there was still one more change—and this was the greatest of all. With America embroiled in a global war, the army had accelerated matriculation at the military academy. The Class of 1943 had become the Class of January 1943 and the Class of 1944 became the Class of June 1943. Christl's class—formerly the Class of 1945, originally scheduled to graduate in June of 1945—now became the Class of 1944 with a new June 6, 1944, graduation date on the calendar.

For Christl's Class of (now) 1944, the change meant that three years of academics had to be crammed into two. Nevertheless, the academic authorities remained determined that the cadets would complete their minimum requirements for their bachelor of science degrees, and so almost all subjects except those relating to engineering were eliminated. Most social science courses were curtailed; English was cut out completely. Even the sciences suffered. The cadets completed their course in chemistry without a single day in the laboratory.[19]

On top of such measures, almost all leaves were cancelled or curtailed. "No relaxation in the rigidity of our regimen resulted from our stepped-up activities," one of Christl's classmates remembered. "The wartime aspects of West Point were simply piled on top of them. And yet in all of this we were unable to complain, at least in public. Under normal circumstances we would have felt free to howl; but since men were fighting and dying overseas, we restrained our protests."[20]

Despite the increased operational tempo, the academy still graced the cadets with leave at Christmas. Christl departed West Point on December 19, 1942, for his first trip home to Minnesota in 18 months. "It seemed hardly more than an elongated weekend," the *Howitzer* lamented about the short 15-day respite, but Christl probably enjoyed every moment of his hard-earned freedom.

The upper classes returned to West Point on January 3, 1943, and, in short order, watched the former Class of 1945 graduate 18 months early on January 19, 1943. During that spring semester, Christl earned a spot as a yearling on the academy's varsity basketball squad—no mean feat in light of the heavy academic load now crushing him and his classmates. But some of those classmates took on even more challenges. As the end of the semester approached, 256 of Christl's classmates—the ones who had opted to become "air cadets"—boarded a train on April 20, 1943, for subsequent dispersal to airfields across America's South for primary flight training.

Other than the distractions of the former Class of 1944's early graduation in June, the summer of 1943 brought little in the way of a break for Christl. On June 2, 1943, he and his fellow future second lieutenants—the ones not attending flight school—journeyed by train to Fort Knox, Kentucky, where, two days later, they were welcomed by the US Army Armored Center's commander, a color guard, and a band playing the "West Point March." At Fort Knox, the cadets participated in tank crew drills, fired the 37-mm guns of M3 Stuart light tanks and the 75-mm guns of the M4 Sherman, and were awed by the spectacle of an armored regiment, with combined-arms support, mount a mock attack across Fort Knox's range.

On June 8, the cadets departed Fort Knox for Fort Benning, Georgia, the army's home of infantry, this time enduring a hot, uncomfortable ride in the rolling stock of the Southern Railway. There were no overnight berths, only uncomfortable rattan seats that had clearly seen better days. The cadets arrived at Fort Benning tired, disheveled, and generally disgusted with the turn of events. There was no fanfare upon their arrival at the Georgia post; rather, the cadets simply drew field gear and, divided into two groups, were inserted into an ongoing Officer Candidate School training cycle. For ten days, the cadre and soldiers at Benning put the visiting cadets through their paces with lessons in patrolling, infantry in advance, and other tactical elements.

"Our instruction followed a cycle," the *Howitzer* reported. "The bleachers for a lecture, the woods for work, the bleachers for critique."[21] At the end of the visit, a demonstration of a large-scale paratrooper attack impressed the cadets to the same degree as Knox's armored assault. Less impressive were the cadets' discovery that "the Georgia clay and bushes teemed with chiggers, microscopic red devils foreign to Yankee cadets."[22]

Continuing with their combined-arms tour, the cadets next visited Camp Davis, an artillery and antiaircraft artillery training base some 20 miles up the North Carolina coast from Wilmington. "The stay at Davis was almost a vacation," the *Howitzer* remembered happily. "There was little work; most of the instruction was demonstration, which included the actual use of radar in conjunction with firing. We fired the guns from 50 caliber to the 90 mm. Most memorable events were the daily jaunts to the warm North Carolina surf after knocking off work at 11:30 and 4:30."[23] Whether it was the excitement of the seeing the big guns blasting away or the daily trips to the beach, Christl formed a favorable opinion of the branch its members proudly called "the king of battle."

After its time at Camp Davis, Christl's class took on different roles. Approximately half of the class returned to West Point to become instructors at the academy's encampment at Lake Popolopen, where they taught such topics as fortifications, patrolling, and demolitions, or, back in garrison, to man the so-called Beast Detail, where they worked to whip the summer's fresh crop of new cadets into shape. For the Beast Detail, theirs was a tall task. Congress had doubled the wartime size of the Corps of Cadets, and that summer the largest class of new cadets ever—1,075—had arrived for Beast Barracks.

The other half of the Class of 1944, however, reported for duty with various replacement training centers—Fort Bragg, North Carolina, for field artillery units; Fort Eustis, Virginia, for antiaircraft units; Fort Belvoir, Virginia, for engineer units; Fort Monmouth, New Jersey, for Signal Corps troops; or Camp Wheeler, Georgia, for infantry and cavalrymen. There, either by shadowing platoon leaders and noncommissioned officers or, in some cases, assuming the role of platoon leaders themselves, they experienced firsthand the role of a second lieutenant in actual combat units.

At the end of the summer of 1943, Christl and the entire Class of 1944 regrouped for a final two weeks of training in upstate New York at Pine Camp with the rest of the Corps of Cadets. There the Corps's stay was divided into two phases. During the first week, the Corps conducted its own maneuvers, pitting the 1st Regiment against the 2nd. Then, in the second week, cadets were assigned to units of the 5th Armored Division. Plebes and yearlings served as fillers in companies or batteries, and the firsties were assigned as second lieutenants in branch units that matched with their earlier training at the replacement training center.

Again, the *Howitzer* offered a contemporary view of the experience: "Immemorable [*sic*] lessons—we will always remember the liquid ice showers, our retreat in the mud until 1:00 am, and chilly dawn attacks. Welcome letters, poncho forms resting against trees, 'C' rations, weary feet, happy departure, home!"[24]

Once back at West Point in the fall of 1943 for what would be his final academic year, Christl was chosen by his classmates to chair their Election Committee and, on September 4, 1943, joined with the rest of his class in receiving their class rings. He also drew duty as the company's supply sergeant for Company H-2, began varsity basketball practices under Coach Kelleher, and, if he was like most upperclassman, occasionally called upon a nearby plebe to "pop off" with a piece of plebe knowledge known as "The Days."

"Sir, the days!" the hapless plebe would bellow. "Today is _____! There are ___ and a butt days until Christmas leave! There are ___ and a butt days until 100th night! There are __ and a butt days until graduation and graduation leave for the Class of 1944, sir!"[25]

Left unsaid in "The Days" was what would come after graduation leave: officer basic training, assignment to a troop unit, and embarkation for a distant battlefield. But those days were still in the distant future. Now, for Christl, and his fellow firsties Bob Faas and Jack Hennessey, it was time to play basketball.

CHAPTER 3

The Garnet, the Red Raiders, and the Redmen

If "Big Ed" Christl was Coach Kelleher's likely choice for Army for the opening jump ball against Swarthmore College, then Swarthmore's center, Ray Winch, of Collingswood, New Jersey, would probably have been the Garnet's pick to match up with the tall cadet. A three-sport athlete who played football and was a high-jumper in the track and field events, Winch stood 6′4″, matching his counterpart Christl inch for inch. The Swarthmore center had started his collegiate career at Rutgers University but, after his freshman year, had joined the Navy's V-12 program and, upon arriving in Philadelphia, had found himself on Coach Stetson's basketball squad.

With a blast of the referee's whistle and a toss of the ball toward the field house's rafters, the Army-Swarthmore contest began. Almost instantly, Ed Kelleher's game plan was revealed. Capitalizing on his team's superior height and athleticism, he overwhelmed the Garnet with a suffocating man-to-man defense that seemed to leverage every turnover into points for the Cadets.[1] Much to the home crowd's delight, West Point had built a suffocating 35–6 lead by the time the first 20-minute half ended.

For Army, Bob Faas was on the court for the first time in six games—not counting a token appearance in last season's tilt against Navy. Faas had suffered a season-ending broken wrist against Pittsburgh halfway through the 1943 season, and so the Swarthmore game was his first return to full-blown competition—and the speedy forward made the most of it. By the end of the game, the firstie had logged 10 field goals and a free throw to lead Army with 21 points before Kelleher pulled him from the game. Meanwhile, second classman Dale Hall, the athletic phenomenon from Parsons, Kansas, seemed intent on matching his 4.0 GPA in the classroom with seven field goals and three perfect trips to the foul line. For his part, Ed Christl seemed to pick up where he had left off the previous year, logging a dozen points in the matchup.

As the lopsided contest progressed, Kelleher pulled his starters and began dispatching players from his bench. That evening, even the plebes on the team had a chance to make their West Point debuts in front of their fellow fourth classmen in the field house. Pete Molnar checked in and notched a field goal and a free throw, while Bobby Dobbs, at guard, added six points to the score himself, with classmate Richard Walterhouse logging a single basket.

As the game wound down toward an 80–29 Army victory, the only unhappy face on the Cadets' bench may well have been that of first classman Jack Hennessey. Nicknamed "Three-Star" for his exploits on three of the academy's varsity squads—football, basketball, and baseball— the cadet from South Chicago was widely considered to be the best all-around athlete in the Class of 1944. On the basketball team, he was the mainstay of the Cadets' defense, but on a night like this it seemed like everyone in a black and gold uniform was capable of contributing an Army bucket to the blowout—except, that is, for Hennessey. For whatever reason, Hennessey's first game of his final season was, personally, a disappointing one. At the end of the game, the scorebook recounted not a single point in Hennessey's row.

Otherwise, however, Army's win over the Garnet was one for the record books. West Point's 80 points in the game set a new record for the Academy Field House. But with their studies awaiting and a predawn accountability formation scheduled for the next morning, there was little time for the Cadets to celebrate. Besides, their next game, against Colgate University, was only three days away.

*****

On Saturday afternoon, January 15, a convoy of cars carrying an exhausted and battered Colgate team was waved through West Point's gates by a military policeman and entered the academy. Two days earlier, en route to the team's first game on this two-game road trip—a contest with Rensselaer Polytechnic Institute—one of Colgate's team cars had overturned, injuring three Red Raiders. Then the game against RPI went down to the wire before Colgate, after losing two of its players to injuries, squeaked out a 53–52 victory over the Engineers. A road trip from Troy, New York, to West Point followed the next day to deliver Coach Karl Lawrence and his team—like Swarthmore's, heavily leavened by V-12 personnel—to the academy and their appointed clash with the Cadets.

Looking at his battered squad, Coach Lawrence could at least take some solace as he counted the talented Bobby Wanzer, a former Seton Hall player now in Colgate's US Marine Corps V-12 program, among his players as a six-foot point guard. Wanzer, with his peerless work ethic and deadly free-throw accuracy, would one day earn a place in the NBA's Hall of Fame thanks to his years with the Rochester Royals (today's Sacramento Kings). But could Wanzer carry the day for Colgate?

Coach Kelleher's Cadets soon provided an answer. Despite Colgate's travails, the Cadets showed no mercy to their visitors in this second game of the season. For the first few minutes, Colgate, led by Wanzer and fellow guard John Sandmann, managed to keep matters close. But then West Point broke the game open. The Cadets posted 20 unanswered points, and at the half the score stood at 38–16. Kelleher's man-to-man defense had stifled Colgate's repeated efforts at fruitless fast breaks.

As play resumed, Colgate's Wanzer posted the first score of the half with a free throw. But Bob Faas responded with a free throw of his own, and the Wisconsin native added a long field goal for good measure. Then Colgate's rangy center, Ed McLaughlin, drew a foul and claimed a free throw. Moments later, however, McLaughlin's teammate Bob Dewey fouled plebe Bobby Dobbs, sending Dobbs to the free-throw line to capitalize on the opportunity.

Undeterred, Dewey took the next shot offered and posted two points for Colgate. "Three-Star" Hennessey quickly flipped the court on the Red Raiders and passed the ball off to Dale Hall, who sank the ball for two points. Then it was Wanzer's opportunity, which he used to sink a shot from the side of the court. Wanzer's marksmanship, however, was matched by Christl, who drove in and scored from close range.

For the next few moments, the back-and-forth continued unabated. Army's Hall fouled Jack Kearns, who took the resulting opportunity to sink a free throw. Faas, fouled in turn, also swished one from the foul line. But Wanzer responded in kind, only to be matched by a field goal launched at distance by Hall. Now it was Colgate's turn, and both Wanzler and teammate Neil Dooley posted field goals. At this juncture, West Point's Bill Ekberg was in the game at center, giving his fellow big man Christl a breather. With a delicate touch that seemed out of place with his 6'6" frame, Ekbert put up a one-hander to bring the nascent Colgate rally to a futile end. Halfway through the second half, the score was Army 51, Colgate 28.

In the final 10 minutes of the game, the Cadets coasted comfortably to a 69–44 victory over their visitors. The scorekeepers credited Hall with 18 points, Kenna with 10, and the seemingly irrepressible Faas with 11. Christl added 8 to his total at center, with Ekberg right behind at 7. But, once again, Jack Hennessey merely logged three goose eggs in the box score—zero field goals, zero free throws, and zero points. The senior could only look forward to the upcoming game against St. John's University—four days away, on Wednesday, January 19—for redemption.[2]

*****

In West Point's third game of the season—the match against the Redmen of St. John's—Army's coach faced a familiar foe. Kelleher had begun his college coaching career at the St. John's campus in Brooklyn over two decades ago, and, in the much more recent past, it was St. John's that had knocked his Fordham Rams out of the NIT last year. The Army coach may have felt some sympathy for the outmatched Swarthmore Garnet and maybe a twinge of sorrow for Karl Lawrence's Red Raiders, but one wonders at Kelleher's mind-set as he squared off against the Redmen and a man who was already a legend of this era of basketball—Coach Joseph Lapchick.

Three decades earlier, Lapchick—the son of Czech immigrants who had settled in Yonkers, New York—had left school and his subsequent $15-a-day factory job to hustle what money could be earned playing in various pickup basketball games and leagues in New York. By the age of 19, he was making $75 a game—a tidy sum for 1919—and four years later the rangy 6′5″ center joined the barnstorming Original Celtics. A decade of playing for the Original Celtics and later the Cleveland Rosenblums in the American Basketball League followed before he took the head coaching job at St. John's in 1936. And it was as the coach of St. John's that Lapchick had edged out Kelleher's Fordham Rams last year on the way to claiming the NIT championship.

Perhaps, therefore, there was some legitimacy to Kelleher's demeanor when he convened with Lapchick and a collection of other collegiate coaches at Toots Shor's Restaurant at 51 West 51st Street in New York City for the Metropolitan Basketball Writers Luncheon the day before the match with St. John's. "My team isn't too hot," Kelleher warned sportswriter George Coleman, although Coleman's subsequent litany of the talented football players on his bench signaled that the journalist did not completely share Kelleher's despair.

Nevertheless, as Coleman chewed over the upcoming match for the *Brooklyn Daily Eagle*, he put his faith in the St. John's cagers. "Adroit Redmen Figured to Beat Burly Army Five," the paper's headline read that morning. The game "promises to be the roughest and hardest fought scramble of the college season," Coleman told his readers. "Both teams are loaded for bear."

But "the Army plays for keeps," the sportswriter warned. "When an Army cager starts to go underneath for a layup, nothing but a stone wall or stealing the ball will stop him from ending up under the basket. When the Army stops a shot, the shooter is stopped too! … The whistle is seldom blown, and all opposing fives expect a rough, Army style of competition."

Such competition aside, Coleman still foresaw a St. John's victory. The Redmen, he assured his readers, "are expected to outsmart the Cadets. The Indians may arrive home a little tired, but many fans think they should bring the bacon with them."[3]

As St. John's tipped off against West Point in the Academy Field House, it was clear that Lapchick's squad, led by the diminutive but talented guard Hyman Gotkin, complemented by teammates such as

Dick McGuire, Ivy Summer, and Bill Kotsores, was ready for action. They faced Kelleher's almost airtight man-to-man defense, reinforced with the Cadets' fast-breaking offense, with the confidence of the team considered to be the best among New York City's colleges. Gotkin and his teammates deployed a smooth passing game, accompanied by almost flawless shooting and, despite the size differential, mounted a staunch defense of their own. But for one moment where Mississippian Doug Kenna, one of Kelleher's moonlighting football players, sank a layup to give Army a brief 18–16 lead, the Redmen dominated the first half.

By the half, the score was St. John's 20, West Point 18, although the Redmen had never been able to claim a greater-than-five-point surplus over their opponents during that half. If true to legendary form, Coach Lapchick would have been pacing the bench line throughout the period, a veritable train wreck of nerves as he suffered each foul call and bemoaned each missed shot. The loss of McGuire, his sturdy right guard, only 10 minutes into the game must have spiked his blood pressure even higher. Meanwhile, sitting at the end of Army's bench, Coach Kelleher worked to keep his own fabled composure intact. As the halftime buzzer sounded, Kelleher called his team over to him. The forecasting of the *Brooklyn Daily Eagle* aside, he was not about to let the Redmen outsmart his Cadets.

"Ease up on the guarding," he told the Army squad. "Stand back a bit. Don't let them get around you." Kelleher could see that the physicality of the game was taking its toll on the St. John's players and, in a calculated gamble, bet that the tired Redmen would be off on their long shots.[4]

The wily Kelleher was right. As the Cadets held St. John's to a single foul shot, Dale Hall, at forward, tore loose with a one-man scoring rampage. In the span of 10 minutes, he single-handedly rang up 10 points. Even as Hall slowed down, Ed Christl stepped up. Using his big frame to his advantage, he came alive in the final 10 minutes of the second half. Time after time, he snagged offensive rebounds, posting seven straight points before he fouled out. Subbing in for Christl, Bill Ekberg ultimately added four points of his own to the Cadets' total as West Point pulled away from St. John's minute by minute, ultimately doubling up on the visitors on the scoreboard.

The Redmen tried to respond as best they could, but, frustratingly, it seemed as if every Redman's run on the basket hit a stone wall. Only when Lapchick sent in Don Wehr to assist the weary Hyman Gotkin did his team put together a string of four baskets to challenge Army's late-game dominance. But by then it was too little, too late. When the final buzzer sounded, the score was Army 49, St. John's 36.

With the victory, West Point notched its third win of the season—although, once again, Jack Hennessey had been held scoreless. What, "Three-Star" Hennessey probably wondered, would the upcoming road trip against Columbia University bring? Kelleher and the Cadets leaned heavily on their right guard's steady defensive work, but for a competitor like Hennessey an absence of points on the scoreboard must have stung. Perhaps a balm would be found on the road.

CHAPTER 4

Bob Faas

In the winter of 1943–44, it was a rare event for West Point's athletes to travel off campus for games. In those trying times, the military's budget was seemingly better spent on Sherman tanks and artillery shells than road trips for the basketball team to Swarthmore or St. John's. But on the morning of January 22, 1944, Kelleher and his Cadets nevertheless entrained for New York City to take their three-game winning streak on the road to Columbia University. If one of them had opened the *New York Times* to the sports pages as the train clacked south along the Hudson's western bank, he would have read the headline "Army Five Here Tonight—Unbeaten Cadets, Led by Hall, to Invade Columbia Court."

Coincidentally, a much more literal invasion had already taken place that very morning, some four thousand miles to the east. In the predawn darkness, the Allied forces in Italy launched Operation Shingle, an amphibious landing at Anzio conceived in the hope of opening a new avenue to German-occupied Rome. Maj. Gen. John P. Lucas, West Point Class of 1911, directed the Allied invasion force as the commander of VI Corps. Col. William O. Darby, West Point Class of 1933, commanded the collection of US Rangers and British Commandos that complemented Lucas's corps. In all likelihood, it would have been a rare reader of the *New York Times*, or any other paper that Saturday morning, who would have dwelled on the sports pages. The big story was Anzio and whether or not the fall of Rome was imminent.

Nevertheless, by that Saturday afternoon, attention had again returned to pursuits closer to home, and in upper Manhattan the Columbia Lions awaited Kelleher's team at the school's Morningside Heights gymnasium. Columbia's basketball team, which had kicked off its season in November, sported a modest 6–5 record. Columbia was, however, riding a two-game winning streak and could take some heart in the fact that it had beaten the Cadets last year. Columbia's coach, Elmer Ripley, was, like St. John's Joe Lapchick, a former Original Celtic and an alumus of the American Basketball League who had traded his court shoes and jersey for a coach's clipboard. A respected coach in his own right, he was destined to one day coach teams as diverse as the Harlem Globetrotters, Israel's Olympic team, and, from 1951 to 1953, Army. But as far as the challenge immediately before him was concerned, Coach Ripley only had to break open a copy of Friday's *Columbia Daily Spectator* to consider what his squad faced.

"Paced by their high scorer Dale Hall, who caged 21 points against St. John's at West Point, Army will bring their fast-breaking offense and airtight man-to-man defense to Morningside in quest of their fourth straight victory," the paper's scribe warned. "The soldiers combine height with speed, and their control of the backboards was one of the decisive factors in Wednesday night's triumph."[1]

To counter Kelleher's Cadets, Ripley and the Lions leaned heavily on Walter "Boards" Budko, Columbia's sophomore center who stood at 6'5". One day Budko would play professionally for the Baltimore Bullets and be able to claim to have been the first Columbia player to score a thousand points in a season. That night he led teammates Vince Lolordo, Wayne Morgan, Otto Apel, and Bruce Gehrke onto the floor to try to snap West Point's winning streak. To support their home team, a raucous crush of blue-and-white-clad fans packed the crowded stands from court to rafters, their shouts and cheers punctuated by the horns and drums of a rabidly enthusiastic pep band. Only as the game's referee called Budko and West Point's Christl to center court for the opening jump ball did the partisan crowd and the bandsmen quiet for a brief moment.

The opening seconds of the game kept the crowd silent—at least initially. Christl pulled up and sank a field goal. Faas, fouled by a Lion, went to the foul line. His subsequent free throw shots netted one point.

In less than a minute, much to the chagrin of the Columbia faithful, the score was 3–0, Army.

At that point, West Point's shooters went cold. In response, Columbia's band came back to life. So did the Columbia fans. Ten minutes ticked off the clock as Army failed to muster a single basket, with one shot after another banging off the rim. The Lions' shooters did little better, although they did manage to claim a pair of baskets, which brought the score to Columbia 4, Army 3.

The Lions, energized by the scrappy rebounding of their guard Morgan, gamely kept the contest close as each squad battled for hard-earned baskets. Bit by bit, however, the Cadets pulled ahead, only to see the score tied at 14 when Columbia's Jim Cumisky dashed in for a layup. But Army's Pete Molnar was having one of his best games of the season, and with lethal accuracy the plebe sank two quick field goals to send the Cadets to the locker room at intermission with a 20–14 lead. Ed Christl's work at center was responsible for nearly a third of West Point's points.

As play resumed after the intermission, Ripley's Lions went on the offensive. In short order, they claimed a basket and three free throws to bring Columbia to within a point of Army. The partisan Morningside Heights crowd and their spirited band poured their collective hearts and voices into the escalating rally.

But West Point had not come to New York City to lose, and team captain Christl rose to the occasion in his usual unflappable manner. With a practiced eye and a steady hand, he arched a pair of shots in for a total of four points, with Molnar and Doug Kenna each adding to the total themselves. At the end of the Cadets' run, the score stood at Army 30, Columbia 19.

At that point, Dale Hall, who had already contributed a bucket to the scoring run, launched a one-man attack on Columbia. Scrambling on defense and running down-court pell-mell on offense, he appeared to be everywhere at once. "The ball seemed to roll off his fingertips and into the basket," marveled James Robbins, who was covering the contest for the *New York Times*. "He was like a flash down the court and his tosses were uncannily accurate, at times. They were so well thrown they looked easy."[2] He ultimately posted 17 points in the game, with most of them scored in the final 10 minutes of play.

"Boards" Budko and his Columbia teammates responded as best they could, battling on and never once slowing down, even as Army's scores continued to mount. In the end, though, even the gutsiest of efforts could not put more time or points on the scoreboard. Coach Kelleher and his Cadets finally succeeded in quieting the Columbia faithful with a final score of Army 55, Columbia 37. Army's record for the season was now 4-0—even if, yet again, Jack Hennessey had failed to appear in the score book.

On the following Monday, down in Baltimore, readers of the *Evening Sun* picked up their daily paper and read the prognostications of Paul Menton, the paper's sports editor. "Already the New York basketball writers are speculating on the possibility of the United States Military Academy officials approving an invitation for Army to participate in the invitation tournament for the top-ranking teams of the nation in mid-March."[3]

Meanwhile, overseas on the Anzio beachhead, the Allied invaders had high hopes for the coming days as well. Rome was seemingly nearly within grasp at the price of an operation that had only cost 13 Allied lives. In London, BBC broadcasters predicted that Rome would be reached within 48 hours.

History, of course, would prove differently. The Anzio beachhead would, in the days, weeks, and months to come, ultimately become synonymous with military frustration, lost opportunities, and squandered lives. The following month, General Lucas would be relieved—his West Point pedigree notwithstanding—and replaced by Maj. Gen. Lucian Truscott, a former Oklahoma schoolteacher who had, in large part, bluffed his way into a commission during World War I. Meanwhile, back stateside, only time would tell if West Point's young campaign on the hardcourt, seemingly so promising at the beginning, would come to similar disappointment. If West Point's next opponent—Penn State—had anything to do with it, that would be exactly what happened. The Nittany Lions had a date at Army in four days.

*****

On Wednesday, January 26, Coach John Lawther and Penn State's basketball squad made the long journey from State College, Pennsylvania, to West Point. The Nittany Lions boasted a 5–4 record but were coming off a home loss to Colgate. Lawther had coached collegiate basketball for 17 seasons and had never posted a losing record; his sliding-zone defense was the bane of most opposing coaches and teams. The sliding-zone, although effective, was "un-American," hissed Rhode Island coach Frank Keany. "The idea of the game is to win, isn't it?" Lawther had retorted.[4]

In the winter of 1944, Lawther needed every stratagem he could muster, un-American or not. Like most universities, Penn State's student body had been decimated by the war, with its male students volunteering or being drafted in droves. For a coach such as Lawther, attempting to field a basketball team in such times was difficult, so he secured some relief by culling the ranks of Marine Corps officer trainees present on campus for the V-12 program. Accordingly, the Nittany Lions squad counted among its ranks Don McNary, a 6'5" center from George Washington University; Monty Moskowitz, who had played ball at Western Reserve; and Bud Long, of Washington and Jefferson University. Army's 4–0 record might seem daunting, but the combination of talented future Marines, artfully deployed into Lawther's infamous defense, promised a stern challenge for Kelleher's Cadets.

As the game began, Penn State's defense rewarded Lawther's hopes and confirmed Kelleher's fears. The lead seesawed back and forth, and, by the time the buzzer sounded to close out the half, Penn State had claimed a 23–18 lead. For the second time in five games, the Cadets trotted into the locker room trailing their opponents, with the spectators left wondering if West Point could find a solution to Lawther's frustrating zone defense.

There were no reporters in Army's locker room who recorded what may have been a motivational exhortation delivered by Kelleher to his team or who noted any crafty changes in the coach's game plan. Maybe Kelleher did such things; maybe not. Perhaps the players themselves simply gathered their wits, girded their loins, and decided that they would not let Penn State visit the team's first loss on them at home. Or maybe, on that team of future combat leaders, someone rose from the sweaty locker-room ranks and spurred his teammates to action. If so, that Cadet was, quite possibly, team cocaptain Bob Faas.

*****

Like his classmate Christl, Faas was a son of the Midwest—in his case, La Crosse, Wisconsin, 125 miles downstream on the Mississippi River from Christl's hometown of Minneapolis. Faas attended La Crosse Central High School, where he starred on the basketball and tennis teams, was elected president of the Class of 1939, and earned honors as the school's valedictorian. "Bobby's greatest desire is to attend West Point," his high school year book noted, but at the time there was no congressional appointment to West Point to be secured. Accordingly, Faas enrolled at La Crosse State Teachers College (today's University of Wisconsin–La Crosse) in the hope that his opportunity for a nomination would eventually come.

In college, Faas made the most of the next two years—playing tennis and basketball on the school's intercollegiate teams, logging additional hours on the basketball court for the Tausche Hardware Company's squad in the city's Industrial League, serving as his college class's president, and, according a school newspaper reporter not encumbered by this century's social sensibilities, "ha[d] hordes of delectable femininity worshipping at his shrine." Despite such distractions, Faas stayed true to his ambition of attending West Point and, with a nomination from Congressman William H. Stevenson, ultimately joined the Class of 1944 for Beast Barracks in the summer of 1941.

Once at the academy, Faas excelled both academically and athletically. "One of the outstanding men of his class," the *Howitzer*, proudly declared. "An all-around swell guy ... a composed leader and a sincere friend."[5]

At West Point, Faas wasted little time in finding his way onto Army's basketball squad, earned his "numeral" as a member of the squad while still a plebe, and lettered the following years. To Coach Kelleher, Faas was "a speed boy, and naturally a key man in [Army's] fast-breaking offense."[6] To sportswriter Chip Royal, Faas was "the diminutive forward

[who] makes up for what he lacks in height with unusual speed and shooting."

But basketball was merely one aspect of Faas's time at the academy. He also played intercollegiate tennis, tutored his fellow plebes, boxed in the annual plebe boxing smoker, staffed the Corps's 2nd Regiment as the regimental training officer, served on the school's Hop Committee, qualified as a rifle sharpshooter, was elected president of the Class of 1944, and still placed in the top half of his class academically. Other than during his plebe year and his time on the regimental staff, Faas was assigned to cadet Company C-2, an outfit formed on August 17, 1942, to help the Corps absorb the wartime influx in cadets. It was, according to the *Howitzer*, a somewhat schizophrenic company, an amalgamation of the "hard runts" of H Company and the men of I Company—"the home of indifference and contentment."[7]

Faas was also one of the academy's air cadets. In the summer of 1942—just after Faas had finished his plebe year—the army had established the Army Air Forces Basic-Advanced Flying School at Stewart Field, about 15 miles north of West Point. In a nod toward the new era of warfare, qualified West Point cadets could choose to become air cadets and pursue flight training—and approximately 40 percent of them did just that.

The air cadets' number included Faas, and so, on April 20, 1943, as his second year began to draw to a close, Faas and 255 classmates entrained at West Point's station. Their orders dispersed them, in groups of a couple dozen, to airfields in Bonham, Brady, Coleman, Corsicana, Fort Worth, and Stamford in Texas; to Chickasaw, Muscogee, and Oklahoma City in Oklahoma; and to Pine Bluff in Arkansas. There they entered the primary phase of flight school, in which the cadets would each log at least 60 hours in the air. Primary was a definite change from the rigor of West Point, and "the air cadets thrived on it," the *Howitzer* reported. "After two weeks, most of us had soloed and were working on chandelles, eights on pylons, lazy eights, and other elementary maneuvers. The last month brought acrobatics with even greater thrills."[8]

Left unmentioned by the *Howitzer*, however, was the cold fact that not every cadet survived primary. On May 26, the aircraft of Faas's classmate Everal Lemley smashed into the ground outside of Brady, Texas. The crash took his life and that of his instructor, Marion McLauren. Another 85 cadets simply washed out of flight school at some point during the training.

Such tragedies and disappointments aside, by the end of June, primary had been completed, and Faas and his fellow air cadets returned to West Point or, to be more precise, Stewart Field. At Stewart, they embarked upon the nine weeks of the army's basic phase for flight school—transitioning into the more powerful trainer aircraft, learning to fly relying solely on instruments, and mastering formation flight. Meanwhile, on the ground, they took classes in meteorology, navigation, and code—and, of course, physical training. By August they were ready to cap their training in the basic phase with cross-country flights and a "wing-fling" hop at the Stewart Field gymnasium.

As Faas's third and final year at West Point began in the fall of 1943, his flight training continued. Now it was time for the advanced phase, also conducted at Stewart Field. 129 of the air cadets, tabbed to be future bomber or transport pilots, were assigned the twin-engine Beechcraft AT-10 Wichita; 29 others, destined to fly fighters, would train in the single-engine North American Aviation AT-6 Texan.

Faas found himself in the latter group, confronted for the first time with the now legendary AT-6. "We called it an AT-6 or a '6'; Navy and Marine pilots called it an 'SNJ'; British and Canadian flyers called it the 'Harvard'; … and no one called it a Texan except journalists, promotional writers, book authors, and people who never flew it," explained one World War II instructor pilot.[9] The AT-6 was an all-metal, full-cantilever, low-wing monoplane, with tandem seating in its closed cockpit, where the student pilot typically sat in the front (except during instrument training) and the instructor pilot behind him. With a Pratt & Whitney 9-cylinder, 600-horsepower, radial air-cooled engine and capable of a cruising speed of 150 miles per hour and a flight time of some four hours, the AT-6 was a challenging but welcome step up from the basic and primary trainers Faas has piloted previously.

An article in *Flying* magazine detailed the grueling daily routine endured by Faas and his fellow air cadets in those days as they learned to put their AT-6s and AT-10s through their paces:

5:50	First call for reveille
6:00	Reveille
6:30–7:00	Breakfast
7:00–7:55	Preparing room for daily inspection
7:55–9:20	Class in military engineering
9:30–10:40	Study Period
10:40–12:00	Class in ordnance and gunnery
12:05–12:45	Lunch
1:00–1:45	Bus to Stewart Field
1:45–4:00	Flying
4:00–5:00	Ground school
5:15–6:00	Bus to West Point
6:20–6:55	Dinner
7:15–10:00	Call to quarters for study periods
10:00	Taps

On alternate afternoons, when Faas was not flying, his schedule would have looked like this:

1:00–2:00	Study period
2:00–3:00	Class in law or economics
3:15–4:30	Class on unit administration
4:30–6:20	Free time
6:20–6:55	Dinner
7:15–10:00	Call to quarters for study periods
10:00	Taps[10]

The Class of 1944's 50-year memorial book painted an equally grim picture: "Weather cycles made flying infrequent and progress in the autumn was agonizingly slow. The weather was cold and flying in fleece-lined trousers and jackets and boots restricted cockpit mobility and contributed to aircraft accidents."[11]

In short, once November came, there was precious little time—and only on every other day—for Faas to join his teammates on the hardcourt.

Otherwise, he spent his afternoons behind the controls of an AT-6. Most of September was devoted to simply transitioning to the new aircraft and mastering its powerful engine—and remembering to lower the retractable landing gear when coming in for a landing. Then in October came opportunities for cross-country flights to cities such as Allentown and Wilkes-Barre in Pennsylvania and Rome in upstate New York. As winter set in, Faas not only began basketball practices under Coach Kelleher but also started instrument training in the AT-6. Suffice it to say, therefore, that Faas was no stranger to pressure. So perhaps it was Faas who rallied the troops in the locker room on that Wednesday evening.

Or perhaps not. Regardless, whatever or whoever provided the reason or the motivation, it seemed to be a different West Point squad that emerged for the second half. In the first half, Dale Hall had not lodged a single field goal; now, working from the right side of the court, he unleashed a barrage of lethally accurate shots that, one after another, dropped through the rim. In a matter of minutes, he had netted five field goals, complemented by the fast footwork and steady eye of Faas at right guard and the dominating presence of Ed Christl in the paint. The Cadets quickly established a 10-point lead, 39–29.

Their zone defense compromised, the Nittany Lions try to make up for lost ground on the offensive boards. Moskowitz rolled in a pair of layups, followed by a field goal from McNary, to cut Army's lead to four points with seven minutes left. But, basket by basket, the Cadets soon pulled away. By the end of the game, Army's second half rally had beaten back Penn State 49–38. The manager's scorebook credited Hall with 14 points and Christl and Faas with a baker's dozen each. West Point's record was now 5–0, with the Bears of the Coast Guard Academy inbound from New London, Connecticut—and Jack Hennessey hungrier than ever for his first basket of the increasingly long season.

CHAPTER 5

Jack Hennessey

With the arrival of the US Coast Guard Academy's team at West Point on Saturday, January 29, 1944, the stage was set for a cadet-on-cadet clash. And although the Coast Guard Academy might have not enjoyed the same cachet in sporting circles as the more storied programs at its brother academies at West Point and Annapolis, Coast Guard, had, nevertheless, fielded a formidable basketball squad in 1944. Scarcely anyone on Coast Guard's team stood under six feet, and the team strode into the Academy Field House with the confidence born of a 4–2 record—with the last two games won on the road. Coach Nelson "Nels" Nitchman helmed the squad (now that his coaching duties as the Coast Guard Academy's football coach were behind him) and, true to form, had compiled an extensive dossier on each of the West Point players, which he had shared with his own cadets.

As soon as referee David Tobey tossed up the jump ball to begin the game, the cadets of the two academies leapt at each other's proverbial throats. In the opening half, the lead changed so many times, and so quickly, that three different newspapers reported different tallies as they tried to chronicle the game. And, amid the hustle and clashing of bodies on the hardcourt, a Coast Guardsman fouled Jack Hennessey. As the 22-year-old first classman picked himself up off the floor, rose to his full height of 6'2", and took the ball at the foul line, the field house fell silent. Now, finally, after five fruitless games, "Three-Star" Hennessey had a chance to break his four-game scoring drought.

Hennessey had grown up on 91st Street in the Chicago neighborhood known as South Chicago, in a modest two-story brick house a stone's throw from Bessemer Park, "where the gangs of that day—blacks, Mexicans, Polish, Hungarians, and Irish—all had their neighborhood turf and athletic teams." In Hennessey's case, the team was, not surprisingly, the Shamrocks. "We played each other in all sports [and] I worked summers at the Carnegie Steel Mill about a mile away—doing the swing shift, 11:00 pm to 7 a.m.," he reminisced. "That kept me off the streets."[1]

So did school. Hennessey attended first St. Patrick's Elementary School and then Mount Carmel High School, a Catholic parochial school. At Mount Carmel, he carved out a reputation as both an honor student and a star football player in the city's Catholic High School League as well as earning letters in track, swimming, and tennis.

Graduating from Mount Carmel in 1938, Hennessey entered St. Mary's College in Winona, Minnesota, at the young age of 16. At St. Mary's, he lettered in football, baseball, and basketball. In addition, he made the honor roll, was elected class vice president, soloed in the school's glee club, and, as a nod to his majoring in the Greek language, earned the nickname "Greek."

On one memorable day in Minnesota, Hennessey and a fellow student were walking into Winona when a car of local high school girls drove past and then, taking note of them, slowed to a stop. One of the girls knew Hennessey's companion and the car's driver, Mary J. George, in a gesture typical of those days in Winona, offered the two St. Mary's students a ride into town. Mary, the daughter of a local attorney, was an auburn-haired beauty and, wasting no time, Hennessey climbed happily on board. Before the ride was over, he leaned over to Mary and asked, "Hey, Red. How about a date?"

"Mom was a little surprised at how confident he was," Mary's daughter Katie Barbour would later recall.[2] Mary overcome her surprise, however, and accepted Hennessey's bold offer and. Before long, the two were a couple.

Despite Mary's charms, St. Mary's was but a stepping stone to Hennessey's ultimate goal—admission as a cadet at West Point. In those days, he seemed to harbor an additional goal as well, for, in 1940, he signed up for the Civilian Aeronautical Association's Civilian Pilot's Training Program. The CPTP reflected the US government's ambition to begin to build a cadre of pilots capable of manning the kind of air force that Hitler's Luftwaffe was proving, in Europe, to be a decisive factor in modern warfare.

But on October 24, 1940, while practicing forced landings with his 20-year-old instructor pilot, Hennessey crashed along the banks of the nearby Mississippi River. Hennessey suffered, cuts, bruises, and a lacerated kidney; his instructor pilot died of his injuries in the hospital. The crash ended Hennessey's football season, although, fortunately, it did not prevent him from passing his physical exam the following spring when Congressman Raymond S. McKeough nominated him to West Point. In June of 1941, Hennessey headed for New York, leaving Mary to finish her final year of high school. Earning acceptance to Sarah Lawrence College in Yonkers, New York, Mary would make her way to the East Coast the following year.

According to the collective memories of the Class of 1944, Hennessey was among a group of future cadets who spent their last night of freedom at New York's Piccadilly Hotel in Times Square. The Piccadilly, and particularly its colorful Piccadilly Circus Bar, operated under the benevolent oversight of the legendary Ed Wallnau, the hotel's vice president and manager, who took an avuncular interest in visiting cadets, midshipmen, and servicemen. The hotel and its watering holes were renowned as a place where soon-to-be-cadets could enjoy a final round of fun and libations before reporting to West Point. If memories are correct, then it was Hennessey and a contingent from the Piccadilly Hotel that crossed the Hudson on the Weehawken ferry and boarded the very last train to West Point that day to report to West Point. As one might have expected, the Beast Barracks cadre was, by then, primed for the final train of new cadets, and Hennessey and his comrades were met with a veritable roar as their R-Day began.[3]

A week and a half after arriving at the academy, as a Saturday afternoon offered a brief respite from the rigors of training and the hazing upperclassman, the new cadet put pen to paper and wrote home to

"Dear People." "This morning we had our weekly Saturday inspection," Hennessey reported. "We stood at attention for an hour. The tactical officer inspected each plebe individually. We wore our dress gray outfits, caps, breast plates on white shoulder belts, bayonet on waist belt, white gloves, and carried our rifles. After that was over, we stood at attention for another 15 minutes while the officers inspected our room. It's quite a grind."

The next paragraph of the letter, however, revealed that, even at the academy, Hennessey's sense of humor was still undaunted:

> Last night at bath formation, we had a lot of fun. After we take our baths we form and report to the cadet seniors that we "are bathed and fully clothed as ordered, sir." Well, every time I came up to report the senior snickered a little and I'd burst out laughing each time and I'd have to go in and take another shower. So I took four showers last night.

Even so, Hennessey was smart enough to recognize what would spell the difference between success and failure during Beast Barracks. "The keynote of success up here is brains, smartness, and neatness," he concluded. "We really have to keep ourselves and our rooms spoony"—"spoony" being cadet slang for "neat in personal appearance."[4]

In that same letter, Hennessey related that he had an afternoon game with the company's baseball team, and indeed the new cadet wasted no time in carving out an impressive athletic record at West Point. "Jack is one of those rare all-around athletes who have made West Point teams famous," the *Howitzer*, reported, reflecting on his seasons spent with the school's football, basketball, and baseball squads. Hennessey netted letters in each sport, as well as earning stripes as a cadet lieutenant in Company H-2 and election as the vice president of the Class of 1944. He also served on the committee that bore the responsibility for designing and procuring his class ring.

"This son of Eire," the *Howitzer* continued, "who comes from the tough South Side of Chicago, is blessed with a typical Irish humor which wins him innumerable friends wherever he goes and is certain to win a strong feeling of devotion from his men."[5]

Fortunately, as a cadet blessed with a sense of humor, Hennessey had the good fortune to be assigned, as a plebe, to M Company. Here,

Hennessey found himself in the same company as Ed Christl. Despite the outward appearances of staid uniformity, many of the cadet companies were blessed with their own internal culture, and M Company was certainly one of them. The company was housed in a set of barracks known affectionately as "the Lost Fifties," which consisted of a set of narrow four-story structures with the upperclassmen on the lower three floors and the plebes perched up on the fourth floor, all connected by one staircase leading from one floor's landing to the next. These barracks' relative isolation and layout contributed to a certain relaxed attitude in M Company that was envied by plebes in other companies—and, occasionally, led to some episodes of rather free-spirited behavior by the barracks' occupants.

In each of M Company's barracks room, a footlocker sat at the foot of each cadet's bunk, per standard cadet issue and regulations. On one particularly boring evening, as Hennessey and his two roommates looked about their bleak confines, one roommate bet the other that he could squeeze himself into his footlocker. The other roommate took the bet, and, after dumping the collection of extra clothes and gear onto the floor, the first roommate, with a series of impressive contortions, managed to squeeze himself into the footlocker.

At that point, the other roommate, with an evil grin, slammed the top of the footlocker shut and, in a flash, dragged the footlocker out of the barracks room and to the top of the stairway. Then, ignoring the muffled protestations emanating from the footlocker, he shoved the footlocker down the flight of stairs toward the upperclassmen's floor.

With a series of crashes and bangs, the footlocker rocketed down the top flight of stairs, only to detonate into the waiting wall below, whereupon the dazed roommate crawled out of the splintered footlocker and pulled himself erect. Viewing the carnage, Hennessey and the other roommate laughed uproariously at the stunt—that is, until a pair of upperclassmen attracted by the commotion emerged from their third-floor rooms below.

In many companies in the Corps of Cadets, such high jinks would have earned the perpetrators a score or more hours marching "punishment tours" on Central Area—the large swath of paved interior courtyard between the barracks—in full dress, under arms, with their rifles on their shoulders. And, for a moment, as Hennessey and his roommate quieted and as the third roommate's battered head cleared, the three plebes must have wondered if that was going to be their fate as well. But in response the two upperclassmen simply burst out laughing themselves. Fortunately, for Hennessey, the perpetrator, and his battered roommate, theirs was not a company inclined to let military discipline get in the way of a good prank or a healthy sense of humor.[6]

Six games into the 1944 season without a basket was, however, probably beginning to test even Hennessey's sense of humor. As a guard, he knew that Coach Kelleher leaned on him for his defense while looking at Christl, Faas, Hall, and Kenna to rack up the points. Nevertheless, as Hennessey toed the foul line, he wanted a basket, and so did the cadets crowding the stands.

Today, one can almost imagine the moment. West Point forwards Bob Faas and Dale Hall, along with center "Big Ed" Christl, edge up against the free-throw lane, elbowing for position with the tall Coast Guardsmen, while guard Doug Kenna hangs back defensively near half court. Referee Tobey, satisfied with the alignments of the teams' players, tosses the ball to Hennessey. Hennessey bounces the ball in front of him twice or thrice, eyes the rim, and, in a fluid motion, arches the ball skyward with a practiced snap of his wrist. The crowd of spectators holds its collective breath for a split second and then, as the ball swishes cleanly through the net, lets out a thunderous roar.

After Hennessey's successful trip to the foul line, the first half continued in nip-and-tuck fashion, with Coast Guard pulling ahead by a basket as intermission approached. But in the waning seconds of the half, one of the West Pointers streaked in for a layup and, after being fouled, added a free throw. At halftime, the score was Army 25, Coast Guard 23.

West Point's lead only survived the intermission, however, as Coast Guard's Jack Dorsey tied up the game with a corner shot to begin the half. But pressed by Coach Kelleher's man-to-man and likely worn down by their third road trip in as many games, the Bears began to succumb to the Cadets' relentless assault. Even Johnny Austin, Coast Guard's talented forward, was bottled up. He ultimately posted 10 points for his academy's squad, but, as the second half ticked away, the game was all Army's affair. Nitchman's squad only managed a single basket in the final nine minutes of play. With West Point players Kenna, Hall, Faas, and Christl claiming 11, 9, 8, and 6 points, respectively, Coast Guard was simply overwhelmed. With a final score of 55–37 (four of those points coming from Jack Hennessey's work), Coach Kelleher and his Army team not only claimed their sixth straight win of the season but, with the victory, eclipsed last season's total of wins. In 1944, the Kelleher era was looking promising indeed.[7]

*****

For at least one man on the West Point sidelines, however, the ebullience of the win over Coast Guard was tinged with a cold reminder of the deadly serious business that awaited the team's firsties beyond the confines of the Academy Field House. Lt. Col. Kenneth Dawalt, currently a professor of physics at the academy, had drawn additional duty as the officer in charge of the basketball squad. Army's selection of the professor to join the Cadets on their bench was a logical choice; Dawalt had captained West Point's cagers when he was a Cadet himself in 1936.

On the morning of the game against Coast Guard, therefore, Dawalt would have easily recognized the name Robin Epler in the morning's news dispatches. Epler, West Point Class of 1933, had captained the basketball team when Dawalt was but a plebe and, most recently, had been the deputy base commander of Eglin Air Base in Florida. But it was not for basketball that Epler had made the news the morning of January 29, 1944. Rather, the newspapers reported that the previous day, an A-20 Havoc bomber he was flying had lost power in both of its engines and crashed into a field outside of Crestview, Florida. Epler's body was found catapulted out of the wreckage.

*****

Even as Epler's widow was making arrangements to bury the former basketball team captain at Arlington National Cemetery, Christl and his teammates were preparing for their next opponent: West Virginia University. Under first-year coach Harry Lothes, the Mountaineers limped into West Point on February 2, 1944, with a 5–5 record, playing their fourth road game in a row.

Despite the long road trip, West Virginia still showed plenty of fight as the contest commenced. The lead changed hands a half-dozen times in the first six minutes of play as the Cadets and the Mountaineers battled one another. But a competitive six minutes seemed all that West Virginia could muster, and Dale Hall and Doug Kenna, two of Coach Kelleher's footballers, turned the evening into a showcase for their basketball talents. Hall posted nine field goals for 18 points on the evening; his classmate Kenna added 15 points. By halftime, the score was 32–17, Army.

In the second half, with victory seemingly assured, Kelleher began rotating in his second- and third-stringers. By the time the night was over, even firsties such as Spike Geltz and Alan Weston were making rare appearances during a game, much to the delight of their classmates. When the buzzer finally sounded, the score was 58–31, and Army was the owner of a seven-game winning streak—and, once again, due for a road trip to a hostile venue.

*****

The last time West Point had opened a season with seven straight wins, it was 1938, with that streak broken by Yale in the eighth game. And with West Point embarking on a rare road trip for the eighth game of the 1944 season, the University of Rochester hoped to play a similar role as spoiler. Indeed, the blackboard in Rochester's locker room read "Ambush Army," and the team welcomed Colgate head coach Carl Lawrence's assurances to his fellow upstate civilian collegians that the Cadets were overrated.

Bob Gebhardt, who was enjoying a breakout season as one of Rochester's forwards, needed little such motivation. He had kept the bench warm last year at Fordham back when Ed Kelleher was his coach; now he would like nothing better than to prove that Kelleher had overlooked him at Rose Hill. After all, he had, most impressively, scored 52 points in his last two games. Rochester's captain, Bob Mulvihill, was also a former Fordham player, as was Johnny Bach.[8]

Rochester's home court was the River Campus Palestra, built 14 years earlier. As Kelleher and his traveling squad of 12 cadets arrived in Rochester early in the afternoon of Saturday, February 5, for their 8:30 p.m. evening game against the Yellowjackets, dark gray clouds, pregnant with the threat of snow, hung overhead. The temperature registered in the thirties, but, with a brisk wind coming off of Lake Ontario, Rochester felt even colder.

At game time, however, the temperature inside the Palestra was almost tropical, as a record-setting sold-out crowd of three thousand Rochester faithful packed the arena. The bookies were carrying the Cadets at nine-point favorites, but apparently they had not shared their doubts about Rochester with their starting five.[9] From the tip-off, the Yellowjackets lived up to their name, swarming and stinging the interlopers who had invaded their home court.

Clearly determined to make his presence known to his former coach, Rochester's Gephardt recorded the game's first two points with a pair of free throws. But Ed Christl may have had an axe of his own to grind that evening. After all, Gebhardt's Fordham teammates had drubbed Christl's team 68–42 the previous year, and a competitor like Christl had a long memory, even when an opponent was in a new uniform. Christl responded by seizing a rebound and banking in a basket and then punctuating Army's first score with a long field goal from the corner. Teammate Doug Kenna, who played fullback for West Point's football team, then plowed in for a layup to bring the score to 6–2, Army.

Undaunted, Gebhardt replied with a pair of baskets from the corner, tying the game. Dale Hall, displaying his own remarkable athleticism, slammed a rare dunk to bring the score to Army 8, Rochester 6, only to give up a pair of baskets to Gebhardt and his fellow Fordham refugee Johnny Bach and, in doing so, lose the lead.

But now Hall came alive—never a good development for a team opposing West Point. The Army forward scored with a layup and a pair of other baskets, complemented by another score from Doug Kenna. In a matter of moments, the score was Army 16, Rochester 12—but not for long. Again, Gebhardt and Bach scored, knotting the contest at 16–16.

Hall responded to the challenge by dropping in a pair of shots to move the score to Army 20, Rochester 16. But Rochester's center, Howard Werner, was fouled and claimed a free throw. Then again Gebhardt and Bach scored, giving the Yellowjackets a 21–20 lead. By now, the game, fast-moving and furious from the start, slowed down with a series of fouls called on Rochester. Bill Ekberg, who was spelling Christl at center, capitalized on the opportunity and sank a trio of free throws to give Army a 23–21 lead as the Yellowjackets' starting center fouled out and took a seat on the bench.

Paul McKee, Rochester's second-string center, embraced the opportunity fate had presented in front of the sell-out crowd in the Palestra. He was a Marine Corps V-12er who had formerly starred on Syracuse University's football team (and who would one day play for the Washington Redskins). In short order, McKee executed a layup to tie the game once again, and, when Army responded with a set shot from Hall and a free throw from Harle Damon to pull ahead by three, he countered with three free throws to knot the score once more. But with a minute left in the half, Ekberg pivoted from the center to net a basket, complemented a moment later with a pretty one-hander by Hall from beyond the foul line. At intermission, the score stood at Army 30, Rochester 26.

Army returned to the floor after the halftime break and quickly took full control of the game. For the final 20 minutes of the contest, Dale Hall continued to add to his point total (he would eventually claim 23 for the night), complemented by the work of speedy Bob Faas and Jack Hennessey. The latter used the occasion to add a pair of field goals and a free throw to his season's total. But, other than Hall, Army's standout was center Bill Ekberg. With 14 points, the tall Minnesotan had his best game of the season so far. And although Gephardt would ultimately be able to post 18 points for the Yellowjackets, supplemented by 10 from McKee, it would not be enough. In the end, Army powered to a 57–43 victory.[10] The Cadets' season now stood at a remarkable eight wins and no losses.

CHAPTER 6

Panthers, Statesmen, Quakers, and Wildcats

Returning to West Point after the Rochester road trip, the Cadets next faced the University of Pittsburgh on February 9 on Army's home court. The legendary H. C. "Doc" Carlson had run Pittsburgh's basketball program since 1922. Sportswriters had long enjoyed reporting on the physician's unorthodox techniques with his teams. Hoping to coax the best possible performances out of his players, Carlson's experiments had ranged from feeding his players ice cream in the locker room at halftime to giving them oxygen on the bench. But in 1944, with a 5–5 team comprising mainly untried freshman and sophomores that he had christened his "Tiny Toughies," it would take far more than vanilla ice creams and inhalation of oxygen to best Kelleher's Cadets.

Army's squad, clearly bigger and stronger than Carlson's, never let the Panthers earn a lead. The Tiny Toughies, led by team captain Walt Jones (who was wearing a mask to protect a broken jaw), battled as best they could, however, and, eight minutes into the game, the score was only 12–6. Nevertheless, bit by bit, the Cadets pulled away, aided by the Panthers' woefully inaccurate shooting. Yet at halftime the scoreboard showed Army 25, Pittsburgh 10.

The second half only brought more bad news for the Pitt Panthers. With their erratic scoring efforts—despite the best efforts of feisty Bill Cieply at guard—shut down by Army's stalwart defense, Carlson's squad faded quickly as Ed Christl, Dale Hall, Doug Kenna, and Harle Damon combined, by the end of the game, to share 53 points among the four of them.

"Cadets Whip Pitt, 66–32—Some Army!" the next day's *Pittsburgh Press* declared unapologetically. The *Philadelphia Inquirer* was even more brutal: "Army Slaughters Pitt Panthers."[1]

*****

In the wake of their drubbing of Pittsburgh, the Cadets, now 9–0, were scheduled to host the Hobart College Statesmen for a Saturday afternoon game on February 12, 1944. Chip Royal, the sports features editor for the Associated Press, was already on campus. In short order, he hammered out a story that was soon dispatched nationwide via the AP wire.

"You can't set foot inside this military reservation these days without hearing about the Cadets' great basketball team," Royal reported. "Yes sir and ma'am, the Army is really rolling on the shiny courts."

"The West Pointers credit it all to Ed Kelleher, the civilian coach they imported from Fordham University," wrote Royal. "Kelleher says no. He points out that he inherited a veteran team … and that it was due to click anyway this year. Maybe so, but the cadets still give all the credit to the new coach."

"Ed has taught the boys a fast break they didn't have last year," Royal admitted, "has developed a defense that is a tough nut to crack, and has helped the shooters on the fine points of caging the round ball."[2]

With sportswriters such as Royal on the scene at West Point, Kelleher's Cadets did not disappoint at game time the following day. For a quick moment at the beginning of the contest, the Hobart Statesmen took the lead, but the lead was fleeting. Once again, the footballers from the Class of 1945, Doug Kenna and Dale Hall, amassed a crushing collection of points—in this game, each scored 20. Hobart's entire team was unable to match that output, and the 13 points that Bob Faas added to the total only salted the wound further. At the end of the contest, Royal's fellow sports scribes reported a final score of Army 69, Hobart 36—and duly noted that Army's 10-game winning streak was the longest it had enjoyed in 20 years.[3]

*****

On February 16, it was time for the Quakers of the University of Pennsylvania to try to their luck against the red-hot Cadets. As the afternoon game time approached, Penn's coach, Don Kellett (football fans might recognize him as a future general manager and president of the NFL's Baltimore Colts), must have taken some comfort from his team's four-game winning streak, including a pair of home-and-away wins against Columbia. In fact, Penn boasted a 9–3 record here in this final stretch of its season.

In addition to momentum, Kellett could also count on sophomore forward and team captain Frank Crossin. A native of the blue-collar town of Luzerne, in northeastern Pennsylvania, Crossin had earned the nickname "Chink" for the sound that his frequent baskets made on Luzerne's playgrounds as he sent the ball arching accurately through chain-link hoops. He had arrived on Penn's campus in the fall of 1942 after claiming the record for the state's highest-scoring high schooler. And, three weeks before that day's game against Army, he had set a new Penn record when he posted 29 points against Swarthmore College.

But Army was no Swarthmore, and Kellett had just lost his other star player, Tom Mears, to naval flight training. Nevertheless, for the first eight minutes of the contest, the Quakers hung gamely as they and the Cadets swapped the lead three times. But, at the 10-minute mark, the scoreboard read Army 17, Visitors 8. By the intermission, Kelleher's Cadets had established a 31–17 lead.[4]

Crossin and company, however, were not ready to admit defeat, and the Penn forward came out from the halftime break to swish a quartet of one-handed shots in short order. An increasingly nervous crowd in the Academy Field House watched Penn pull within five of the home team by the time six minutes had elapsed on the game clock.

But then, as so many teams had seen happen before, Army slowly began to pull away. Halfway through the second period, the Cadets had a 41–31 lead, and, in the words of the *Philadelphia Inquirer*, "the final ten minutes proved a nightmare for the Quakers. The lid was clamped firmly on their basket, while almost everything the Cadets threw up came swishing through the hoop."[5] Once again, the third classmen on the Army squad dominated. Dale Hall recorded 18 points for the evening, Doug Kenna posted 17, and West Point notched a 55–38 victory. But, for the firsties, Bob Faas logged three baskets and a free throw, while Jack

Hennessey put eight points on the board. And even though Ed Christl did not score, he still garnered a laudatory sketch and accompanying prose from famed sports cartoonist and writer Tom "Pap" Paprocki, who was exercising his creative talents for the Associated Press.

"All season the cadets have played the same brand of basketball," Paprocki wrote. "A fast-breaking team, they have run their opponents ragged and then exploded with a scoring spree that smothered the opposition."

"While the Army basketball team has been romping through its all-victorious campaign, the spotlight has been focused on the individuals whose names became familiar to sports fans because of their deeds on the gridiron last fall," he observed. "The Cadets' captain, Ed Christl, moved along without fuss or fanfare to set up the plays that were to fashion the long string of triumphs."

"Christl isn't the spectacular type at all," Paprocki reported. "He does his job efficiently and, if he misses the headlines, he has the satisfaction of knowing that his teammates appreciate what an able performer he is."[6]

"Undefeated West Point Quintet Routs Pennsylvania for Eleventh Victory," shouted the *Hartford Daily Courant* in the wake of the Army win.[7] But Ed Kelleher knew that he was facing another tough opponent that coming Saturday—the Wildcats of Villanova University.

*****

On February 19, Villanova took to the court at West Point. Alexander Severance—who held a law degree from Temple University and also taught business law at Villanova—coached the visitors and, in his seven years as head coach at Villanova, had never seen a losing season. His Wildcats had even made it to the Final Four of the inaugural NCAA Championship Tournament in 1938.

But 1944 had proven to be a difficult year for Villanova. Severance filled the team's schedule with games against both traditional opponents and teams born of the exigencies of the current conflict—the US Marine detachment at the Philadelphia Naval Yard, the recruits of the Sampson Naval Training Station in Geneva, New York, and the soldiers of Fort Dix, New Jersey—and the military teams had proved as challenging as their civilian counterparts. By the time the Wildcats reached West Point, they were dragging a hard-earned 9–8 record with them.

In the winter of 1944, however, West Point was no place for a battered team to find a respite. Nevertheless, as Severance's team began its game with Kelleher's Cadets, they showed no sign of a squad looking for relief or sympathy. They scored first and, for the first full 11 minutes of the contest, kept Army scoreless. With seven minutes left in the half, the score registered Villanova 10, Army 6, as Wildcats guard Phil Jakeway led the visitors' assault on West Point.

Unfortunately for the visitors, Jakeway soon ran into foul trouble, and, with him slowed, Army capitalized on the opportunity. Working together, Dale Hall and Harle Damon combined to ultimately push the score to Army 13, Villanova 12 at the half.

The game's second half began at a furious pace, with the two teams' netting a total of 16 points within five minutes. In that time, the lead changed five times as Hall, with help from Ed Christl, bringing the score to Army 23, Villanova 18. But fouls eventually sidelined Jakeway, and, in the final twelve minutes of the game, the Wildcats offense sputtered to an ignoble end. As the Cadets continued to add to their lead, Villanova managed to add only a pair of baskets. As the game ended, the final score was Army 34, Villanova 22. West Point had logged its twelfth win.[8]

The victory, however, threatened to be a costly one for the Cadets. The game had been hard fought by both teams, and, in the course of the contest, Ed Christl had suffered a broken right thumb.[9] Fortunately, West Point's schedule showed a week-long hiatus before Army's next game—against New York University—and Kelleher undoubtedly welcomed a quiet week to let his star center's thumb begin to heal.

*****

Overseas, however, the ensuing week would be anything but quiet. The day after the Cadets' win over Villanova, Lt. Gen. Carl "Tooey" Spaatz (West Point Class of 1914) unleashed Operation Argument against strategic bombing targets across Nazi Germany and occupied Europe—particularly those factories and facilities that supported the production of enemy aircraft. Just the previous month, Spaatz had taken reins of the newly formed command United States Strategic Air Forces in Europe. After his fliers had endured weeks of lousy weather, he finally had his chance to unleash his B-17 Flying Fortress and B-24 Liberator bombers against his German foe when the skies cleared on February 20.

For six days, massive formations of US bombers pounded enemy targets. At times, as many as a thousand Flying Fortresses and Liberators, escorted by scores of P-38 Lighting, P-47 Thunderbolts, and P-51 Mustang fighters, were in the air, complemented by nocturnal bombing missions flown by Great Britain's Royal Air Force. By the end of the operation—which became known as "Big Week"—US airmen and their RAF brethren had flown 6,200 sorties and dropped some nineteen thousand tons of bombs on enemy airfields, airframe assembly facilities, and ball-bearing plants.[10] The effort cost the Allies 370 heavy bombers and 38 fighters, but at this point the strategists knew that in the developing war of aerial attrition, even losses as heavy as that would ultimately overwhelm the Luftwaffe.

Of course, none of those air strategists asked Bob Faas or any of the other 169 air cadets in the Class of 1944 what they might have thought of such grim arithmetic—or bomber losses in such operations that numbered one out of every ten. In the words of the poet, theirs was not to reason why. Besides, as Big Week drew to a close and the Allies tallied destroyed targets and lost aircraft, Faas had a far more urgent matter at hand: Saturday's basketball game against New York University.

CHAPTER 7

Army Versus Navy

With New York University scheduled for West Point's opponent for the Cadets' 13th game on February 26, superstitious Army fans might have fairly wondered if it was time for Kelleher's luck to run out. And if anyone was capable of tripping up the Cadets' winning streak, it was NYU head coach Howard Cann, the 6'4", 217-pound former Olympic shot putter who had coached the team for the last two decades. In those 20 years in Manhattan, Cann had suffered only a single losing season; nine years earlier, he had witnessed his team crowned national champions by the Helms Athletic Foundation – which, while neither a foundation nor blessed with any particular credentials, had managed to self-assuredly establish itself, for a time, as the arbiter of national sporting titles.

Thirteenth game or not, Kelleher did not believe in bad luck. Instead, he put his faith in his man-to-man defense, fast breaks, and aggressive rebounding. Ten minutes into the first half, the score was Army 12, NYU 5. The Cadets remained in control for the remainder of the half, and at halftime the score read Army 25, NYU 14, despite the best efforts of NYU stars Sid Tanenbaum (destined to play for the New York Knicks) and freshman John Derderian.

"The deadly eye of Cadet Dale Hall was enough to carry the soldiers' colors to victory," reported the Associated Press, "as he poured in long set-shots and under-the-basket maneuvers for eighteen points to garner high-scoring honors."[1] In the end, the Cadets clinched a 46–36 victory, although Cann's players claimed a moral victory in keeping West Point's margin of victory to only 10 points—its lowest of the season.

*****

After NYU came the Terrapins of the University of Maryland. "Veteran coach Burton Shipley thought he would never see the day when 17-year-olds would grace an Old Line varsity quintet, but, with the loss of all but one of his lettermen, the court mentor had little choice." So reported 1944's *The Terrapin*, the yearbook for the University of Maryland. As it suggested, Burton Shipley, in the gathering twilight of his 27-year coaching career at Maryland, found himself in an almost impossible situation.

"Armed service demands blasted cage personnel off Maryland's campus as effectively as Allied air force block busters are wiping out German cities," lamented Baltimore's *Evening Sun*. "There isn't a varsity man left from last year; indeed, only one squad member remains, six-foot Ermy Engelbert, who is the tallest man on the Richie Coliseum floor."[2]

By the time the Terrapins arrived at West Point, the Terrapins were already on their way to an embarrassing 4–14 record, and Coach Shipley, having suffered fractures of both of his legs when his daughter's skittish new pony threw him from its cart and into a gatepost, had been sidelined. The university's lacrosse coach, Al Heagy, had drawn the unfortunate duty of the taking the young Terrapins to West Point to face unbeaten Army.

In short, Maryland did not appear to be a difficult opponent for Army, but, in this second to the last game of the season, Kelleher was not prepared to let his guard down for a second. He knew that after Maryland his cadets would face the Naval Academy and that, for West Point, the annual tilt against Navy constituted a season in and of itself. The prospect of an overconfident Army squad looking past the Terrapins—and perhaps even being upset—was not a possibility that Kelleher wanted to consider.

Fortunately for him, the opening moments of the Army-Maryland game on Wednesday, March 1, 1944, quickly put those fears to rest. Ed Christl was still out nursing his broken thumb, but his replacement, Bill Ekberg, more than made up for his fellow Minnesotan's absence.

Ekberg posted a season-high 17 points for the game—but even that total paled in comparison to Dale Hall's 32 points. When one added such sums to the points rung up by Doug Kenna, Jack Hennessey, and Bob Faas—8, 6, and 5, respectively—it was no wonder that West Point set a new scoring record that afternoon. By the end of the contest, the score was West Point 85, Maryland 22. The more statistically attuned scribes noted that, with 832 points for the season, West Point had surpassed its old record of 765 points in 1922's 18-game campaign.[3] West Point's record now stood at 14–0. But there was still one final game to play: the climactic battle against the Midshipmen of Navy.

*****

Back in 1943, the Cadets had arrived at the Naval Academy for their annual tilt with Navy burdened by a 4–10 record and, to make matters worse, with Faas nursing a broken right wrist. The Midshipmen, at 6–7, were hardly enjoying a stellar season themselves that year but, on their home court, were favored over the visitors. But, hungry to claim a victory and redeem their season, the Cadets had played their collective hearts out on the court at Annapolis and, in the end, humbled Navy 56–45.[4]

On March 4, 1944, however, it was Army's turn to play host. This time, the Midshipmen entered the Academy Field House—packed to capacity with 5,500 cadets, newspapermen, and other spectators—as the underdogs. Nevertheless, as anyone familiar with the rivalry knew, it was anyone's game to win or lose. On one hand, the momentum of Army's winning streak was oiled with a desire to revenge the previous fall's humiliating 14–0 football loss on the gridiron to Navy. Vengeance was a powerful motivator for Cadets such as Hennessey, Hall, and, in particular, Kenna, whose injured knee had kept him sidelined against the Middies during the fall football contest.

On the other hand, Navy was enjoying a stellar season itself in 1944. Captained by Ken Longnecker, its only losses had come to the University of Pennsylvania and the college-veteran-leavened ranks of the Bainbridge (Maryland) Naval Training Station and North Carolina Pre-Flight teams. Furthermore, it could count on the veteran leadership of head coach

John Wilson, a master diagnostician who had helmed Navy for the past 18 seasons with the fierce demeanor of a Marine Corps drill sergeant.

Playing with a fury seemingly saved for this very moment of the season, the Cadets tore into their Navy counterparts. The game marked Christl's return to the hardcourt after missing the past two games with his fractured thumb, and he clearly intended to leave his mark in the Academy Field House during his last game in the Army black, gray, and gold. Within 10 minutes, thanks to Christl's pivot work and aggressive rebounding and Hall's and Kenna's deadly accurate shooting, Army had netted 20 points.

Navy, on the other hand, only managed to post a measly four points, garnered by a basket forced by Navy plebe Dick "Monster" Duden and a pair of free throws. Jack Hennessey was the bane of the Midshipmen's offense—"turning in his usually unnoticed workmanlike job of tipping potential Navy baskets as they left the shooters' hands and generally keeping the sailors from breaking under the hoop."[5]

By the halftime break, the score was Army 29, Navy 11, and, after the halftime break, Army picked up where it left off. Hall and Kenna both sank set shots, bringing the score to 33–11. At this point, the game threatened to become an embarrassing debacle for the visiting squad.

Allison Danzig, a courtly reporter for the *New York Times* known primarily for his coverage of tennis—he was the journalist who had coined the terms "Grand Slam" and "ace" in that sport—was on hand for the game. "The cadets' speed, ball handling and marksmanship … were too much for Navy," he wrote. "The midshipmen were off in their shooting and unlucky in the many shots that rolled out of the hoop."[6]

But back at the Naval Academy, a flag emblazoned with the words "DON'T GIVE UP THE SHIP"—a treasured artifact from the War of 1812—had hung for decades, and Navy's basketball squad had no intention of surrendering without a fight. And when Jack Hennessey incurred his third foul and Coach Kelleher pulled him from the game rather than risk a fourth (which, under the rules of the day, would have been his final foul), Navy, saw its opportunity.

"Without three-star Johnny, the change in Army was unbelievable," declared *Chicago Tribune* scribe Dick Young, a tough sportswriter legendary for his refusal to pull punches. "Navy charged through at will, breaking for clean cracks at the hoop and getting away unharried shots from the outside."[7]

Applying relentless pressure both offensively and defensively, Navy added five points to the scoreboard, suffered a basket from Hall, and then, in reply, added another five. Suddenly, it seemed, the score was Army 37, Navy 21, and the Middies seemed to be mounting an improbable comeback. But thanks to Kenna's hard-nosed play and accurate shooting, the Cadets managed to keep the them at bay as the score climbed to 43–28. For a moment, the home crowd drew a collective sigh of relief, even as the fatigue began to show on the faces of the scrambling Army cagers.

Determined to smash the visitors' hopes, Kelleher dispatched Hennessey back into the game—only to see his star defensive player immediately collect his fourth and final foul.

"Then, the Army lads plummeted like a released blockbuster," Young wrote. "With Longnecker and Duden breaking in for layups, practically unmolested, the Middies converted an apparent rout into a sizzling battle." Within a matter of minutes, Navy clawed its way back into the game, bringing the score to Army 44, Navy 36. "The once confident Army band, which earlier seemed only concerned with rubbing in the rout, was now fighting frantically to preserve its margin," Young reported.[8] In the stands, Army's fans—particularly the cadets—were in an uproar, shouting and stomping as they implored the home team to hold on for a victory.

At this point, with the ball in hand, the Cadets went into a solid freeze at midcourt, forcing valuable time off of the clock. Then Kenna, seizing on an open look, dropped in a field goal. He drew a foul on the play and added a free throw to the effort. Now the score, with barely a minute left, was 47–36.

Even then, however, Navy was not yet done. Christl fouled Longnecker, which sent Army's team captain to join Hennessey on the bench with four fouls. Christl's Navy counterpart capitalized by sinking his two free throws. Now the score stood Army 47, Navy 38.

Scrambling for the ball in the ensuing possession, Longnecker again pushed in for a basket. With only twenty seconds on the clock and the

Cadets wisely giving him a wide berth to avoid another foul, he rolled in an easy layup. The basket brought Navy to within seven.

But that was as close as Navy would get. With the final seconds ticking down, the Midshipmen were simply out of time. The game ended with a score of Army 47, Navy 40.

"A terrific roar of triumph went up from the stands as the game ended and the cadets poured out onto the floor to congratulate the team and Coach Kelleher, for Army's most successful season in 20 years," Danzig reported.[9]

"Army's swift-striking, high-scoring basketball battalion is the only major undefeated basketball team in the nation this morning—and they can thank Cadet John Hennessey, who has averaged fewer than two points a game," wrote Young for his readers the next day back in Chicago. "Never was the value of an overlooked, unpretentious guard more strikingly illustrated than in the tingling tussle at West Point yesterday. …Throughout its spectacular season …, the mantle of glory was draped on the muscular shoulders of sharpshooting Dale Hall, who has set an academy scoring record. But, though Hall yesterday added 13 markers to complete his terrific total at 273, the crowd finally realized that it has always been Hennessey who has meant the difference between victory and defeat. And they realized it as Hennessey was notching just three points against the Midshipmen yesterday."[10]

*****

For the first time since 1923, and the last time in the 75 years since, West Point's basketball team had completed the perfect season. As Dick Young, Allison Danzig, and sportswriters across the country noted, the Cadets were the only major college basketball team to run the table with an undefeated record in 1944. But there were plenty of universities and colleges who could look back on their seasons with justifiable pride—and, in fact, not count their seasons as yet completed. Schools such as Oklahoma A&M, Canisius College, DePaul University, Muhlenberg College, the University of Kentucky, the University of Utah, Bowling Green State University, and Army's recent adversary, St. John's University, all earned invitations to the NIT—considered in 1944 the premier postseason tournament in college basketball. In addition, a cohort consisting of Utah (invited when a car accident injured two University of Arkansas players) and seven other schools—Catholic University, Dartmouth College, Ohio State, Temple University, Iowa State, the University of Missouri, and Pepperdine University—earned berths in the sixth annual NCAA tournament. St. John's would ultimately claim victory in the NIT; on March 28, 1944, the University of Utah won the NCAA's trophy.

But Ed Christl, Bob Faas, Jack Hennessey, and the rest of West Point's undefeated 1944 basketball squad were absent from both of those tournaments, even though a slew of invitations to national and regional tournaments had been tendered.[11] And even though the Helms Athletic Foundation crowned West Point the nation's top collegiate basketball team for the 1944 season, the accolade, in the absence of an NIT or NCAA tournament appearance, likely rang as hollow to the Cadets in 1944 as it probably does today. With respect to the champions of 1944, today's record books speak of St. John's and the University of Utah; Army is, at best, a footnote. So why did West Point not take up the gauntlet thrown by the NIT and NCAA selection committees and battle for a national championship in 1944?

Although research has uncovered no single conclusive document or comment from West Point's or the Army's top brass of the day on the topic, the absence of such a "smoking gun" may well be because West Point's participation—or, more precisely, lack thereof—in such postseason tournaments was such a foregone conclusion that it did not in the day merit much discussion at all. After all, in 1942 and 1943, even the national spectacle of the annual Army-Navy football games had been moved from Philadelphia's Municipal Stadium to be played, instead, at Annapolis and West Point, respectively. In those days, civilians on the American home front faced, among other wartime realities and challenges, gasoline and tire rationing, mandatory 35-mile-per-hour speed limits intended to conserve both gasoline and tires, and the arm-twisting dictates of the Office of Defense Transportation (ODT) that, among other measures, divided travel into three distinct categories: "necessary," "permissible," and "nonessential." The final category—"nonessential"—was defined as "travel that cannot in any way help us win the war." Among its examples:

"trips to sport events." "The pleasure and convenience of normal travel which we must give up now are among the 'real' costs of the war—like the meat we do not eat and the shoes we cannot buy, these are things we cannot have while the war lasts," lectured the ODT in a pamphlet titled *How Can We Win the Battle of Transportation?*[12]

Obviously the ODT's strictures did not prevent the playing of the NIT and the NCAA tournaments—or prevent their participant teams from traveling to the tournaments' venue, Madison Square Garden in New York City. But perhaps West Point's leadership was not so much worried about what ODT dictated, or did not dictate, in black and white what colleges could or could not do. Perhaps, instead, West Point's leadership was attuned to the public relations challenges that could arise from its students appearing in the Garden instead of on the battlefields of Europe or the Pacific. After all, as cadets themselves, they had memorized a script of "plebe knowledge" titled "Schofield's Definition of Discipline" that declared, in part, "He who feels the respect which is due to others cannot fail to inspire in them respect for himself. While he who feels, and hence manifests, disrespect towards others, especially his subordinates, cannot fail to inspire hatred against himself."

Would playing one, two, or three more basketball games at the NIT or NCAA tournaments have been considered, in certain quarters, the kind of disrespect—to service personnel and their families—that "Schofield's Definition of Discipline" was warning against? Perhaps. Or perhaps not. Perhaps the academy's athletic budget simply did not stretch to cover a week for the basketball team in New York City. All that can be said for sure is that in the wake of Army's exciting win over Navy, Army's athletic director, Col. Lawrence "Biff" Jones, confirmed to the media that Army had "refused all invitations for post-season games" and that, in particular, "the invitation to play in the Garden invitation tournament [the NIT] could not be accepted."[13]

*****

If the end of their collegiate basketball careers on March 4, 1944, stung Christl, Faas, and Hennessey, perhaps they drew some relief from the promise that in a hundred days they would be graduating from West Point. As fate would have it, Kelleher's seniors were, that same Saturday night, able to cap their win over Navy by enjoying their class's 100th Night Show.

For the Class of 1944, the 100th Night Show marked a tradition that dated back to 1884. Put on by the first classmen, the show generally consisted of an irreverent collection of skits, musical numbers, and performances, usually tied around a common theme of inside jokes and begrudging nostalgia—and, given the composition of the all-male Corps of Cadets, invariably a number of cadets in drag to play any requisite female roles. Such was certainly the case with the Class of 1944's show, which, in case of foreshadowing that West Point could not have appreciated at the time, envisioned the West Point of the year 2000—a West Point, they jokingly imagined, that would include female cadets in its ranks.

After the show, those first class cadets fortunate enough to have dates—or "drags," in the cadets' jargon—would have escorted the young ladies to the evening's hop—the 100th Night ball. Their numbers may have likely have included Hennessey, escorting Mary George, who had, since Hennessey's arrival at West Point nearly three years earlier, remained his "OAO"—his "one and only."

Mary was more than simply Hennessey's OAO, however. By now, she was his fiancée. The two had long discussed marrying as soon as Hennessey graduated from West Point and, one evening in New York City, had continued such conversations as they rode through Central Park in a hansom cab. To Mary's surprise, Hennessey, who had been having similar conversations with his parents, shared an unwelcome piece of news with her.

"My parents think we are too young to marry," Hennessey said unhappily.

"Well, you can do what your parents say and we'll just forget about this," Mary replied. She then ordered the cab to stop, jumped down, and strode off. Hennessey followed her in close pursuit and, in short order, the couple set a wedding date of June 10, 1944, which would shortly follow Hennessey's graduation.[14]

At the time, Christl had his own OAO – Virginia Johnson, a hometown girl from Minneapolis. She had graduated from the Academy of Holy Angels, an all-girl Catholic parochial school in Minneapolis, before attending the University of Minnesota. One suspects that Faas, based on his reputation, was not dateless to the hop either.

Another part of West Point's storied traditions was a repertoire of songs learned by each cadet as part of his plebe knowledge. Among those songs, the old tune "Army Blue"—which dated back to the Class of 1865—would have seemed particularly poignant on an occasion such as 100th Night. Perhaps, therefore, in various nooks or steps or stoops on the academy grounds, groups of First Classmen gathered to serenade their dates or maybe just to amuse one another as they sang the old song. In the modern khaki and olive-drab world of 1944, the title was charmingly anachronistic, but the sentiments it expressed would have resonated nevertheless with the soon-to-graduate cadets:

> We've not much longer here to stay,
> For in a month or two,
> We'll bid farewell to "Kaydet Grey,"
> And don the "Army Blue."
> Army Blue, Army Blue,
> Hurrah for the Army Blue,
> We'll bid farewell to "Kaydet Grey,"
> And don the "Army Blue."
> With pipe and song we'll jog along.
> Till this short time is through,
> And all among our jovial throng,
> Have donned the Army Blue.
> ...
>
> To the ladies who come up in June,
> We'll bid a fond adieu,
> Here's hoping they be married soon,
> And join the Army too.
> ...
>
> 'Twas the song we sang in old plebe camp,
> When first our grey was new,
> The song we sang on summer nights,
> That song of Army Blue.
> ...

Now, fellows, we must say goodbye,
We've stuck our four years thru,
Our future is a cloudless sky,
We'll don the Army Blue.
Army Blue, Army Blue,
Hurrah for the Army Blue,
We'll bid farewell to "Kaydet Grey,"
And don the "Army Blue."[15]

CHAPTER 8

Graduation and Invasion

With the departure of Ed Christl, Bob Faas, Jack Hennessey, and the rest of Kelleher's basketball squad at season's end, the Academy Field House fell silent—but not for long. Branch Rickey dispatched his Brooklyn Dodgers north to Harriman State Park, where they enjoyed $2.75 filet mignons at the Bear Park Inn and, when the weather was too bad for outdoor practice, hopped into station wagons for the short ride to West Point. Up at the academy, the now-vacated field house provided the Dodgers with an enviable indoor training facility.

Despite the presence of the Dodgers on campus, the firsties put their noses back in their books and grinded through their last months of classes. In Hennessey's case, he had a final sports season to complete. "Three-Star" Hennessey traded the hardcourt for first base on the baseball diamond. The team took advantage of the Dodgers' presence on campus for a series of spring practice games, emerged none the worse for wear, and then embarked on a 9–2 season marred only by losses to Columbia and Navy.

In addition to baseball, academics still demanded attention, of course, but, on the military side of the ledger, Faas continued with his flight training—at least when the unruly spring weather permitted. He followed instrument training with combat maneuvers and, in May, began flying P-40s—obsolete fighters but actual fighters nevertheless. That same month, he and the other air cadets moved out to Stewart Field.

For their part, Christl and Hennessey and other "ground cadets" journeyed to New York City to observe air defense units in and around the city. The defensive array they inspected ran the gamut from World War I–era barrage balloons above Coney Island to 90-mm guns in revetments along the beaches, with a wide variety of 40-mm Bofors guns, .50-caliber machine guns, height finders, and radar sets thrown in the mix as well.

As the semester wound down and graduation approached, the Class of 1944 enjoyed more restful diversions. Hops were held each weekend at the cadet gymnasium, movies showed each Saturday and Sunday afternoon, and musicians such as Fred Waring came to campus to play gigs.

Then came Branch Night. Christl, Hennessey, and the other 297 ground cadets assembled in the auditorium at the Department of Military Topography and Graphics, where they were confronted by a huge blackboard chalked with branches and vacancies for new lieutenants as determined by the War Department. The air cadets such as Faas knew, of course, which branch they had selected, but for the ground cadets the selection of a branch was deadly serious business. And since branch selections were not only limited by the number of slots available in each branch but also done by order of merit, the cadets with the higher class rankings were at a decided advantage.

Traditionally, the Corps of Engineers was the most sought-after branch, and for the Class of 1944 it was no exception. Even though there were 54 engineer slots available, by the time John Tkacik, ranked 82nd in the class, came up to make his pick, there was only one left. He happily took it.

From then on, as selections continued down the roster by class standing, fewer and fewer cadets were able to select the branch of their first, or even second, choosing. Nevertheless, Ed Christl was able to pick Field Artillery. John Hennessey selected Infantry.

By the end of the process, the selection process came down to the last two cadets and only two slots left, in the Coast Artillery Corps. In peacetime the Coast Artillery had been deemed a desirable assign-ment—who would not want to be stationed in Charleston, Pensacola, or on the Virginia coast instead of at some dusty fort in the Southwest? But in wartime no one wanted to be relegated to some operational backwater—thus the remaining Coast Artillery slots. And so, for the last two cadets in the order of merit, their selections were foregone conclusions. They were destined for the Coast Artillery.

Nevertheless, sticking to formality, the officer in charge called out Robert Cowherd's name. He was met with a stony silence from Cowherd (who was perhaps irritated at being bested in the class rankings by his twin brother Richard, who, at the rank of 99, had long since chosen the Armored Cavalry), and the second-to-last Coast Artillery slot was quietly assigned to him.

Then, the officer finally called the name of the class "goat"—the cadet who was, at the time, at the very bottom of the class in order of merit.

"James Adamson," the officer called.

"Engineers, sir!" Adamson answered irreverently, drawing a wave of laughter from his classmates.[1]

For the Class of 1944, the final tally on Branch Night (in addition to Faas and the other 169 air cadets) was Corps of Engineers 54, Field Artillery 67, Cavalry 6, Infantry 120, Ordnance 13, Signal 6, Chemical 3, Quartermaster 1, and Coast Artillery 29.[2]

Soon thereafter, as occurred each spring, a bevy of civilian suppliers—Luxembourg, Horstman, Jacob Reed, Rogers Peet, and others—descended upon the academy for the traditional "uniform show." The event presented the soon-to-be second lieutenants with an opportunity to purchase uniforms for the upcoming transition to the army. "Don't buy dress blues," the tactical officers warned their cadets. "No use in wartime. Buy just one tailor-made set of pinks and greens; the quartermaster-issued uniforms were cheaper and would serve for most occasions."[3]

The officers' list of recommendations continued: Don't buy long or short beaver overcoats; instead, get a good raincoat, preferably the alligator-green oilskin coat, and a trench coat with a liner. And buy one of Morry Luxembourg's service caps—he was known throughout the army for making the best caps. But in particular the tacs emphasized that a second lieutenant's pay was only $150 a month. No one should go into debt to cover his uniform costs, they warned.

By the final two weeks of May, the momentum toward graduation was seemingly inexorable. The first class cadets began selling back old textbooks, received shipping crates to dispatch their meager belongings to their first duty stations, and completed their last rounds of vaccines and inoculations at the hands of the academy's medical staff. For the Class of 1944, graduation was within an arm's reach, and it was as if nothing could go wrong.

But then word reached the academy of the death of John W. "Bill" Guckeyson, another member of the seemingly ill-fated Class of 1942. A remarkable athlete in his day, Guckeyson had played football for four years at the University of Maryland and, after earning All-American honors, had turned down an offer from the Philadelphia Eagles to come instead to West Point. At West Point, his classmates elected the irrepressibly popular Guckeyson as their class president. No longer eligible for football, he captained the academy's soccer team, lettered in track, basketball, and baseball, and was heralded by sportswriters as the greatest Army athlete of his generation.[4] After graduating, Guckeyson became a P-51 Mustang pilot and soon found himself in combat in Europe, flying missions out of bases in England. In this role, he continued to make news as he steadily amassed a string of enemy aircraft kills. But on May 21, 1944, his luck ran out as he strafed a locomotive near Stendal, Germany. His death provided yet another somber reminder of the deadly stakes of the contests that awaited even the best of West Point's athletes after graduation.

Sobering though it was, such news could not succeed in over-shadowing the excitement of June Week when it finally arrived. On Thursday, June 1, 1944, Christl, Faas, and Hennessey took their final exams, even as families, friends, and OAOs began checking into guest rooms at the Hotel Thayer on the academy's grounds to be present for the week's festivities. The first of a week-long series of hops took place that evening. Perhaps Mary was there for Hennessey; perhaps Virginia was there for Christl.

By Saturday, June 3, June Week was in full swing, and the day was marked with an event unprecedented in the academy's storied annals. That morning, Christl, Hennessey, and the other ground cadets, attired in their khaki uniforms, formed up and marched out onto the Plain in front of a waiting crowd of five thousand. The cadets wore or carried full field equipment: M1 Garand rifles, helmets, field packs, and combat boots.

Meanwhile, at Stewart Field, a total of 117 single-engined AT-6 Texans (one of which was piloted by Faas) and twin-engined AT-10

Cadet John Joseph Timothy Hennessey, Cadet Company H-2, 1944. (Courtesy of the U.S. Military Academy Library)

Cadet Robert William Faas, Cadet Company C-2, 1944. (Courtesy of the U.S. Military Academy Library)

Cadet Edward Charles Christl, Jr., Cadet Company H-2, 1944. (Courtesy of the U.S. Military Academy Library)

In 1942, cadets still paraded in traditional full-dress uniforms, even as their military training took on a decidedly more modern bent. (Courtesy of Library of Congress)

At meals, plebes' duties included serving the upperclassmen – and memorizing their beverage preferences. (Courtesy of the U.S. Military Academy Library)

A New Cadet learns a lesson in posture from an upperclassman, June 1941. (Courtesy of the U.S. Military Academy Library)

Standing 6'2", Jack Hennessey was assigned to M Company, one of the Corps of Cadets' "flanker" companies, for his plebe year. (Courtesy of John Hennessey, Jr)

From left to right, Officer in Charge Lieut. Col. Kenneth F. Dawalt, Ed Christl, Coach Edward Kelleher, and Team Manager Elmer Anderson. (Courtesy of the U.S. Military Academy Library)

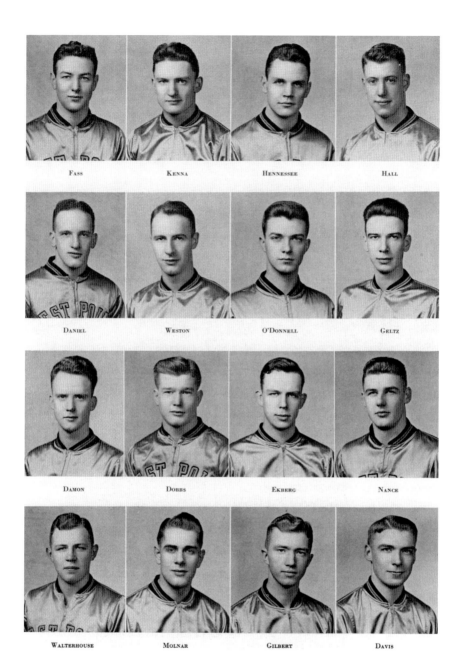

FASS   KENNA   HENNESSEE   HALL

DANIEL   WESTON   O'DONNELL   GELTZ

DAMON   DOBBS   EKBERG   NANCE

WALTERHOUSE   MOLNAR   GILBERT   DAVIS

A composite of West Point's 1944 basketball squad's roster. (Courtesy of the U.S. Military Academy Library)

West Point's basketball team for the 1944 season. Front row: Dale Hall, Jack Hennessey, Ed Christl, Doug Kenna, Bob Faas. Second row: Pete Molnar, Edwin O'Donnell, Alan Weston, Bill Ekberg, Theodore Geltz, Charles Davis, Robert Dobbs. Rear row: Elmer Anderson (team manager), Coach Edward Kelleher, Harle Damon, William Gilbert, Richard Walterhouse, Lieut. Col. Kenneth F. Dawalt (Officer in Charge). (Courtesy of the U.S. Military Academy Library)

Christl pushes up for a basket against Villanova. (Courtesy of the U.S. Military Academy Library)

In this group of First Class Officers from the Class of 1944, Robert Faas (Class President) is seated front row center and Jack Hennessey (Class Vice President) is seated front row right. These cadets are attired in their "full dress" uniform. (Courtesy of U.S. Military Academy Library)

In this group of the Class of 1944's Election Committee, Ed Christl, the Committee's Chairman, is seated fourth from the left. The cadets are wearing their "dress gray" uniforms. (Courtesy of U.S. Military Academy Library)

On June 10, 1944, Jack Hennessey married Mary George in Winona, Minnesota. (Courtesy of John Hennessey, Jr)

Jack Hennessey's teammates Ed Christl (center) and Bob Faas (right) were among the groomsmen at his wedding to Mary. (Photo courtesy of Hope Hennessey)

Jack Hennessey was one of 120 members of the Class of 1944 who branched Infantry. (Courtesy of John Hennessey, Jr)

Jack Hennessey poses during a break during summer training at West Point, likely during the summer of 1943. (Courtesy of John Hennessey, Jr)

Soldiers at Camp Shelby, Mississippi, train with their 105mm howitzer. These men may have been assigned to the 868th Field Artillery Battalion, which Ed Christl joined at Camp Shelby in the fall of 1944. (Courtesy of the Mississippi Armed Forces Museum, Camp Shelby)

During the Advanced phase of flight school at Stewart Airfield, Bob Faas and the other pilots destined for fighter training flew the AT-6 Texan. (Courtesy of the United States Air Force History Program)

A group of air cadets walk past a row of AT-6 Texans on the flight line at Stewart Airfield. (Courtesy of U.S. Military Academy Library)

Soldiers of Hennessey's 276th Infantry Regiment, 70th Infantry Division, rehearse an impending assault near Grossbliederstroff, France, circa February 1945. (Photo: T/4 Todd, 163rd U.S. Signal Corps, courtesy of the 70th Infantry Division Association, www.trailblazersww2.org)

Soldiers of the 70th Infantry Division escort German prisoners to the rear in the vicinity of Diebling, France, February 17, 1945. (Photo: T/5 J. Rutberg, 163rd U.S. Signal Corps, courtesy of the 70th Infantry Division Association, www.trailblazersww2.org)

Troops of the 70th Infantry Division take cover in German-built trenches as they advance on Spichern, Germany, February 22, 1945. (Photo: T/5 Brazle McCroby, Jr., 163rd, U.S. Signal Corps, courtesy of the 70th Infantry Division Association, www.trailblazersww2.org)

At Craig Army Air Field, Bob Faas mastered the P40 Warhawk. (Courtesy of the United States Air Force History Program)

Based on Ie Shima, Bob Faas flew the P-47N Thunderbolt, designed and built for long-range fighter-bomber operations. (Courtesy of the Smithsonian National Air and Space Museum)

In the Pacific, Bob Faas was assigned to the 1st Fighter Squadron, 413th Fighter Group. The squadron was nicknamed "The Fighting Furies," and its unit emblem depicted Miss Fury, a comic-book superhero from the era. (Courtesy of the United States Air Force History Program)

Wichitas swarmed into the air from the field's four concrete runways. The single-engine trainers rendezvoused over Galeville Field; the twin-engined aircraft linked up over Montgomery Auxiliary Field. Then the air armada crossed the Hudson River two miles north of Newburgh, turned south, and, paralleling the river, flew at two thousand feet over Mount Beacon and on to West Point. "One of the greatest aerial spectacles in mid-Hudson Valley annals," army brass assured the press, and in this case the hyperbole seemed justified.[5]

To the delight of the hundreds of spectators, just as the ground cadets began to pass in review, the swarm of cadet-piloted aircraft appeared overhead. "Probably the most dangerous flying I have ever done or been a part of was that Air Cadet fly-by over The Plain on 3 June 1944," recalled Faas's classmate Lee Smith. "We used up a lot of Heavenly Grace and Favor that day."[6]

Another hop at Cullum Hall followed that evening. Then, on Sunday, the cadets assembled in the Cadet Chapel for the baccalaureate service and the dedication of a class window. Even with the presence of families, girlfriends, and fiancées, most of the Class of 1944 elected to sit together, filling the chapel's pews with rows of gray-uniformed young men.

Chaplain John B. Walthour, an Episcopal priest who had been ordained 13 years earlier, had become West Point's chaplain in 1941. Known to his spiritual charges as "Father Jack," he presided over the service that Sunday morning and gave a sermon that at least one member of the Class of 1944 kept for posterity:

> You will be saying to the men who follow you what I now say to your Class. Men should always pray, and never lose heart or give up. For when a man seeks definitely, expectantly, and preservingly [sic] to know and to do the will of God, his prayers will be answered. Don't pray that you will find life easy and undemanding. Pray that you may become stronger, finer, cleaner young men. Don't pray that no task may come to you that is beyond your capabilities. Pray instead for capabilities that will enable you to perform any task that comes to you. Pray always, and, knowing the God to whom you pray, believing in Him and His responsiveness to your desire, you will never lose heart; you will never give up. For you will have, welling up within you, a never-failing source of spiritual power.[7]

That Sunday afternoon was a busy one, filled with first a reception at the superintendent's quarters—the same white house that had once been home to Robert E. Lee and Douglas MacArthur—and then a lengthy parade for the Corps' Stars and Awards Presentation, as top-performing cadets were awarded sabers, swords, books, watches, certificates, and other tokens of appreciation, achievement, and accomplishment. It was at this parade that Jack Hennessey was awarded the Army Athletic Association Award as the best all-around athlete in the Class of 1944.

On the morning of Monday, June 5, the Class of 1944 attended memorial services at the Cadet Chapel or a requiem mass at the Catholic chapel, followed by their swearing-in by their tacs as second lieutenants in the United States Army. Then, at 11:00 a.m., the Corps of Cadets assembled for the Alumni Review, with the 1st Regiment on the eastern side of the Thayer Monument and the 2nd Regiment on the western side. The monument commemorated Col. Sylvanus Thayer, the "Father of the Military Academy."

As the academy's band played "Tenting Tonight" and "Tramp, Tramp, Tramp, the Boys Are Marching" at a slow tempo, the alumni in attendance trooped the line. Then the tempo picked up with "Over There," "Let the Rest of the World Go By," and other songs from the World War I era. The oldest graduate present—George Morgan, Class of 1880, who had earned the Medal of Honor fighting Apaches in Arizona as a horse cavalryman—placed a wreath at the foot of the Thayer Monument, the West Point Choir sang the "Alma Mater" and "The Corps," and the "old grads" moved to the reviewing stands. A parade in their honor followed.[8]

For Bob Faas and the rest of the Class of 1944's air cadets, their penultimate moment at West Point came that afternoon. Assembled in formation at Trophy Point, they received their hard-earned silver pilot's wings, pinned onto their uniform blouses by parents or OAOs. It was a measure of the remarkable expansion of the American military that Maj. Gen. Robert W. Harper, the US Army Air Forces assistant chief of air staff training and Class of 1924, oversaw the ceremony. Only three years earlier, that same Harper had been a lowly captain serving as a tac in Beast Barracks.

That evening, the graduating class had a final dinner in the mess hall, accompanied by families and guests. Then the festivities moved to the academy's theater for a final hop, where the music was provided by none other than Glenn Miller and his band. Graduation would come the next day, and, with their mattresses already turned back in to the quartermaster in order to facilitate a more speedy departure, many a cadet spent a restless night atop the bare springs of his bunk.

Graduation day—June 6, 1944—dawned as a beautiful morning. But even as the Class of 1944 blinked away the cobwebs of the previous night's festivities and scurried to prepare for the impending ceremony, a remarkable piece of news detonated in the barracks that, for a moment, overshadowed even this day of days. From their first day—July 1, 1941—at West Point, Christl and his classmates in the Class of 1944 had felt themselves carried along a surging tide of history. And now, on graduation day, the tide seemed to be pouring them through a veritable cataract. For even as they awoke to their last day as cadets, the news wires from Europe were already abuzz with momentous news.

On this very morning, from their bases in England, the Allies had finally launched their long-anticipated invasion of Nazi-occupied France. For the Class of 1944, June 6, 1944, was the day of their graduation from West Point. But for the rest of the world, June 6, 1944, would forever be known as D-Day. In a remarkable coincidence, the invasion's supreme commander, Dwight D. Eisenhower, was not only a fellow West Point graduate but also the father of John S. D. Eisenhower, a member of the Class of 1944.

Understandably, Cadet John Eisenhower's father was not present for his graduation. His mother, however, was at West Point for the big day. Like most of the graduates' parents, Mrs. Eisenhower was staying at the Hotel Thayer; unlike most other parents, she was awakened by a phone call from a reporter at the *New York Post* that morning.

"The invasion? What about the invasion?" she asked the reporter.

"Well, it's started," he explained.

"Please forgive me," Mrs. Eisenhower replied politely. "Did you say the invasion had started? I'm still rather asleep, you know."[9]

*****

Overseas, the D-Day invasion, although carried on the backs of the citizen soldiers of the American republic and its allies, provided yet another reminder of West Point's role in what was now being called the Great

Crusade. General Eisenhower had graduated in the Class of 1915; his classmate Omar Bradley commanded the American landing forces (and, in another coincidence, was the future father-in-law of the Class of 1944's Henry Beukema). Lawton Collins (Class of 1917) commanded Bradley's VII Corps; Collins's division commanders included Raymond Barton (4th Infantry Division, Class of 1912), Matthew Ridgway (82nd Airborne Division, Class of 1917), and Maxwell Taylor (101st Airborne Division, Class of 1922). And although Bradley's V Corps was commanded by a Virginia Military Institute graduate (Leonard Gerow), Charles Gerhardt (Class of 1917) commanded Gerow's 29th Infantry Division on Omaha Beach.

For basketball players such as Christl, Faas, and Hennessey, whether they realized it that particular morning or not, their connections to the unfolding Normandy landings ran deeper than most. As plebes, they had shared the basketball court and team dining tables with their team captain, Ernest J. "Dirty Ernie" White of the Class of 1942. But on this particular morning, White, now flying P-47 Thunderbolt fighter-bombers at the head of the 359th Fighter Squadron, had lent his and his squadron's heft to air support for the D-Day landings. So had his classmate and teammate Richard M. Maffry, a B-26 Marauder pilot. Other former teammates in hostile skies over Normandy that morning included Charles Hardy (Class of January 1943), another B-26 pilot; his classmate Robert Whitlow, a B-24 Liberator pilot; and, from the Class of June 1943, Eber "Suitcase" Simpson, a P-47 pilot.

But it was Harold Parfitt, Class of June 1943, who was the former teammate with the closest—and most unpleasant—look at the D-Day landings that fateful morning. Parfitt, who had played guard for West Point's cagers a little over a year earlier, was now a platoon leader with the 147th Engineer Combat Battalion. His battalion had landed shortly after 7:00 a.m. onto the chaos of Omaha Beach. Before their LCTs had even reached the sector of beach known as Dog White, plunging German artillery fire wrecked two of the battalion's LCTs and killed some 45 men. Parfitt was among the lucky survivors, but as he reached land he realized that his unit was scattered hopelessly up and down the beach.

Hoping to find members of his platoon, Parfitt began picking his way along the beach toward the rocky highlands of Pointe du Hoc. He probably never heard the German mortar shell that exploded nearby and, for a moment, knocked him senseless. As he recovered his wits, he saw that his left thumb was hanging by a thread of ligament.

Parfitt bandaged his bloodied hand as best he could and continued down the beach, gathering up engineers. It wasn't until the next day that a medic examined his wounded hand and told him he had to be medically evacuated to England. Parfitt's protests were to no avail, and by the following evening he was back across the Channel. He would recover from the wound, however, and be back in action as a company commander with the 149th Engineer Combat Battalion within two months.[10]

*****

Even as their bloodied teammate Parfitt was battling for his life on Omaha Beach, Christl, Faas, Hennessey, and the rest of the Class of 1944 formed in Central Area in order of academic rank and marched down to the field house—the site of 13 of their 15 triumphs in basketball the past season. There, they found seats marked with their names while, in the stands above them, breathless families and fiancées crowded together to watch the ensuing spectacle unfold.

As the graduation ceremony began, Gen. Brehon B. Somervell, commanding general, Army Service Forces, and West Point Class of 1914, stepped up to the podium to deliver the Class of 1944's commencement address. A brusquely brilliant three-star general, Somervell had battled bandits in Mexico, Germans in the trenches of World War I, and, during the Great Depression, malingering labor activists during his stint as the head of the Works Progress Administration in New York City.

"This is a historic hour," intoned General Somervell. "Today, these walls, these hills, the very shadows of Battle Monument take on a new meaning and a deeper significance. Only a few hours ago the mightiest undertaking ever attempted by our Army was launched against enemy entrenched along the shores of France."

"Today our forces began that grim, tough and bloody march from the shores of the Atlantic to Berlin," he continued. "Many of you will join in that march. Many of you will become a part of the sweep in the Pacific that will lead eventually to the destruction of Japan."[11]

In response to those words, the Class of 1944 leapt to their feet and "shook the steel rafters of the Field House with their applause." It went on and on until, finally, the commandant of cadets stepped forward and quieted his charges.[12]

As Somervell continued his speech, the ears of Christl, Faas, and Hennessey must have pricked up with attention as the general recited what the soldiers they would soon lead most valued in their leaders: ability, interest in the welfare of their men, promptness in making decisions, ability to give instructions, good judgment, common sense, an ability to "get things done," avoidance of "rank-heavy" behavior, soldierly bearing, courage, and industry. To those attributes, Somervell reminded the graduating class of the paramount importance of one's character.

"The record of the graduates of West Point has been engraved in the history of our country," Somervell concluded. "The record of its graduates in this war is now being written in that same history. A part of it is in your hands."[13]

At the end of Somervell's remarks, the front row of cadets stood, and the academy's adjutant, Col. L. S. Smith, began to read the name of each graduate in the order of his class standing. First came James Franklin Scoggin Jr., top of his class and destined for the Signal Corps. Like all the men behind him, he walked up onto the dais, saluted General Somervell, took his diploma from the superintendent, and returned to his seat. And so it continued, name after name. To John Eisenhower's embarrassment, a tremendous burst of applause greeted the calling of his name—such was the excitement about D-Day.

Then, finally, came the name of William Benjamin Tuttle Jr.—the last man in the Class of 1944's order of merit. James Adamson had apparently managed to pull ahead of Tuttle in the last round of final exams, and so it was Tuttle who would go down in posterity as the class "goat." As was tradition, the class irreverently rewarded its loudest applause for Tuttle's accomplishment. Tuttle, it should be noted, was seemingly undeterred by the ignominious beginning to his military career. He quickly obtained a branch transfer to the Infantry, joined the 82nd Airborne Division, and carved out a 30-year military career that saw combat in three wars.

Those days, of course, were in the future. Of much more immediate interest were the Superintendent's, General Wilby, final command to the Class of 1944: "Class of 1944, dismissed!"

With those words pronounced, Christl, Faas, Hennessey, and their 471 classmates joyously hurled their white service caps toward the rafters. After three tough years, they had done it—they were now part of the Long Gray Line. They were graduates of the United States Military Academy.

Later, as the new second lieutenants pulled out their diplomas from the white pasteboard tubes, they would find a particularly unique memento of the day's historic events. It was a message from General Eisenhower himself:

> The American Armies in Europe are delighted to join in welcoming into the commissioned ranks of the Army the West Point Graduating Class of 1944. Clearly and soberly recognizing the sternness of the tasks still ahead of us in this war, we face them calmly and with confidence because of our trust in Divine Providence and our faith in America and in her young leaders, upon whose shoulders the heaviest battle burdens habitually fall. We know that in the soldierly qualities of devotion to duty, character, and skill, you will measure up to the high standards and examples daily being set by your contemporaries from all walks of life, and who are now carrying on the work in which you will soon be engaged. May the traditions of your Alma Mater sustain you, and good luck be with you always.[14]

And so, with their diplomas, their new uniforms, their shiny second lieutenant's bars and branch insignia, and the well wishes of General Eisenhower in hand, Ed Christl, Bob Faas, and Jack Hennessey set out from West Point. For those three men, one season of life was over. But another one, even more challenging than the last, lay ahead.

PART II

Battle

"Also I heard the voice of the Lord, saying, Whom shall I send, and who will go for us?

Then said I: Here am I; send me."

—ISAIAH 6:8

CHAPTER 9

Trailblazers

With the exception of their classmate John Eisenhower, who crossed the Atlantic to join his famous father in England for the month of June, the rest of West Point's Class of 1944 paused to enjoy a well-earned month of graduation leave. Two dozen new second lieutenants, prohibited by West Point regulations from marrying while cadets, commenced their month of graduation leave as newlyweds after weddings on graduation day.[1]

Unlike those couples, Jack Hennessey and his OAO, Mary George, decided to be married in her hometown. And so, four days after graduation, the couple wedded in Winona, Minnesota, on June 10, 1944. Their groomsmen included Hennessey's teammates Christl and Faas. During this same time, perhaps caught up in the ongoing barrage of romantic gestures, Christl proposed to his hometown sweetheart, Virginia Johnson.

Sprinkled across the upper Midwest, Hennessey, Christl, and Faas made the best of the time at hand. Despite wartime rationing on the home front, they probably enjoyed their share of good meals—whether it was Hennessey and his new bride making their first forays into a shared kitchen together or Christl and his fiancée Virginia enjoying a steak dinner at Jax Café in downtown Minneapolis or, in Faas's case, grabbing a cheeseburger at one of his old college haunts in downtown La Crosse. For them and their fellow Americans, June 1944 was a month of John Wayne and Susan Hayward starring in *The Fighting Seabees* at the local movie theater (where a ticket cost 25 cents), the National League's Boston Braves battling the New York Giants on the baseball diamond, and Bing Crosby dueling with Harry James and His Orchestra for air time on the radio. But each morning, newspapers peppered their readers with war news headlines about the ongoing fight for the Normandy beachhead and others such as "Super Fortresses Bomb Japan; Yanks Land on Saipan," "Russ Launch New Drive on Eastern Front," and, as the first mysterious V-1 rockets hit London, "Robot Raiders Strike Britain 2d Night in Row."[2]

Today, even in peacetime, the standard two months of graduation leave, coming on the heels of years at West Point, pass in the blink of an eye for a freshly graduated second lieutenant. And so one can only imagine how a quickly a month of such leave, carved out during wartime, must have passed for couples such as the Hennesseys and Christl and his fiancée Virginia. The days probably passed no more slowly for the bachelor Faas—and they screeched to a halt on Thursday, July 6, 1944, as graduation leave came to an end and the second lieutenants reported to their new duty stations.

*****

As he was an infantry officer, Hennessey's first active-duty station was Fort Benning, Georgia, on the eastern bank of the Chattahoochee River, where he reported for the Infantry Officer Basic Course. That July the course's student body consisted solely of Hennessey and the other infantry lieutenants from his class at West Point. For eight weeks, through a series of conferences/lectures, demonstrations, and practical exercises, the cadre of the Infantry School tried to impart to them how to manage an infantry platoon in garrison and, more compelling, lead that same platoon in combat. Some of these skills were common to all army lieutenants, irrespective of their branches, and encompassed such things as the basic aspects of military law, first aid, qualification on personal side arms, radio and field communications, and, of course, the proper completion of paperwork and reports. Other skills were decidedly more focused on the martial tasks at hand: how to organize and run a motorized convoy, to lead a patrol at night, to set up a platoon in defense, to conduct a river crossing under fire, and to work with artillery and armor support.

John Eisenhower, back from his three-week visit with his father in Europe courtesy of a 36-hour flight aboard a B-17, was one of the lieutenants in the course. Of the Infantry Officer Basic Course, Eisenhower had the following observations:

> At Benning we were learning the non-academic nuts and bolts of the infantry trade at platoon and company level. We qualified in the important infantry weapons and benefited from the experiences of officers who had been overseas and brought back the latest of techniques in tactics, mine warfare, and enemy habits. Military training at West Point had included a good deal of theory and had covered the general functions of all branches; here we were learning a single technique—how to be infantry unit commanders in a specific war.[3]

Normally the Infantry Officer Basic Course would have lasted three months, but combat operations were chewing up young lieutenants with a seemingly insatiable appetite. According to one set of statistics, the average life expectancy of an infantry lieutenant in the late summer and autumn of 1944 in Western Europe was just 10 days.[4] Accordingly, the army shortened Hennessey's Infantry Officer Basic Course to two months, and he finished his time at Fort Benning on September 4, 1944. Then, he and his new bride Mary enjoyed 10 days of leave between the completion of the course and Hennessey's next assignment at Fort Leonard Wood, Missouri—an army post in the Ozark Mountains that wags had soon christened "Fort Lost in the Woods."[5]

After finding a room for Mary in a motel in nearby Rollo—dependent housing was practically nonexistent at Fort Leonard Wood, which had been constructed from the ground up for the war—Hennessey reported for duty with the 70th Infantry Division. The division had been activated slightly over a year earlier, on June 15, 1943, at Camp Adair, in Oregon's Willamette Valley. Camp Adair was, more or less, located at the terminus of the Oregon Trail, and the division's staff had quickly seized on the connection to nickname the division "the Trailblazers." As the division G-2 (the officer in charge of intelligence) wrote in the division's introductory pamphlet for new arrivals to the division:

> First plans of this Division were made at Fort Leavenworth, Kansas, which is located at the start of the Oregon Trail. The selection of Camp Adair as the place for training the Division makes the name "Trailblazer" more significant. This area is the terminus of that famous trail. We too have a trail to blaze that might well be called the "modern Oregon Trail." Whether it extends to Tokyo or Berlin,

every member of the Division will have to possess that same indomitable will to win as was characteristic of the early pioneer.[6]

In the modern Trailblazers' case, the modern Oregon Trail to Berlin (or Tokyo) apparently ran through Missouri, for, in July of 1944, the division had entrained for Fort Leonard Wood to complete its training there. And although the division had originally not expected to deploy overseas until the summer of 1945, its new commander, Maj. Gen. Allison J. Barnett—who had enlisted as a 15-year-old in the Kentucky National Guard three decades earlier—received word that autumn that overseas deployment from Fort Leonard Wood would be sooner rather than later.

General Barnett and his staff responded by bringing the division's training to ever-heightening intensity, even as they lost soldiers as individual replacements for units denuded by combat overseas and as they gained new men to fill the gaps. The latter included a collection of former Army Air Forces personnel no longer needed by that particular branch, individuals culled from infantry replacement training centers, and a batch of former college students unceremoniously ejected from the nation's campuses when the army curtailed its Advanced Specialization Training Programs. The new arrivals also included Hennessey and a cadre of classmates from West Point such as George Blanchard, Abraham Glass, Ralph Hollstein, and Walter Snelling, who joined the 70th Infantry Division at the Missouri post in October of 1944.

Upon his arrival, the division assigned Hennessey to the 276th Infantry Regiment, commanded by Col. Albert C. Morgan, an Alabama native and a member of West Point's Class of 1918. Blanchard was assigned to a sister regiment—the 274th. But one suspects that the directive received by Blanchard from his regimental commander, Col. Samuel "Shooting Sam" Conley (Class of 1924), was similar to what Hennessey's own commanding officer told him. "Listen, Blanchard, one day I will call on you," Colonel Conley warned Hennessey's classmate. "I expect more from you as a West Pointer than I do from OCS or ROTC men. I'll treat them more considerately. When I call on you, you'd better be ready."[7]

In the 276th, Hennessey drew duty as one of the regiment's infantry platoon leaders in Company G, 2nd Battalion. This was a typical tasking for a new second lieutenant and the one for which the Infantry Officer

Basic Course had tried to prepare him. "Three rifle squads and a small headquarters cell together comprised the infantry rifle platoon, which was commanded by a lieutenant—for as long as he survived."[8] Various attachments enhanced the 41-man rifle platoon—a medical aid man from the regimental medical detachment, a mortar observer or observation team from the company's weapons platoon or the battalion's heavy mortar platoon for specific missions, or perhaps even one or both of the company's two .30-caliber light machine-gun teams.

In G Company, Hennessey's commanding officer was Capt. James R. Michael, who had graduated from West Point in the Class of January 1943. The captain, who had played football at the academy and commanded Company A-1, was "likeable, square shooting, efficient, and possessed plenty of horse sense"—certainly desirable attributes for a commanding officer.[9] Michael's company was one of the four rifle companies that made up the regiment's 2nd Battalion. In total, three rifle battalions made up a regiment; in turn, three regiments, complemented by various support units, constituted an infantry division.

Under Michael's leadership, Hennessey trained with his platoon and then, as October passed into November, worked with his platoon sergeant to prepare his men and their equipment for the pending overseas deployment. The division was tight-lipped as to their ultimate destination, but the stencils issued to mark their packing crates—which read "Boston Point of Embarkation"—nevertheless offered a clear signal as to the general direction they were heading.[10]

In the third week of November, the division began pulling out of Fort Leonard Wood. Overseas, the fighting in Europe was becoming increasingly brutal, grinding through infantry units at a disturbing rate on battlefields ranging from Germany's Hürtgen Forest to the French fortress city of Metz, and American commanders in Europe were clamoring for infantry units. In response, the army first dispatched the 70th Infantry Division's three infantry regiments—Hennessey's 276th and its two sister regiments, the 274th and the 275th—in the division's vanguard for the "secret" point of embarkation in order to get the infantrymen deployed for the fight as soon as possible. The three infantry regiments, traveling without the division's field artillery battalions, engineers, signal or ordnance companies, or other supporting units, were led by Brig. Gen. Thomas W. Herren, a career officer from Alabama who was now the Trailblazers' assistant division commander.

The 274th was the first regiment to depart from Fort Leonard Wood; the 275th and 276th soon followed, rolling out on troop trains on November 19 and 20, 1944. By the evening of November 22, 1944, Hennessey's train was pulling into an unidentified encampment only later identified as Camp Myles Standish, some thirty miles south of Boston in the Massachusetts city of Taunton.[11]

After the regiment's tired soldiers, aching and stiff from the lengthy journey, climbed down from their train cars into the cold New England air, their new hosts subjected them to a stern orientation briefing as they stood impatiently in formation. Following an hour of warnings about the post's regulations and the need for secrecy, the companies were dismissed to their billets. Their one-story wooden barracks were heated by a single pot-bellied coal-burning stove placed strategically, if ineffectually, in the middle of each barracks and seemed to accomplish little but to permeate the men's uniforms, gear, and blankets with the odor of coal smoke. "One could stand near a stove and char his rear-end while his nose froze," one sergeant remembered.[12]

For the next two weeks at Camp Myles Standish, the men of 276th performed their usual soldierly duties: KP, latrine detail, barracks police, and standing guard duty in the sleet and snow. They also endured a series of lectures (ranging from security measures to safety procedures aboard a troop transport), received issues of supply for operations in Europe (including a pair of combat boots and shoe pacs [a cold-weather boot], one lightweight standard gas mask, one sleeping bag, two pairs of ski socks, and one wool sweater), and practiced assembling and dissembling their newly issued M1911A .45-caliber semiautomatic pistols, M1 Garand rifles, and M1 carbines. They also enjoyed a welcome one-day pass into nearby Boston or Providence. By now, it was clear that movement overseas was imminent—it was clearly just a matter of time.

And that time came on the morning of December 6, 1944—six months to the day after Hennessey had graduated from West Point. A short trip by rail brought both his regiment and the 275th to Boston's harbor, where they detrained and, as the sergeants tried to restore order to the ensuing chaos, queued up at the gangplanks that connected the docks to the biggest ship (if not, in some cases, the only ship) most of the soldiers had ever seen. Before the war, the twin-stacked ocean liner, measuring over seven hundred feet in length, had been named the SS *America* and was once the proud flagship of the United States Lines. In her prewar years, she could carry 1,202 passengers; after being acquired by the US military and retrofitted as a troop transport, she could carry 7,678 personnel. And, as such, she not only acquired a new mission—the ship acquired a new name as well. Coincidentally, she was now the USS *West Point* (AP-23).

As the companies formed up on the dock in the shadow of the *West Point*, a band summoned for the occasion struck up "Oh! Susanna," the official march of the Trailblazers. And as the band played, the steel-helmeted Trailblazers, burdened by their 40-pound field packs and with weapons slung over one shoulder and 30-pound duffle bags over the other, converged on the gangplanks. As they did, a solicitous group of American Red Cross women moved among them, passing out coffee, doughnuts, and ditty bags of cigarettes, playing cards, candy, chewing gum, and German and French phrase books.

Once at the gangplanks, the soldiers shuffled across. As they did, they called out their names, ranks, and serial numbers for each company's first sergeant. By early afternoon, both the 275th and the 276th Regiments were on board. At approximately 4:00 p.m., the *West Point* lifted anchor and set out from Boston harbor. The 274th was already on a similar voyage, on the SS *Mariposa*, a passenger liner that had been requisitioned from the Matson Lines for war service.

As the East Coast began to recede into the distance, many of the regiments' soldiers crowded along the railings on the upper decks to catch a final glimpse of the United States—and to hope it was not their last. For many, it was a somber moment—until one soldier remembered that, as a requirement for leaving Fort Myles Standish, he, like every soldier leaving the post, had been issued a handful of condoms at the post gate. The soldier quickly concluded that he would have little use for condoms on a troopship packed with several hundred other infantryman, and so he irreverently inflated his collection of rubber prophylactics and tossed them into *West Point's* foamy wake.

"The idea soon caught on, and in just a few moments, hundreds of the balloon-like objects were rising above the wake of the USS *West Point*," Staff Sgt. Frank H. Lowry remembered. "It did not surprise anyone when the ship's officers and the army officers failed to manifest any humor in the incident."[13]

For the next seven days, *West Point* steamed east/southeast across the Atlantic at high speed, sailing alone and relying on her speed and zigzag maneuvers to avoid any German U-boats. Belowdecks, Hennessey's platoon battled seasickness, stood in hour-long lines for chow twice a day, continued with their European orientation training, conducted daily "abandon ship drills," cleaned and prepared their weapons, tried to stay clean in the ship's uninviting saltwater showers, and do their best to avoid the company first sergeants looking to fill work details. Otherwise most of their days were spent whiling away the hours on their narrow canvas bunks, tiered four or five high and tightly packed alongside one another. At least the close proximity lent itself to the inevitable game of poker and the seemingly interminable bull sessions. Meanwhile, Hennessey and the other officers had the decided benefit of bunking in the upper-level staterooms—shorn of their prewar luxury but a marked improvement over the crowded troop deck nevertheless.

By December 13, the *West Point* was passing the Rock of Gibraltar and entering the Mediterranean Sea. She sailed on, now accompanied by a destroyer escort and, by the morning of December 15, 1944, had reached Marseille's harbor, on the southern coast of France. Landing barges soon pulled alongside the *West Point*, and, in a long line that snaked through the ship, Hennessey and his platoon disembarked through lower hatches to cross unsteady gangplanks and board one. Once full, the barge steamed for shore, beaching with enough violence to topple its occupants and unleash a profane chorus of curses. By now, dusk was falling on the French port. A biting rain began to fall, chilling the men to the bone as they marched off the barge's ramp onto the French beach and, harkening to the shouts of their sergeants, fell in to a company formation. For Hennessey and his platoon, it was an inauspicious welcome to Europe.

CHAPTER 10

The Battle-Axe

As Jack Hennessey and the rest of the 70th Infantry Division's vanguard of infantry regiments stepped ashore in southern France in December of 1944, Ed Christl was still back in the United States—for the moment. Five months earlier, sporting the crossed-cannons insignia of the Field Artillery on his new uniform's lapel, he had reported for duty at Fort Sill. Fort Sill was a dusty army post in southwestern Oklahoma that dated back to the Indian Wars. Since 1911, however, the fort was where the army dispatched officers such as Christl to learn the artillery trade, and, in the scrubby hills and dusty plains of Fort Sill, the new lieutenant did just that as a member of Artillery Officer Basic Course No. 125. The official postwar history of Fort Sill's artillery school outlined his course of study: field artillery tactics, administration, combat orders, maps and map substitutes, logistics, reconnaissance, staff duties, fire direction, observed and unobserved fire, operation of a firing battery, matériel, and motor transport.[1]

But what that same history failed to relate is that hundreds of miles from the nearest ocean, Christl found himself, metaphorically, on the crest of a doctrinal tsunami just as it was crashing to shore. In his case, the earthquake that had caused the tsunami was born of an argument waged at the Field Artillery School throughout the 1930s. The debate rifted the school's officers along an intergenerational fault line. One group of thinkers, tied to the prewar doctrine of World War I (and earlier conflicts), had long argued that the fires of the artillery battery should be directed solely by the battery commander positioned with his guns. "The artillery lends dignity to what would otherwise be a vulgar brawl," one Napoleonic general had once supposedly sniffed, and, in the century that followed, few battery commanders, accustomed to their traditional positions of command and control, were inclined to disagree with him.

The other, younger group of officers, drawing on hard lessons learned in the trenches and revetments of World War I, argued that with changes in fire control, the artillery could be an even more potent force on the modern battlefield. Throughout the 1930s, they had experimented with such measures as relying on forward observers (who could actually witness the relevant shell bursts on—or off—target) instead of battery commanders to adjust indirect gunfire and, to complement the forward observer's work, utilizing observed-fire charts, range-deflection protractors, and a dedicated fire-direction center to enable the forward observer to not only timely adjust the fire of one but also even multiple batteries simultaneously. "With the introduction of these new fire direction techniques, the artillery made what can fairly be described as a quantum leap in its ability to participate in mobile warfare," one officer observed.[2]

Nevertheless, the dispute between the two schools of thoughts, fought in the lecture halls of Fort Sill, in the cool confines of the post's officers club, and in the pages of the journal *Field Artillery Notes*, continued to rumble and tremor for over a decade. But in 1941, the fault line decisively split when the army's chief of staff, Gen. George C. Marshall, witnessed a demonstration of massed fire by a division directed by the new techniques. Not coincidentally, the army, in the following February, incorporated the concept and use of a fire-direction center and associated measures into its official doctrine as published in *FM 6–40: Field Artillery Field Manual; Firing*.[3]

If the shift in doctrine was the earthquake, then the resulting tsunami carried along its crest battalions' worth of young lieutenants such as Christl, destined to crash them ashore onto foreign battlefields. Had they arrived at Fort Sill five years earlier, the tradecraft they mastered would have been markedly different from the doctrine and operational measures that now made up the syllabus of their course work at Fort Sill. One can fairly wonder how many a World War II battle would have ended but for the effective new doctrine and tactics Christl and his comrades mastered at Fort Sill.

Christl's Artillery Officer Basic Course ended on September 30, 1944, but for him the day was easily overshadowed by another moment in his life. That afternoon, he married Virginia in the post chapel. Virginia's parents, Mr. and Mrs. Roy J. Johnson, traveled from Minneapolis for the wedding, accompanied by Virginia's sisters, Mrs. L. H. Derksen and Marguerite Johnson, as Virginia's matron of honor and bridesmaid, respectively. Hennessey's West Point classmate 2nd Lt. Robert Murphy stood alongside Christl as his best man.

With his training at Fort Sill completed, army orders dispatched Christl from Oklahoma to Camp Shelby, deep in the piney woods of southern Mississippi. In late 1944, the camp was, with approximately one hundred thousand soldiers and civilians on base, the largest city in Mississippi, and the extensive acreage of the adjacent De Soto National Forest—turned over to the army for training purposes for the war—provided ample room for maneuvers and firing ranges. Only Fort Benning could claim to be larger or have more troops assigned to it. But Virginia Christl would not add to the camp's population or that of nearby Hattiesburg; instead, she returned to Minneapolis to live with her parents.

At Camp Shelby, Christl reported for duty with the 65th Infantry Division and was joined in the division by a number of West Point classmates with similar orders. They included fellow artillerymen Jim Blandford, George B. Brown, John Grimmeison, and David Ott. The division's infantry regiments welcomed other classmates—men such as John W. Carley, Fred Keifer, Frank Moore, P. W. Phillips, and Jimmy Stewart.

At Camp Shelby, the division assigned Christl to the 868th Field Artillery Battalion. In an infantry division such as the 65th, each division contained three battalions of light artillery and one battalion of medium artillery. The latter, equipped with 155-mm howitzers, operated in general support of all three regiments, shifting its heavier, longer-range firepower where need was greatest.[4]

Christl's 868th Field Artillery Battalion, however, was one of those three light battalions, comprising three four-gun "firing batteries." In combat, such battalions would generally operate in direct support of one regiment, and in that manner its affiliation to a particular infantry regiment would generally became habitual. These battalions' batteries were equipped with the M2A1 105-mm howitzer, capable of firing a 33-pound high-explosive projectile to a range of about seven thousand yards. To unprotected soldiers on flat terrain, a 105-mm round was lethal to most within 30 yards of its impact. Even men as far as five hundred yards away were in danger of being wounded by the 105-mm shells' shrapnel.[5]

Once at Camp Shelby, Christl discovered that the 65th Infantry Division's shoulder patch depicted a white halberd—a medieval weapon that combined an axe blade with a spear point—against a blue background and that the division's nickname was, understandably, "Battle-Axe." The design had been picked because a halberd—a particularly lethal weapon in Europe's Middle Ages—was an implement of warfare designed for cutting through an enemy's resistance.[6] Unfortunately, it seemed as if the 65th, despite the best efforts of its commander, Maj. Gen. Stanley E. Reinhart (Class of 1916), was not the sharp weapon of war that its insignia suggested.

A little over a year before Christl's arrival at Camp Shelby, the army had activated the 65th Infantry Division at the camp on August 16, 1943. Individual unit training had begun in early 1944—about the same time Christl's last basketball season had commenced back at West Point. For a time, all looked promising for the Battle-Axe. The division made a good showing on its mobilization training test, and training proceeded satisfactorily. Personnel turnover was inconsequential, equipment was plentiful, morale was good, and squads and platoons began to take shape as teams.[7]

But then, in the latter part of May 1944, with the cross-Channel assault on Normandy imminent, hard fighting continuing in the Italian theater of operations, and American forces pushing farther west into the Pacific, the need for individual replacements for infantry units overseas interrupted the division's training. Whether singularly or in groups, soldiers were plucked from Camp Shelby and dispatched as fillers to battalions overseas or to units scheduled for impending deployment. By

July, some of the divisions' platoons—with authorized strengths of 41 men—numbered barely 20. By the end of July, the division—which, at full strength, would have had some 14,250 officers and men in its ranks—had lost 7,000 of them.[8]

The loss of the division's lieutenants and captains from the infantry regiments had been particularly hard. "We didn't keep platoon leaders very long," one battalion commander remarked that summer. "We have had about four complete turnovers since January. In one of my companies the 2nd Platoon has had three commanders and the 1st Platoon has had six. In another company two platoons haven't had an officer for two months; platoon sergeants have been in command."[9]

Matters were equally difficult at higher levels. That summer, the division's G-1 (the officer in charge of personnel), Lt. Col. David H. Arp, reported that the division had endured a 100 percent turnover in regimental and battalion commanders in six months and a 50 percent turnover in general staff officers. "In one of the regiments," Arp said, "one battalion is commanded by a major, in another, two, and in the third, all three."[10]

Not only did the departing soldiers denude the Battle-Axe's existing formations, but their preparation for overseas replacement (POR) processing—qualifying with prescribed weapons, completing immunizations, and clearing the vast pile of paperwork—also placed a heavy burden on the dwindling corps of experienced officers and NCOs. "Lights frequently burned far after midnight in the offices of the division G-1 and adjutant general, and regimental personnel staffs worked in shifts on a 24-hour basis," a history of the time related. "Platoon and company leaders spent many extra hours at night and on Saturday afternoons to get outgoing men through [POR]."[11]

Adding to the challenges was the need to absorb the replacements for the men lost. Over the course of the summer, the replacements arrived from disparate sources—some 1,100 former aviation cadets, a 1,000-odd group of 18-year-olds from replacement training centers, and approximately 3,000 other replacements from disbanded antiaircraft artillery and tank destroyer units. Several hundred more came in from overseas units. Colonel Arp was unimpressed with the last group.

"Overseas commanders send their 'eight-balls' to us under the rotation plan," he observed. "Most of the men are very bitter. They feel like they have done their share. They are a bad influence on the other men." And as for the ones who were identified as "infantry volunteers," Arp was no less enthused. "In every case ... [they] have been men who were dissatisfied in other branches—men who did not like their commanding officers, who wanted a change of station, or who were falling down on their jobs," the G-1 recalled. "In some instances, pressure has been put on them to volunteer. ... An officer will say to a misfit or ne'er-do-well: 'You're apt to lose your rating if you stay here. You've got a good chance to keep your stripes by joining the doughboys. My advice is for you to take it.'"[12]

General Reinhart echoed his G-1's concerns. "Replacements have been inferior in quality to the original fillers. Some of them have been kicked about from unit to unit. We did not have an opportunity to indoctrinate them as we did the original fillers, to imbue them with the spirit of the organization."[13]

Even in the face of such challenges, Reinhart and his commanders worked to put the battalions through their unit training, and, in some fashion, such training was completed in July. But some of the battalion exercises were held with fewer than two hundred men, "and the few regimental problems that were undertaken were not deserving of the name."[14] For example, the infantry and artillery "went through the motions of combined training" for approximately two weeks, but, with understrength formations and inexperienced officers, the regimental combat team exercises were so limited that when later the division's final status report was submitted, no combined training was even credited.[15]

The absence of such combined-arms training was worrisome—to say the very least. As a collection of military historians who crafted a case study of the division at this time recognized, "infantrymen needed to develop confidence in teammates of other branches—in the artillerymen to place supporting fire in the right place at the right time, in the quartermaster company to get supplies to them, in the engineer battalion to clear roads for their advance, in the ordnance company to keep their weapons in fighting condition, in the signal company to maintain the flow of communications, and in the medics to treat their wounds." "This confidence could come only from long acquaintance," they declared, "and from working together on various levels from individual training to large-scale maneuvers."[16]

In an effort to at least bring its individual soldiers up to speed, the division initiated a six-week program of modified individual training in late July, with special schools set up under the division G-3 for the new officers. But even as Reinhart implemented such measures, he continued to lose enlisted personnel. In August, for example, the division lost a tenth of its enlisted strength to transfers.[17]

Even the arrival of the new lieutenants from West Point by way of Fort Sill caused consternation. Christl's classmate David Ott—a future lieutenant general and commandant of the Field Artillery School—remembered the situation in the class's 50-year anniversary book. "From on high the decision was made that we would all be sent to battalions in divisions still in the United States," Ott recalled. "In other words, no one was to go to a corps artillery (separate) battalion or enter the replacement stream for Europe or the Far East. This was to insure we served in fighting divisions in which we had trained."

"The problem," Ott continued, "came from another pair of decisions that we would all go overseas with the battalions we had joined, and no battalion would go over-strength in lieutenants. As it turned out, all of us joined battalions and were assigned to firing batteries that were already up to strength, so we were excess lieutenants."

"When the battalions got overseas orders, it was other lieutenants who had to leave," Ott admitted. "All had been there longer than we and fervently desired to go with the unit with which they had trained, with the people they knew and trusted. "They were bitter, angry, hurt, and rightfully so. Up went the cry: "The West Point Protective Association has struck again!"[18]

If Ott's memory was correct, then, Christl's arrival at Camp Shelby in mid-October of 1944 may have been less than warm. Nevertheless, Christl met the circumstances with his characteristic eagerness and good-natured confidence. Even at the best of times—and these were certainly not those—the most junior officer in a battery was assigned the most onerous extra duties and menial tasks to perform. This was certainly the case for Christl as he arrived to join the 868th. But, as a fellow officer later noted, "It made no real difference to Ed that he was the only second lieutenant in our battery. ... Each job to him was an important rung to climb upward toward the big job ahead."[19]

By the time of Christl's arrival, the division had progressed to a level of modified unit training—and with a heightened level of focus and energy spurred by orders for the division to have its equipment ready for overseas deployment by January 3, 1945.[20] The news had come as a shock to the division staff; previously, they had believed that it would not be until the summer of 1945 that they would be deployed. Nevertheless, those same orders provided a sense of purpose and a corresponding boost to the unit's morale, even as the revolving door of transfers and replacements continued to spin. Reinhart and his staff welcomed the opportunity to rid the division of some one thousand physically deficient personnel, but the corresponding burden of undertaking the 11th-hour training of their replacements presented its own challenges.

Over the course of the next two months, the 65th Division endured a series of contradictory and disruptive orders. Pack and separately deploy your infantry regiments in November, one order read. Then, even as the infantrymen were loading their equipment onto freight cars at the end of October in obedience, that earlier order was suspended. A follow-on order directed the infantry to travel with the rest of the division but also moved up the division's deployment date to early December, presenting the division with the challenge of somehow simultaneously unpacking equipment, conducting critically needed last-minute battalion field exercises, and packing and otherwise preparing for overseas movement.[21] This was the state of affairs for Christl in mid-December, even as his classmate Jack Hennessey was landing with his infantry platoon at Marseille.

Finally, on Christmas Eve, 1944, Christl and the rest of the 65th Division began to board trains for movement from Camp Shelby to the New York port of embarkation. The last element of the division followed on New Year's Eve. Before the first week of January was over, the division was at sea, sailing for Europe. And as an official US Army history noted, "If the plans for the building and training of this division had been carried out as originally laid down … when it moved overseas in 1945 might have been the most battle-worthy of the long line of divisions produced by the Army Ground Forces. For into the planning of the organization, training, and equipment of this unit was poured the accumulated experience of four years' intensive effort. But, mainly because of personnel exigencies …, the 65th was about the least ready for combat of all divisions trained in World War II."[22]

The history continued. The division's regiments, it recounted, "had never worked with their supporting battalions of artillery in field exercises. The division commander had never maneuvered his command as a unit; in fact, the division had never been together, except for reviews and demonstrations, and its composition had changed greatly from one assembly to another. In the infantry regiments only one man in four had been with the division for a year, and almost every fourth man had joined his unit in the past three months. The division was more of a hodge-podge than a team."[23]

For his part, General Reinhart did not disagree. As he complained to an Army Ground Forces staff officer at the time:

> The Division that I gave basic training to is no longer here…. The last time I checked up on personnel turnover, this Division had furnished over 10,000 men for other duties and had sent out enough officers to fill one and one-half divisions…. Personnel turnover prevented the making of a team out of this Division. Our situation is comparable to that of a football coach who has to turn over his team to other institutions a few weeks before the playing season starts. He wires for replacements. He gets two players from one college, three from another, and so on down the line. The pickings are so bad at this late date that he gets a miscellany of misfits and culls. He has to put backfield men in the line and linemen in the backfield. He can't be expected to make a team under such circumstances.[24]

But Reinhart, his staff, his commanders, and his NCOs had indeed made a team. It may not have been ideal or the team for which he had hoped, but it was a team nevertheless. And now that team, led at its lowest levels by young lieutenants such as Ed Christl and their platoon sergeants, was bound for combat. Christl's former teammate Jack Hennessey was already there.

CHAPTER 11

Task Force Herren

Jack Hennessey and his men had arrived on the beach at Marseille on December 15, 1944. Once ashore, they and the rest of the 276th Infantry Regiment, joined by the men of the 275th, climbed into trailers towed by a waiting convoy of semi trucks and, standing like cattle, were transported through the narrow, cobblestoned streets of Marseille.

Rain had started as soon as they had hit the beach, and now, as the convoy of trucks rolled through Marseille, the cold downpour intensified. But that did not stop hundreds of French men, women, and children from standing on balconies and street corners or leaning out of windows to wave American and French flags at the passing Trailblazers. For the tired, wet, and cold soldiers and their officers, who had little idea of what to expect from the French, the spontaneous display from the city's residents was a welcome gesture.[1]

An hour later, the convoy reached a bivouac area 16 miles north of Marseille, where the 274th Infantry Regiment had already encamped and darkness was already falling. The site was designated as Delta Base CP (command post) No. 2, and sat atop a "desolate, rocky, treeless, windswept plateau."[2] The muddy ground was barren of vegetation and devoid of structures other than a row of wooden kitchen and storage sheds, about 50 yards apart, along the northern side of the plateau, and, downwind of the sheds some two hundred yards distant, a series of slit trenches surrounded by six-foot posts covered with burlap. These were the latrines.

Advance of 70th Infantry Division through France and Germany, December 1944 to May 1945.

Slipping and splashing in the rainy dark, the troops pulled canvas shelter halves from their packs and pitched two-man tents in a company street formation between the storage sheds and latrines. It was no easy task; the mud was so soft and deep that the tent stakes would not hold. The men collected large stones to use to keep the stakes in place. As they finally hit the sack after the long, wet day, they soon felt the cold mud seeping through their bed rolls. Even exhausted as they were, few soldiers slept until morning. December 16, 1944, their first full day in the European theater of operations, dawned gray, gloomy, and clammy.

As Hennessey's soldiers turned to their tasks at hand that morning, Brig. Gen. Thomas Herren received disturbing news. Herren was in charge of the three Trailblazer infantry regiments, collectively christened Task Force Herren, bivouacked at Delta Base CP No. 2, but, as he conferred with his intelligence officer, he must have wondered how long their encampment outside of Marseille would last. This very same morning, he learned, a massive German force had assaulted through the snowy Ardennes Forest some five hundred miles to the north in Belgium. The German attack had seemingly taken the Allied command and the American units in the area by disastrous surprise. This was the beginning of the massive battle that, as the German advance pushed back the American defenders, newspapermen would soon be calling "the Battle of the Bulge" in recognition of the disturbing protuberance now extending into the American lines toward the critical port of Antwerp.

As Herren and his staff kept up with developments to their north, their soldiers worked to be prepared for whatever contingency might require Task Force Herren's presence on the battlefield. They manned work details to move the regiment's equipment and supplies from the beach in Marseille to the bivouac area, drew rations and ammunition, picked up their allotment of motorized vehicles and antitank guns, received orientation briefings on the shifting strategic situation on the front lines and, of course, performed KP and pulled sentry duty. As the weather turned even colder and the mud froze and the wind bit deeper into their bones, the soldiers scrounged for firewood to keep their warming fires burning. Some squads even received passes for a few hours to venture into Marseille. For the moment, Herren must have hoped that his infantry regiments would be joined by the rest of their supporting units from the division before being cast into combat.

Such was not to be the case, however, and, beginning on December 20, 1944, Herren's regiments began moving north into France. On December 23, it was the 276th's turn. After a brief march to a railhead, the men boarded antiquated French boxcars marked "HOMMES 40—CHEVAUX 8"—meaning their capacity was 40 men or eight horses—as Hennessey joined the other officers in a passenger coach at the front of the train. Despite the French optimism about the number of men the boxcars could hold, each received a complement of 20 American GIs. Fully equipped with packs and weapons, they were nevertheless crowded indeed.

For the next six days and nights, two of these boxcars were home to Hennessey's platoon. For food, each car had been issued crates of field rations, to be warmed by the Coleman heater provided in each car. If a latrine was needed, a sandbox in one corner of the boxcar was to suffice. By mutual agreement among the boxcars' occupants, such facilities were rarely used.

In fits and starts, Hennessey's troop train pulled northwest through the rugged limestone hills of the Alpilles and into the lower reaches of the Rhône Valley at Avignon. From there, the train chugged north up along the Rhône River to the city of Lyon and then, continuing north, to Dijon. It was a laborious journey, interrupted for hours at a time by broken equipment, torn track, and warnings of air raids. Fortunately, the warnings proved unfounded. Even more fortunately, the stops provided the men with an opportunity to stretch their legs, answer nature's call somewhere other than in the sandbox latrine in their boxcar, and try out on the local mademoiselles the phrases helpfully provided in their French phrase books.

At one such stop, a trainman stepped forward from the caboose to advise the officers that the train would be halted for at least a half hour. In response, Hennessey and one of his fellow platoon leaders—Charles Cheezem, an ROTC officer from Clemson University—hurriedly conferred and decided that their soldiers, huddled in cold cattle cars, would surely welcome a taste of the local wine. The two young officers disembarked and, trotting into the nearby town, quickly procured a couple of bags of wine. Then, with their watches showing ten minutes to spare, they returned to the railroad siding—only to see their train chugging away.

Stunned at the sight of their train leaving them behind, Hennessey and Cheezem dropped the wine and sprinted after it—but to no avail. The old French engine picked up steam and steadily put more and more distance between itself and the two lieutenants. Defeated, the two Americans panted to a stop, their labored breath clouding the cold air around them. As they caught their breath, an unsettling thought crossed their minds. They had just missed a troop movement—in wartime, a court-martial offense.

Fortunately, a possible solution soon presented itself with the appearance of another locomotive rolling north along the same tracks. As it pulled into the now empty siding, Hennessey and Cheezem explained their problem—to no avail. Then, they explained it again, this time with their hands resting noticeably on their holstered sidearms. This time, their plea for help was more convincing. In a matter of minutes, they and their commandeered locomotive were in hot pursuit of their regiment's train—if one could call a 12-hour chase a hot pursuit.

"It was a long twelve hours," Cheezem later recalled. But, ultimately, they caught up with their quarry and rejoined their unit no worse for the experience.[3]

Another stop on the journey took on a more reverent note. Somewhere in the vicinity of Dijon, the soldiers awoke to Christmas morning. That afternoon, the trains paused for a half-hour break—long enough for the battalions' chaplains to conduct Protestant services and a Catholic mass for the troops as a light snow began to fall. "Don't kneel, the ground is damp," the Catholic chaplain told his flock. "The air is cold, keep your helmets on. God will understand."[4] After the service, the men reboarded their boxcars and tried to enjoy a lukewarm Christmas dinner of meat and vegetable hash.

In Dijon, the train pulled onto tracks that, fatefully, were pointing northeast—toward the German frontier. And, on Saturday, December 26, the troop train reached its destination—a snow-covered field on the outskirts of the French city of Brumath. With no ceremony, the men disembarked, spreading out at five-meter intervals. As the artillery rumbling in the distance reminded them, they were now, after months of training, within earshot of the front lines. A quick briefing of the officers took place, after which Hennessey returned to his platoon as they shivered in their greatcoats and helmets. "Prepare to move out," he informed his platoon. "The next leg of the journey will be on foot."[5]

The soldiers slipped on their packs, shouldered their rifles, and, falling into a five-meter-interval, single-file lines on each side of the road, moved out behind their scouts. "During their training days at Camp Adair and Fort Leonard Wood, the men went on many forced and endurance marches," a veteran of the regiment remembered. "Some were as long as thirty miles with field packs, but none was nearly as brutal and punishing as the march that day in the frigid Alsace Plain."

For 16 miles, the regiment pushed on at a punishing pace. Dozens of men began to straggle, would catch up at the hourly breaks, and then straggle again. Few were well-rested, some were already suffering from various illnesses, and none had had any appreciable exercise since leaving Boston some three weeks earlier. Before long, the roadside was littered with discarded ration tins, bottles of wine, and even the occasional gas mask case as the regiment, with feet blistering in the ill-fitting rubber shoe pacs, stumbled on.

Late that afternoon, the regiment's soldiers stumbled wearily into the French town of Bischwiller, some five miles west of the Rhine River and the border with Germany. Hennessey's G Company found billets in one of the town's warehouses—unheated and drafty but at least out of the bitter wind. Unfortunately, it was here that the company suffered its first casualty. One of G Company's Browning Automatic Rifle (BAR) gunners—one of the former aviation cadets assigned to the division as last-minute fillers in the summer of 1944—had put his loaded weapon, covered by a blanket, on the floor where a tired soldier tripped over it. The weapon discharged, shooting the gun's owner in the neck. He survived but had to be evacuated to the rear.[6] Then orders came to detach some 20 men to nearby divisions in need of replacements. The casualty and the replacements' unhappy departure meant that G Company, now within five miles of Germany, was already understrength.

In the two days that followed in Bischwiller, Hennessey and his platoon recuperated from the forced march, received extra ammunition, grenades, and additional equipment, and learned more about the situation into which their orders had delivered them. By now, after 10 days of folly, sacrifice, bravery, and luck, the German offensive through the Ardennes had been contained; the Bulge was no longer bulging but, rather, was being reduced. And so here, 150 miles to the southeast, on France's Alsatian border with Germany, the role of the 70th Infantry Division's three infantry regiments was to help the US Seventh Army hold the line while events played out to the northwest.

Herren's 275th Regiment had drawn frontline duty first upon arriving in Bischwiller. On December 29, the 276th Regiment moved forward to relieve them. A seven-mile road march brought Hennessey and his platoon, along with the rest of the 276th, to the vicinity of the town of Soufflenheim, where they occupied a string of outposts overlooking the Rhine River into Germany. For the men, it was bitterly cold duty, with two hours in a foxhole and then four hours off a few hundred yards to the rear in whatever shelter they could find.

The soldiers' discomfort was exacerbated by their realization of just how thinly the American lines were stretched in this area. The US Seventh Army and its subordinate units—a pair of army corps (VI Corps and XV Corps), each consisting of approximately four divisions—had shifted westward and northward to cover ground previously occupied by Lt. Gen. George Patton's US Third Army. Now, Patton's troops were fully engaged in their counterattack into the Bulge, and their counterparts in the Seventh Army were, in turn, left to cover a distressing large stretch of front lines.

Had Hennessey and his men had the benefit of a large-scale map, they would have been further discomfited. Their regiment occupied that corner of France's Alsace province that, following the curve of the Rhine River, juts impertinently into Germany's Baden-Württemberg state. Truth be told, in the European theater of operations that December, there were few American units farther east than Task Force Herren.

Unfortunately, the Germans were equally aware of the Seventh Army's thin defenses along the Alsatian frontier. At half past midnight on New

Year's Day of 1945, they launched Operation Nordwind—destined to be the last major German offensive of the war. Intelligence had warned the Americans of the impending assault, and the Wehrmacht failed to achieve its hoped-for surprise, but, in this particular sector, running along an axis created by the Vosges Mountains, the elite 6th SS Mountain Division, supported by regular army units and those of the Volkssturm (national militia), pushed relentlessly south. As units of the Seventh Army's VI Corps—deployed to the west of Task Force Herren—gave ground before the advancing Germans, not only was the Alsatian capital of Strasbourg threatened, but regiments such as the 276th also found themselves with the enemy to their front and rear. Whether Hennessey and his platoon realized it or not, the year 1945 was off to a most perilous start.

CHAPTER 12

A Cold North Wind

Jack Hennessey and his platoon spent New Year's Day, 1945, extracting themselves from their exposed outposts overlooking the Rhine, boarding trucks, and moving with the rest of the regiment back some ten miles to Oberhoffen. They remained there, apprehensively listening to the muffled booming of artillery to the northwest, for the rest of that afternoon and night. Then, in midmorning the next day, the 276th Infantry Regiment boarded a convoy of trucks and headed west into the forbidding woods of the Vosges Mountains. An icy fog enveloped the trucks as they inched along on the narrow, slippery French roads. As they shivered in the backs of their trucks, they, at their lowly echelons, likely had no idea that their regiment had been attached to the 45th Infantry Division and was being shuttled westward to positions athwart the advancing German soldiers of Operation Nordwind.

Hours later, the 30-mile trip ended in the town of Zittersheim on the afternoon of January 2. The regiment's commander, Col. Albert Morgan, set up his command post in the French town and deployed his three battalions along a roughly east-west axis that stretched from Volksberg on the left through Wingen-sur-Moder and Wimmenau and then on to Ingwiller on the right. The 2nd Battalion, to which Hennessey's platoon, as a part of G Company, was assigned, occupied the right side of the 11-mile regimental front. The 3rd Battalion held the left flank, and, behind Wingen-Sur-Moder, the 1st Battalion rested in reserve.

For the rest of the day and the next, the battalions worked to improve their positions, throwing roadblocks across the mountain roads and chiseling foxholes and fighting positions in the frozen ground. A column of French tanks, gaggles of fleeing villagers, and the occasional firefight with German scouting parties kept everyone on edge, as snow flurries brought the threat of even more snow and cold day gave way to colder night. Apprised of the approaching Germans, Colonel Morgan pulled his regiment's 1st Battalion into the line near Wingen-sur-Moder the evening of January 3 to bolster the 45th Infantry Division's 1st Battalion, the 179th Infantry already garrisoning the small town.

Morgan's deployment of his reserve proved prescient. The next day, in the predawn darkness, two battalions of the 12th SS Mountain Infantry Regiment, 6th SS Mountain Division, artfully bypassed the 179th Infantry's defenses, capturing dozens of its men in Wingen-sur-Moder, and seized the French village. The SS troopers were skilled veterans of three years of heavy fighting against the Red Army on the eastern front and well equipped with *Panzerfaust* antitank weapons and automatic weapons. It would be up to Colonel Morgan's green Trailblazers to oust them from Wingen-sur-Moder, restore the key line of communication running through the Vosges, and ensure that the Germans advanced no closer to the strategic Saverne Gap, 10 miles to the south.

In a brutal house-to-house battle that lasted three days, the 1st and 3rd Battalions of the 276th, supported by the 274th Regiment, wrested Wingen-sur-Moder and the surrounding heights back from the German invaders. By the morning of January 7, the little town best known for its glass-making heritage was, ironically, a broken wreck. Only one building still stood undamaged. For its fight in Wingen-sur-Moder, the 274th Regiment's 2nd Battalion would receive a Presidential Unit Citation. It read, in part:

> In two days, the 2nd Battalion, 274th Infantry, operating under almost insurmountable supply, communication, and evacuation problems, in bitter cold, without food or rest, and with the loss of 130 casualties, destroyed two German SS. Battalions [*sic*], liberating over 250 Americans held prisoner by the German forces, recaptured 32 American vehicles, three anti-tank guns, and hundreds of small arms.
>
> The determined fortitude, courage, and fighting spirit displayed by members of the 2nd Battalion, 274th Infantry, is [*sic*] exemplary of the finest traditions of the American Army and will be inscribed indelibly in the annals of the American Infantry.[1]

Meanwhile, in the 276th, Hennessey's 2nd Battalion, on the left flank of the action, was, for the moment, spared the vicious baptism of fire suffered by its sister battalions in the regiment. Rather, deployed to the west of Wingen-sur-Moder, it stood ready in reserve until, aware of the ongoing infiltration of German units south past the village of Lichtenberg, regimental headquarters directed the battalion to secure the village. On January 6, the Trailblazers did just that, attacking into Lichtenberg and seizing the remnants of the Château de Lichtenberg, a 13th-century castle that had stood in ruins since its destruction in 1870 during the Franco-Prussian War. The next day, they pushed farther north, with limited success against obstinate resistance in the snowy woods and bitter cold. Nevertheless, the Trailblazer regiments had done their part to stymie the German assault. "The green troops of Task Force Herren … had fought with an enthusiasm that belied their inexperience," army historians would later admit.[2]

*****

With the American lines secured and the German Nordwind advance initially stymied, the American commanders moved to ensure containment of the enemy threat and allowed the troops scarcely a day of rest. As the soldiers of the 276th rearmed and resupplied, their battalion and company commanders received orders to prepare for an attack north with the rest of the regiment. The objectives were four hills southwest of and overlooking the small Alsatian town of Baerenthal. Baerenthal was not much of a town, but it sat astride a two-lane road that followed the North Zinsel River out of the Vosges Mountains and back down into the Alsatian Plain. If the Americans did not want another unexpected surge of Germans boiling out of the Vosges, such avenues of approach had to be seized and sealed.

At 7:00 a.m. on January 9, 1945, the 1st and 2nd Battalions of the 276th crunched forward through the snow, moving along a west-east axis toward the hills south of Baerenthal. The 3rd Battalion trailed behind as the regimental reserve. Ahead of them, mountainous hillsides rose precipitously, pierced only rarely by narrow, twisting tracks and one-lane roads. Their rocky slopes were covered with timber, dense underbrush, and a foot or more of snow. Moving into these hills, the soldiers had to sling arms and climb hand over hand to clamber upward and onward. Not unexpectedly, in the rugged terrain, battalions lost contact with battalions, companies lost contact with companies, and platoons even lost contact with platoons.

Three hours later, following a small mountain stream, the regiment came abreast of the village of Obermuhlthal and began taking sniper fire. The advance slowed, particularly on the regiment's left flank, in the 2nd Battalion's sector, as German machine-gun fire and difficult terrain brought the day's movement to a halt. Night fell, and the troops spent a tense night in the frozen forest as friendly and enemy patrols clashed with one another in the surrounding darkness.

Years later, Staff Sgt. Frank Lowery, who fought with A Company, 276th Infantry Regiment, in the Vosges Mountains remembered such nights.

> One who has never experienced a cold miserable night in a frozen foxhole following a long day of intense fighting, cannot possibly fathom the excruciating agony and suffering of the rifleman in that small hole. … Only the infantryman who has lived through it, really knows how it was. All night long a man is tense, scared, and spends the endless hours on the alert staring into the darkness…. His bruised body aches from hitting the frozen ground and rubble and his stomach is in knots from the pangs of dysentery. His ears ache and his hearing is impaired from mortar, tank, and machine gun fire. He is tortured by the intense cold, and his fear is genuine. Not only are his hands and feet near frozen, the extreme cold burns his eyes, ears, lips and cheeks. It burns his throat all the way down to his lungs. He is dead tired and weary but stays alert and dares not fall asleep.[3]

The next day, January 10, Colonel Morgan moved the regimental command post forward to Offwiller, and his battalions' assault continued. The German Volkssturm units, comprising conscripts ranging in age from 16 to 60, displayed "exceedingly low morale" in the face of the Americans' steady advance; the same could not be said of the SS troops, who, according to the 276th's after action report, fought with "the same high morale and fighting spirit as previously."[4] On this day, even heavier German artillery and mortar fire bedeviled the advance, slowing the pace further as the Trailblazers' companies worked to straighten their lines and maintain contact with one another in the knee-deep snow and heavy woods.

As the battle progressed, it devolved into a series of small-unit actions, fought by individual squads and platoons. In such conditions, leadership rest not on the regimental or battalion or even company commanders' shoulders but on that of their platoon leaders, platoon sergeants, and squad leaders. Amid the thick forest, with fir boughs hanging heavy with snow until blasted off by the detonation of a German mortar shell, Hennessey was one such platoon leader.

Displaying heroism "beyond the call of duty," Hennessey "aggressively led his platoon in an attack through heavily wooded hills in bitterly cold winter weather," his Bronze Star citation ultimately read.[5] Exposing himself to small-arms and artillery fire, he moved among his squads, working with his squad leaders to direct their men forward. Each enemy position encountered was met with an aggressive assault, as rifle fire was complemented by bursts of BARs and hurled grenades. Tree by tree and thicket by thicket, Hennessey and his men pushed forward. Elsewhere along the uncertain American line, their fellow soldiers did likewise. But the going was slow, and the cold day ended with the American GIs, wet from crawling through snow and their own sweat, scratching foxholes in the frozen ground. With nightfall, the temperature plummeted below zero, ensuring that the water in their canteens stayed frozen.

Daybreak on January 11 marked the third day of the attack. Once again, German artillery and mortar shells rained down on the Americans as small-arms fire swept across the few open fields and glens. To Hennessey's right, the 1st Battalion, with fixed bayonets and frozen feet, captured Hill 403 and then pushed on to Hill 358, only to be denied its crest by a barrage of heavy artillery fire. The battalion paused, regrouped, and attacked again, ultimately claiming the hilltop but suffering heavy casualties in the process. By then, their prize was littered with broken branches, splintered timber, and pine boughs. The bark of the trees still standing were scarred by artillery bursts, machine-gun bullets, and small-arms fire. On the ground, the snow was stained with dirt, rocks, gunpowder, and, in some cases, blood. "The acrid stench of stale burnt gunpowder and the smell of death that hung in the forest permeated the air," Staff Sgt. Lowery remembered. "The area was littered with bodies, both American and German, parts of bodies, the severely wounded and the dying."[6]

At that point, Colonel Morgan had to cycle in the regiment's reserve, the 3rd Battalion, to continue with the assault and spell Lowery and his fellow soldiers in the battered 1st Battalion. In the meantime, Hennessey's G Company and the rest of the 2nd Battalion were pinned down by heavy machine-gun and small-arms fire. In response, the battalion broke into smaller units and cautiously infiltrated around the German strongpoints. Pushing on through the gathering winter gloom and into the night, they assaulted their objective, Hill 415. Shortly after midnight, the hill was in American hands, and atop it most of the GIs hurriedly dug foxholes. Their less fortunate comrades were dispatched on patrols to keep the Germans at bay.

At 9:00 a.m. on January 12, the Trailblazers stumbled into their fourth day of the attack. Bursts of German artillery fire disrupted the attack and heavy small-arms fire pinned down the 2nd Battalion on the regiment's left flank. For a time, their sister regiment's L Company came to their aid, but all along the regimental front the 276th seemed to have shot its proverbial bolt. By midafternoon, word reached the battalion commanders that the regiment was being pulled out of the attack.

In the wake of the attacks on the hills overlooking Baerenthal, the 276th Regiment's final tally recorded five Trailblazers killed and another 75 wounded in the four-day fight, although those numbers seem difficult to reconcile with the bloody personal accounts set down by individual soldiers who fought in the line.[7] Hennessey's infantrymen—exhausted, hungry, frostbitten, and, in many cases suffering from trench foot and other maladies—would probably have had similar doubts about such arithmetic.

*****

As Hennessey and his platoon recuperated in some French barn or farmhouse in the frigid Vosges Mountains, the affairs of West Point's basketball team were probably the furthest thing from his mind. Had he been back in the States, however, he could have read in a newspaper that the previous day, as he and his platoon were assaulting the snowy heights of Hill 415, his old team under Coach Kelleher had kicked off its 1945 season. As with last season, the game was with Swarthmore College; as with last season, Army's inaugural outing on the hardwoods claimed a resounding victory. In helping his team post a final score of 70–36, Doug Kenna managed to single-handedly sink as many baskets from the field as his Swarthmore competitors combined.[8] Such was the tally for the "fields of friendly strife," to recall Douglas MacArthur's phrase, back at the academy. But, as MacArthur had warned and Hennessey could now attest, the fight had clearly moved to "other fields, on other days"—and more such days, and more such fields, were undoubtedly ahead.

CHAPTER 13

Objective Yoke

Over the course of the next few days, trucks shuttled Jack Hennessey and the rest of the 276th Infantry Regiment to various villages and small towns while higher command seemingly debated its next move. First the regiment shifted east, farther into the Vosges Mountains, where, for three days, it occupied static positions on a line running through the Katzenthal Forest from Jaegerthal to Lembach. Then, in a seemingly change of focus, the higher-ups moved Task Force Herren 50 miles west across the Vosges range and into the Lorraine region of France. Upon its arrival, the regiment, now 335 men understrength after the past two weeks' fighting, stolidly set to work chopping and carving foxholes through the heavy snow and into the frozen ground. Jeep and truck drivers struggled with the icy roads; everyone struggled with the bitter cold.

In his modern-day classic, *The Guns at Last Light*, Rick Atkinson recited a grim litany of the personal agonies suffered by soldiers such as Hennessey's at this stage in the war, in what was recognized as "the harshest winter in decades." If they were lucky, they had an extra quarter-pond of TNT to blow a hole in the frozen ground to start a fighting position's excavation, but woe to the soldier who fell asleep in a slushy foxhole; he would awake frozen in place, with his squad mates having to chip him out of the ice with bayonets. If GIs slept on the exposed ground and raised their heads too quickly, their scalps left patches of hair affixed to the frozen ground. Tiny fires, fueled briefly by the cardboard scraps of K-ration boxes as they heated the congealed hash in an icy can, provided fleeting intervals of what passed for warmth on the front lines.[1]

Here, the German frontier was scarcely a mile away, but whether the enemy was hunkered down in defense or planning for another surprise attack remained anyone's guess. Seeking the answer to that critical question, the Trailblazers pushed out patrols every night—"the most risky and detested duty that infantrymen were required to undertake," as one veteran of those cold winter nights remembered.[2] But those patrols produced no answers, and staff officers worked to ensure their units had a variety of plans in hand—for attack, for defense, and even, if necessary, for a withdrawal.

*****

As Hennessey and his platoon manned their lines in Lorraine, arrayed against their rarely seen adversaries in the woods, Allied ships continued to deliver fresh American units to Europe's shores. On January 22, 1945, the newest such unit—Ed Christl's 65th Infantry Division, the Battle-Axe—reached the harbor of Le Havre, on Normandy's coast. Landing craft shuttled Christl and his fellow artillerymen from the crowded troopship to a point about one hundred yards off the French beach and unceremoniously dropped their front ramps. There was nothing for the new arrivals to do but shoulder their heavy rucksacks above the rolling surf and wade shoreward through the icy waters. Once on the beach, they milled about in the cutting wind and their wet uniforms, awaiting trucks. When their transport arrived an hour later, a miserable ride followed to their bivouac—a massive encampment known as Camp Lucky Strike.

Now, once again, Christl and Hennessey were on the same continent, although more than simply 350 miles separated the two teammates. In Lorraine, Hennessey's world was one of frosted foxholes and tense night patrols. Thirty miles outside of Le Havre, at Camp Lucky Strike, Christl's immediate environment was one of endless rows of olive-drab, snow-covered pyramid tents, muddy latrines, and bad food. A massive staging area with few comforts, it had been left partially uncompleted by engineer units that had been rushed into the fray as reinforcements during the Battle of the Bulge. "It was the middle of winter, cold, and many of the tents lay flat under the weight of snow—a pretty depressing sight," remembered one of Christl's fellow officers.[3]

Almost as soon as they were settled at Camp Lucky Strike, the 65th Infantry Division's various components—the infantry regiments, the signal troops and engineers, the medical section, the ordnance company, and the artillery battalions such as Christl's 868th—embarked upon readying for the front lines in a manner of organization that would have been the envy of Hennessey's division. It had been rushed pell-mell with his division's detached infantry regiments into the front lines after only days in theater.

The Battle-Axe, on the other hand, had the relative luxury—if one could call time spent at Camp Lucky Strike in the dead of winter by such a term—of over a month at the encampment. By this point in the European campaign, the Germans' thrust into the Bulge had not only been contained but was also being grimly reduced, yard by yard. Although the 65th's troops would be badly needed for the next stage of the offensive in Nazi Germany, Eisenhower and his generals were not burdened with the same sense of urgency to rush untried troops into battle that they had suffered a month earlier. This enabled the generals the chance to afford the men of the Battle-Axe time to receive and prepare weapons, equipment, and vehicles, conduct small-unit training exercises, recover the physical conditioning lost over the course of their month-long journey to France, and, through a series of lectures, briefings, and lessons, be oriented to their new theater of operations. Some of the lessons were mundane—such as the importance of caring for one's feet in the wet, cold weather to avoid the agony of trench foot. Others were decidedly more violent—such as when unwary soldiers marched or drove into the score of German minefields that blanketed swaths of the Norman coastal countryside.

Occasionally, there was even time for rest and relaxation. Battle-Axe soldiers wrote letters home, wrangled the occasional pass from their sergeants, and even laid out a muddy softball field for pickup games. Some may have even received a letter or two. If Christl was one of those so lucky, his wife Virginia may have even enclosed some newspaper clips to keep him abreast of his old basketball team's fortunes back at West Point.

If so, the news Virginia shared with Christl would have been initially encouraging, as the Cadets continued their winning streak. After opening the 1945 season with a streak of victories against Swarthmore, Colgate, Columbia, Princeton, and Penn State, Coach Ed Kelleher's squad beat the Coast Guard Academy on January 27, 1945. The Minneapolis *Star Tribune* reported "Army Cagers Score 22nd Win."[4] Clearly Dale Hall and Doug Kenna, now first classmen with their own graduation approaching in June, had picked up where they had left off the previous season.

A win against West Virginia University followed as January came to an end, and then, on Saturday, February 3, West Point faced Yale. Before a crowd of three thousand packed into the academy's field house, Yale stunned Army by battling to a 27–21 lead after the first half of play. In the end, it was up to yearling Bobby Dobbs—who had carved out his reputation on the gridiron as a fullback and who would one day be the head coach for Tulsa University, the Calgary Stampeders, and Western Texas University—to win the game for West Point. With the cadets trailing 43–42 and 40 seconds left on the clock, Dobbs arched a long shot through the basket that gave Army the lead. At that point, Kelleher's vaunted defense froze the court. At the final whistle, West Point claimed a 44–43 victory over Yale and an 8–0 record for the season.[5]

✶✶✶✶✶

As Dobbs and company were battling to keep West Point's winning streak alive, Jack Hennessey and the rest of the 276th Infantry Regiment were preparing for a battle of a far different sort. By the first of February, the weather had warmed, but the change in temperature on the Lorraine-German border had brought with it new difficulties. The snow started melting, and, as rain clouds scudded through the region, the battle positions, staging fields, and roads soon turned to thick, clinging mud.

Meanwhile, American intelligence officers discerned the unsettling news from the German lines that ran through the French cities, towns, or villages of Forbach, Oeting, Behren, and Kerbach—a line that protected the commanding heights above and approaches to the German border city of Saarbrücken. The enemy, it seemed, was steadily reinforcing its positions—and maybe even preparing to launch a counterattack. This information spurred ongoing plans to conduct a raid-in-force against the

German positions in Oeting, even as, after a two-month separation, the rest of the 70th Infantry Division finally reached Task Force Herren. At a minute past midnight on February 4, Task Force Herren was dissolved, and Maj. Gen. Allison Barnett resumed commanded of the infantry regiments, but the change in designation had no impact on the officers and infantrymen in the front lines.

That same morning, a raiding party from the 3rd Battalion, 276th Infantry, pushed into the village of Marienau at daybreak that same morning, encountered no enemy, and soon withdrew with no new intelligence. Even so, the regiment's intelligence officer—the S-2—had a reasonably accurate sense of what the subsequent attack against Oeting would encounter. He warned of a long antitank ditch, 16 feet in depth, stretching across the enemy position and overseen by a separate system of trenches. Triple concertina rolls of barbed wire protected the trenches, complemented by concrete bunkers, dugouts, booby traps, Teller antitank mines, and antipersonnel mines.[6] The Germans obviously sensed that the otherwise unremarkable village of Oeting was the doorway to the small French city of Forbach and its heights overlooking the Saar River. With Forbach secured, the Americans would be one push away from breaching the river and striking into Germany.

On February 6, 1945, at one minute past midnight, the Americans made their move. Companies E and F advanced into the dark night, slogging through the mud and slush. Their objective was a hilltop west of Oeting labeled "Objective Zebra." Within 30 minutes, as they reached the first line of barbed wire, they came under heavy automatic-weapons and small-arms fire. Using bangalore torpedoes, the companies blasted a path through and edged forward. By 2:00 a.m., they were in the enemy trenches. "Here there was furious fighting," Maj. Theodore Mataxis, the 2nd Battalion's commander, recalled. "The enemy was in dug-outs within the trenches and had to be rooted out with bazookas, grenades, and bayonets. Closing with the enemy at close range, there were numerous examples of great personal heroism."

More bitter fighting occurred at the antitank ditch, but by 5:00 a.m. it had not only been breached, but the two Trailblazer companies had also seized Objective Zebra. Now that they possessed it, they had to hold it. The GIs dug fighting positions fast and deep in anticipation of the inevitable German counterattack.

With Zebra secured, it was Hennessey's, his platoon's, and the rest of G Company's turn to attack. Accompanied by K Company on their left, they crossed the assault's line of departure at 6:30 a.m. just as a driving sleet storm descended upon them. Undaunted, they moved toward their goal, a hilltop west of Oeting marked as "Objective Yoke," even as the self-propelled howitzers of the 93rd Armored Field Artillery Battalion began raining shells down in a roving barrage in the path of their advance. The barrage rolled up the long, painfully steep hillside toward the German positions, receded back toward the GIs, and then pushed forward once more. As the bursts began to move back toward the enemy, G and K Company followed in close pursuit, hoping that that artillery would keep the enemy pinned down.

Nevertheless, the Americans came under enemy fire as they advanced up the painfully steep slope—one that soon began exploding as GI boots trod upon German mines undetected despite the best efforts of pathfinding engineers. But the two companies doggedly continued their advance, even as enemy artillery and mortar shells began falling to add to the din. As one barrage started, Staff Sgt. Raymond Brubaker, with G Company's weapons platoon, jumped headfirst into a nearby ravine. "I felt something under me," he recalled four decades later. "It was a dead G.I. who had been killed several weeks before. He was frozen solid. His face was only two or three inches from mine and his eyes were wide open. The bottom part of his body was covered with snow, but the wind had blown the snow from his face. I had dreams about him for many nights after that."[7]

In a lull in the barrage, Brubaker joined the rest of G and K Companies in their grim push uphill. By 1:00 p.m., they had wrested control of Objective Yoke from the Germans, and they, like their comrades on Zebra, dug in for the night. The American-controlled high ground formed a horseshoe around Oeting, running in a curve from southeast of the town to the south and around to the southwest, west, and northwest. The exhausted and bloodied occupants of those hills spent a wretched afternoon under increasing enemy artillery and mortar fire, even as captured German prisoners revealed that reinforcements were being rushed forward to meet the American threat. Meanwhile, the rain and sleet continued to come down. As darkness descended on the evening of February 6, the men of G Company and the other companies were standing in foxholes almost knee-deep in water.

Fortunately, the four American companies spent the night of February 6 in comparative security. The next morning, however, the Germans counterattacked. First, they hammered into E and F Companies atop Objective Zebra. The infantrymen shoved the enemy attack back, even though battling with weapons so mud-clogged that barely one in three could fire. But even though their assault was stymied, the Germans managed to infiltrate units through and between the American units—a development that not only threatened the Trailblazer companies' supply lines but also even isolated them from one another.

Then the Germans turned their attention to Hennessey and the hill the Americans called Yoke. Supported by yet another artillery barrage, they smashed into thin, muddy lines of foxholes that constituted the defenses of G and K Companies. Hennessey's G Company suffered the brunt of the assault, and for a time the issue appeared seriously in doubt. "Again, the gallantry and heroism of our troops was responsible for our ability to hold our ground," Mataxis remembered. "In one instance, a machine gunner whose tripod had been shattered by mortar fire leaped to his feet and fired the weapon from his hip to disperse the enemy charge."[8] Even so, two of G Company's three platoons, beset by enemy units on all sides and out of contact with K Company, pulled back to the regiment's original line of outposts.

Nevertheless, both hills remained in American hands. But the Germans were not finished. Regrouping, they pounded Objective Zebra with artillery, mortar, and rocket fire and then, finding a sector of F Company more lightly secured than the others, attacked once again at 7:00 p.m., supported by a pair of tanks. F Company lost its artillery forward observer to enemy fire, and, bereft of artillery support, the company began to drift toward E Company. This movement, however, left E Company's position perilously exposed, and the regimental headquarters ordered Zebra to be abandoned. At the same time, G and K Companies slipped away from the hill under the cover of darkness and, although hounded by the enemy, executed a skillful withdrawal.

Once back in the comparative safety of their own lines, the regiment's assault companies licked their wounds. They had never been able to implement the third phase of their operational plan—the seizure of Oeting itself—but they took some solace in both the casualties inflicted on the German defenders and on the information on the enemy positions and terrain that the raid had garnered.

*****

In the wake of the Oeting raid, the 276th Infantry Regiment welcomed 10 days of rest and preparation for its next operation, even though the weather remained cold and rainy. The division pulled the regiment's G Company into the division's reserve and used it to implement a new and thorough program of training for the green replacements arriving to replace the casualties of the last six weeks of operations. The training regime included familiarization with all weapons, squad and platoon attack problems (day and night), field firing, scouting and patrolling, and land navigation and compass work.

The regiment's respite was only temporary, of course. Allied plans called for a push on to the German border—and beyond. The 70th Infantry Division's headquarters, in response, crafted a battle plan that tasked Hennessey's 276th Regiment with wresting the high ground above Oeting from the Germans, capturing the town below, pivoting the line of advance to the north-northwest to capture Forbach, and then, if ordered, pushing through the Forbach Forest to seize the high ground overlooking the Saar River and, beyond it, the German city of Saarbrücken. The rest of the Trailblazer Division would be attacking its own objectives, as would the 63rd Infantry Division on the division's right and the 101st Cavalry Group on its left.

At one minute past midnight on February 17, the American troops crept out of their staging areas and moved through the slush and mud into assault positions. At dawn, in the midst of a heavy fog that limited visibility to mere feet, they attacked. The regiment's 2nd Battalion, which included Hennessey's G Company was, at the time, being held in division reserve and was thus spared the opening blows of the battle.

Those blows were soon in coming. The attacking battalions, brushing aside small-arms fire and suffering casualties from land mines, crested the high ground overlooking Oeting. As the men moved forward across the muddy ground, it was clear that they were executing the hard lessons learned on their previous assault on those same hills. In particular, the American units stayed in contact with one another, foiling any opportunities for infiltrative German counterattacks. Doing so, however, was no easy task. "Everyone was covered with mud from hitting the ground and sliding into holes and depressions to avoid the artillery bursts," one of the regiment's soldiers remembered. "It was an extremely difficult chore to keep the mud from fouling up the rifles. Some men put their precious extra socks over the muzzles and some even wrapped them around the receivers."[9] Nevertheless, by midmorning, the regiment's B Company had gained a foothold in Oeting.

At that point, however, a stubborn quartet of German self-propelled 88-mm guns began blasting the Americans. The guns' heavy fire, accompanied by mortars, not only halted the advance but, by the afternoon, had also succeeded in pushing B Company back out of the unfortunate French hamlet, even as the regiment's dispatch of antitank guns to their assistance was stymied by a well-mined road. As darkness fell on February 17, the companies of the 276th Regiment dug in for the night, their positions arrayed for an all-around defense.

The next morning, on February 18, the American attack on Oeting resumed in a rainstorm, with the regiment's attacking battalions moving forward on a northwesterly axis and Hennessey and the rest of the 2nd Battalion still being held in the division's reserve. The attackers cleared Oeting of enemy troops by noon and, as the winter sun began to set, advanced toward their next objective—the small city of Forbach.

Forbach was only two miles distant, but between it and Oeting stood a set of steep hills heavily wooded by the forest known as the Kleinwald. One of those hills boasted the remnants of medieval Schlossberg Castle. From their vantage point atop the castle's red-stoned tower and battlements, German artillery observers called in artillery and mortar fire on the stubbornly advancing Americans. By nightfall, the Trailblazers had seized each of the critical hills—but for the one crowned by the castle. As night descended, the American soldiers dug in while their officers sketched out the next day's assault.

The next morning, February 19, the Americans eschewed the usual daylight assault. Instead, a ground reconnaissance conducted by the key company commanders and forward observers first took place. Then, at 8:00, as the usual morning fog burned off, the 3rd Battalion of the 276th resumed its attack. As if taking a page from the tales of Sir Walter Scott, American infantry stormed the hilltop castle. A nearby barracks complex, still occupied by obstinate German defenders, proved a bastion in its own right. But by midafternoon the castle was in American hands, and, with the heights secured, the men of the 1st Battalion now pushed into Forbach.

In the city, the 1st Battalion faced tough opposition from the Germans. The 3rd Battalion moved to assist but encountered stiff opposition as well. A soldier fighting in the regiment's Company A described the GIs' brutal introduction to urban warfare:

> City fighting was a new and different experience for the Trailblazers. Before their attack on Forbach, their warfare had been entirely in small villages, forests, and mountains. The multi-storied buildings presented different types of obstacles than did the small houses of Wingen. Each building was like a huge bunker, with basement windows that opened onto the streets like pillbox embrasures. The solid stone walls varied from several inches to more than three feet thick. Many would withstand the shells from 105mm artillery.[10]

The city's German defenders, on the other hand, seemed well versed in urban fighting. Intimately familiar with every building, street, alley, and neighborhood square in Forbach, they established strongpoints at strategic locations, defended with rifles, light mortars, and automatic weapons, throughout the city. Adding to the bloody, noisy chaos, German forward observers directed mortar and artillery fire on the advancing GIs with almost supernatural accuracy, while snipers claimed their own toll. "Often three or four enemy soldiers, strategically located, were easily able to hold up an entire attacking platoon."[11]

Nightfall on February 19 witnessed Forbach still in German hands. Maj. Gen. Allison Barnett, the 70th Division's commander, visited Col.

Albert Morgan in the 276th's regimental command post that evening in Folkingen. "Cut, slash, and drive," Barnett directed his regimental commander.[12] He wanted Forbach in American hands.

But even as Barnett was uttering those words, enemy action proved that the capture of Forbach was not a foregone conclusion. German soldiers poured out of Forbach's outlying buildings and surged up the hill toward Schlossberg Castle "with almost fanatical zeal, yelling in the darkness as they came on."[13] The counterattack reached the base of the tower, where some even crossed into the keep's walls. Their only reward for their persistence was a deadly hail of American gunfire. The castle would remain in American hands, even though pummeled for the rest of the night with artillery and mortar fire.

The next morning, February 20, the Trailblazer infantrymen launched their third day of attacks. Heavy small-arms, automatic-weapons, mortar, and artillery fire broke up the American attacks, however, so now Colonel Morgan committed his 2nd Battalion to the fray. Hennessey's G Company was, as the division's reserve, still spared the combat. But with fighting intensifying in Forbach, one could only wonder how long G Company's respite might last.

The following day, February 21, represented more of the same as the Germans pushed their own reinforcements into Forbach. Now the battle for the town became a grinding, block-by-block slugfest, as the American infantrymen wrested one building at a time from an enemy that contested each advance with nests of snipers and fortified strongpoints. Nighttime brought Colonel Morgan some satisfaction as he surveyed the gains his men had achieved on the streets of Forbach, but those same soldiers suffered a long night trying to hold their gains against enemy attacks.

Particularly terrifying to the Trailblazer soldiers were the Germans' liberal employment of the trailered rocket launchers known as *Nebelwerfers*—nicknamed "screaming meemies" by the American GIs. "They made terrifying, eerie, rasping howls like the legs of a heavy table being dragged over a marble floor, amplified a thousand times," one of the regiment's soldiers remembered. "Merely the sound of those rockets going through the air, particularly at night, was enough to send chills up and down an alligator's spine. It was a sound that one did not soon forget."[14]

The next day's dawn brought more fighting, seemingly more bitter and brutal than the days before. The Germans turned houses' basements into pillboxes and defended each position to the very end, even as their own artillery and mortar shells rained down in the streets outside.

Self-propelled assault guns, automatic weapons, and *Panzerfausts* added to the mayhem, as did American air strikes, but by the end of the day on February 22, the GIs had reached the railroad tracks that split the town in half.

Now, for the moment, their commanders were content with their gains, and the Americans eased on their offensive against Forbach. They spent the rest of the month consolidating their positions, mopping up remaining pockets of enemy resistance, beating back persistent counter-attacks, enduring the frequent German mortar fire, and preparing for further action.

Meanwhile, two miles to the rear but seemingly a world away, Hennessey and the rest of G Company stood in the division's reserve in Morsbach. After two months of winter campaigning, the unit had seen several company commanders come and go. Now G Company was led by a first lieutenant from Hamilton, Ohio, named Adrian Bieker. As the divisional reserve, Bieker's outfit was spared the fighting for Forbach. That respite, however, ended on March 3, 1945, when G Company's assignment in the reserve concluded. The final assault to push the Germans out of Forbach was at hand, and G Company would be a part of it.

CHAPTER 14

Philadelphia

As Jack Hennessey's comrades in the 276th Infantry Regiment battled in the steep, snowy hills outside of Oeting and the rubble-strewn streets of Forbach and prepared for the final push to liberate the latter, the infantry lieutenant's former basketball team back at West Point continued its triumphant march through the 1945 season. With Hennessey's 1944 campaign as inspiration, Coach Ed Kelleher's squad looked capable of repeating the previous season's remarkable perfect season.

On February 7, 1945, the cadets hosted the University of Pittsburgh. With a 6–1 record, the Panthers promised to pose a challenge to Army, but their erratic play proved no match for the West Point squad. After the first four minutes of play, Army seized and never relinquished the lead. Dale Hall paced the quintet with 24 points, and, by the end of 40 minutes play, West Point posted a 71–51 victory for its ninth win of the season.[1]

Three days later, on February 10, it was the University of Rochester's turn to face Army. "Unbeaten Army received little more than a workout yesterday afternoon in setting the University of Rochester basketball team, 79 to 42, before a small gathering of cadets and officers in the field house," Rochester's *Democrat and Chronicle* reported dolefully.[2] The Cadets bounded to an 8–0 lead to begin the game and never looked back. Doug Kenna, who had struggled previously due to recurring problems with a knee injured two seasons ago in football, still managed to post 22 points. John Nance, Class of 1946 and a future captain of the squad, contributed 16 from his position at guard. "Army Five Captures 26th Straight, 79–42," headlines reported.[3]

St. John's was West Point's next opponent, and many felt the 13–1 Redmen would be the toughest opponents of the season so far. Coach Kelleher certainly thought so. He went so far as to warn Brooklyn sportswriter Harold Parrott that his team would likely lose the upcoming match. "Of course, my kids will give it everything they have," the "stocky sage" assured Parrott. "They are great kids and they will never stop driving and scrapping. But I don't think they can be expected to win this one."

Pressed to explained by the sportswriter, the coach responded. "Experience, of course," Kelleher said. "St. John's has the know-how. They can control the ball game. My boys may not know what to do if the St. John's kids refuse to give them the ball. We've always managed to get the ball when we needed it. We may not be able to persuade St. John's to let us have it tomorrow."[4]

"Tomorrow" fell on Wednesday, February 14. Although the day was Valentine's Day, no love was lost between the home team and their visitors from Brooklyn. Over the course of the game, 21 fouls were called—a noteworthy occurrence in the basketball of the day—and more than once the referee had to spring into action to keep the two teams from coming to blows. In the end, however, Cadets proved too strong and talented for the Redmen. The final score was Army 56, St. John's 39. By now, West Point had won 11 games in a row and had not seen a defeat in a 27-game streak that stretched over three seasons.[5]

The University of Pennsylvania figured next on the Cadets' schedule. The contest occasioned a road trip to Philadelphia's Convention Hall, where Army faced a Quaker squad that had posted five losses already during the season. A crowd of 11,505 fans packed the venue for the doubleheader (Temple would play NYU in the nightcap), even though most considered Penn to be a "soft touch" for Army. Many of them were likely thinking that this was a rare chance to see a West Point team that, once it beat Penn, had only to handle NYU, Maryland, and Navy to complete the remarkable feat of a second undefeated season.[6]

Penn, however, had a secret weapon on hand: a 6'4" forward named Howie Dallmar. Three years earlier, Dallmar had led Stanford University to victory in the 1942 NCAA tournament, defeating Dartmouth for the championship and claiming honors as the tournament's most outstanding player. Now Dallmar was at Penn as one of its Navy V-7 trainees, playing on Coach Don Kellett's squad for part of a lone season. In fact, tonight's game would be his last before he left campus for further naval training.

At 8:00 that Saturday night, as the largest crowd ever to have seen a basketball game in Philadelphia took its seats, "weeks of anticipation became explosive reality at Convention Hall."[7] "Explosive" fairly described Army's opening moments of the game: in short order, a pair of baskets by John Nance put the score at 4–0 Army; it was soon 8–1. Army's defense kept the Quakers out of the paint while, on the perimeter, Penn's long shots failed to find their mark. At the half progressed, West Point logged leads of 15–4, 17–8, and 23–12. As the half wound down, a late rally by Penn closed the gap to Army 29, Penn 25.

The Quakers managed to keep their momentum even after the halftime break. Freshman Bob Carlson scored on a rebound, and then Dallmar rifled a pass the entire length of the court to another freshman, Phil Harman, who sank one of his eight field goals for the evening. Harman's shot brought the score to a tie at 29–29, but then Army's Kenna drew a foul and hit the resulting shot from the line. Now the score was Army 30, Penn 29 but only for a moment. A quick Quaker give-and-go gave Penn its first lead of the game.

As the second half battle progressed, and the fans screamed themselves hoarse, Dallmar treated the crowd to a veritable passing clinic. "The 22-year-old San Franciscan was surpassing even his incandescent best," gushed Art Morrow of the *Philadephia Inquirer*. "Over his shoulder, under the small of his back, front, side, Dallmar was feeding his teammates from all over the court."[8]

In response, Army scrambled all over the court in increasing desperation. West Point kept the game close for much of the half—with three minutes, nine seconds left, the score was Penn 54, Army 50—but Penn did not take its foot off the gas. By the time the clock showed four seconds left, the score stood at Penn 61, Army 54, and Coach Kellett pulled an exhausted, panting Dallmar off the court. The crowd in the stands gave him a rousing standing ovation that managed to stop play for a full two minutes. Of course, by then, the game's denouement was merely a formality. At the final whistle, West Point's winning streak was over.

"Stunning, amazing, stupendous—adjectives were paled into insignificance at Convention Hall by the facts of the basketball season's greatest upset," trumpeted Morrow.[9]

With three games left in the season, the Cadets could not, of course, dwell on their loss to Penn. Returning to the academy, they rested and regrouped over the course of the following week before taking on New York University on the Cadets' home court on February 24. Army may had lost on the road in Philadelphia, but it still had its home winning streak to protect—and the NYU Violet, heartened by Penn's stunning upset of the Cadets, could smell blood in the water.

With the stakes so high, some five thousand officers and cadets bulged the field house to capacity for the Army-NYU game. Perhaps adjusting from the loss to Penn, Kelleher kept his team at a slow, deliberate pace of play. For the first half, the strategy seemed to work, as West Point went into intermission with a comfortable 32–22 lead. Dale Hall led Army's scorers, ultimately posting 20 points for the game.[10]

In the second half, however, the NYU quintet, led by Sid Tanenbaum, Don Forman, and Al Grenert, began to steadily chip at Army's lead. Then, with two minutes remaining in the game, NYU's center, Dolph Schayes, drew a foul. The future 12-time NBA All-Star capitalized with a basket to pull the Violet ahead, 51–50.

But two minutes was all that Army needed. Hall pushed in for a layup to put Army back on top, and when the Cadets were able to add another basket to raise the deficit to three points, they went into a freeze defense. The game ended Army 54, NYU 51.[11]

Then came the University of Maryland, in second to last game of the season. The Terrapins, limping into West Point with a 2–12 record, promised to be merely a warm-up for the Cadets' tilt against the Midshipmen. Coach Kelleher opted to begin the game with his junior varsity, and after the first half the score stood at 19–19. At that point, he pushed his luck no further. The varsity took to the court for the second half, and, in a span of 12 minutes, Dale Hall put 15 points on the scoreboard. The Cadets' defense shut down the visitors' offense, and by the end of the contest Army had notched a 54–34 win.[12]

Now only a single game remained in the 1945 season. That game, scheduled for March 3, 1945, would be against Navy—and it would be on the road. Navy, like Army, boasted a 13–1 record and, like Army, was prepared to put it all on the line in the season's finale. In the years to come, few of the members of Navy's basketball squad would remember whether their record for 1945 was 14–1 or 13–2. But they would all remember if they beat Army. They had not beaten Army since 1941. They had no intention of enduring yet another loss—particularly on their home court in Annapolis.

The Midshipmen were not the only ones hungering for West Point's visit to Annapolis. Sports pages in papers across the country trumpeted the impending showdown with banner headlines. "Army-Navy Basketball Game Will Be Heard Around World," sportswriter Al Vermeer proclaimed in a syndicated column that ran from New Brunswick, New Jersey, to Brownsville, Texas.[13] "The Army-Navy basketball tussle likely will be the best of the eastern season," predicted columnist Hugh Fullerton Jr.[14]

As team captain Dale Hall—now with a team-high 196 points for the season—prepared to lead Army in the impending contest with Navy, his former teammate Hennessey readied his own men for their next challenge. Forbach had blocked the Trailblazers' advance to the German frontier for nearly a month. For the Americans, that was long enough. March 3 would not only mark the day Hall and West Point took the final fight of their season to Annapolis. It would also mark the day that Hennessey and his comrades-in-arms took their final fight to Forbach.

CHAPTER 15

Across the Saar

In Forbach, France, March 3, 1945, dawned cloudy with enough light rain to reduce visibility on the city's muddy streets to a couple hundred yards. American artillery barraged the German positions. Then, at 8:17, the infantrymen of the 70th Infantry Division, supported by tanks from the 12th Armored Division, attacked. Their objective was not only the remaining German-occupied section of Forbach but the high ground beyond, which overlooked the Saar River and the German city of Saarbrücken.[1]

Initial plans sent the 276th Infantry Regiment's 1st and 3rd Battalions across the railroad tracks that demarked American-controlled Forbach from the half of the French town still occupied by the Germans. For a time, Hennessey's 2nd Battalion stood in the regiment's reserve but not for long. Heavy enemy artillery and mortar file slowed the Trailblazers' advance and cut off their wire communications. For a time, the fog of war was both literal and figurative. It only became foggier as the Americans deployed a smoke screen and pushed the 2nd Battalion forward into the action. Moving surreptitiously, the battalion took position for an assault the next morning on the woods.

The next morning, the attack continued. Led by Lieutenant Adrian Bieker, Hennessey and G Company, along with the rest of the 2nd Battalion, pushed into the woods north of Forbach and toward the Simon coal mine complex while they endured mortar and small-arms fire from both their front and from German infiltrators to their rear and flanks. Meanwhile, the rest of the regiment shoved farther into Forbach, supported by a company of French troops and aided by tanks and tank destroyers that continued to struggle with mined and booby-trapped streets and underpasses.

Fighting continued on the following day, March 5, as passing rainstorms added their own layer of misery to the battle. But by now it was clear that momentum was on the attackers' side, particularly as obstacles and mines were cleared and more armored vehicles were able to pass the railroad tracks and enter the northwestern section of town. By late that morning, the staff of the 70th Division leaned over their maps and marked Forbach as taken.

Determined to retain their prize, the companies of the 274th and 276th Regiments pushed into the town's northern outskirts, shoving back German delaying actions throughout the afternoon. Then, as a misty dusk descended on Forbach, they dug in. The GIs spent yet another long night hunkered down in the cold, muddy ground, arrayed in platoon positions focused on all-around security, as their officers planned the next morning's push.

*****

In such a manner, Hennessey and his fellow Trailblazer soldiers liberated Forbach—at least for the moment. But what of Coach Kelleher, Dale Hall, Doug Kenna, and the rest of the West Point basketball squad's season-ender against Navy? As Hennessey's G Company had spent a fitful night in forward assault positions in Forbach, positioned to strike against the Germans in the woods beyond Forbach in the first day of the Trailblazers' push on the town, the 1945 basketball season's climax played out four thousand miles to the west.

The Naval Academy's historic Dahlgren Hall provided the venue for the game, selling out four thousand tickets in under two hours.[2] Ultimately, the number of spectators would reach five thousand, pushing the facility to its limits and beyond. Looking at the two teams that were both boasting 13–1 records, sportswriters and other prognosticators gave the home team the edge.

To the delight of the home crowd, Perry Nelson wasted no time in scoring the first basket of the game. Soon the forward single-handedly brought the score to 5–0. By the seven-minute mark, the score stood at 11–5, with Nelson responsible for 10 of Navy's 11 points. The score belied the game's terrific pace, and, as the half progressed, Army clawed back into contention. Despite his concerns about Doug Kenna's trick knee, which had troubled him throughout the season, Kelleher deployed him to replace Ed Rafalko on the floor. At that point, Army's fast break began to click. Kenna scored to bring the score to 13–12, Army's advantage, even as the lead seesawed back and forth. At one point, the score was 15–15; at another, it was knotted at 19–19. Then a pair of foul shots by the seemingly irrepressible Nelson made the score Navy 21, Army 19. By the time the first half ended, the score stood 25–24 in Navy's favor.

Kenna struck first in the second half, but Navy's Jack Carroll matched Kenna's basket with one of his own. A right-handed shot from Bobby Dobbs under the backboard earned Army the lead 28–27.

At that point, the game between the two academies evolved into a "brilliant defensive test," according to the Associated Press's Frank Eck, one of the many sportswriters in attendance.[3] Indeed, in the fierce back-and-forth, Navy guard Adrian Back held the vaunted Dale Hall to a single basket. Guarding Back, Kenna returned the favor, keeping Navy's potent shooter to a mere five points himself.

As the second half progressed, the game again knotted, this time at 35–35. At that point, Nelson committed his fourth personal foul, however, and was dispatched to Navy's bench to rest on the laurels of a 17-point game. Meanwhile, on the court, John Nance sank the resulting foul shot. Taking advantage of Nelson's departure, Rafalko, who was now back in for Kenna, dropped in a basket. So did Nance. Their handiwork brought the score to Army 40, Navy 35.

As the timekeeper's clock showed five minutes left to play, the score stood 49–43 in favor of Army. The two teams exchanged a pair of foul shots, bring the score to 50–44 as the back-and-forth tussle reached the game's final minute. Then Navy forward Bobby Howe sank a long-range set shot. Adrian Back, a veteran of two seasons at the University of Kentucky and a future All-American for Navy, did the same. Suddenly, the scoreboard read Army 50, Navy 48.

After Back's last basket, Army cautiously pushed down court. But frenetic defense by the Midshipmen reclaimed the ball for Navy, and, with 20 seconds left, Back took another long shot; it fell short. In the ensuring fracas, however, the Midshipman seized the ball. As the final second ticked off the clock, he launched a desperation shot at Army's goal. Back's shot hit the rim and bounced away just as the final buzzer blasted. The game ended with a score of Army 50, Navy 48. Once again, bragging rights belonged to Army for another year.[4]

With the 1945 season over, Hall would claim All-American honors and be named the *Sporting News* Men's College Basketball Player of the Year. His classmate (and class president) Doug Kenna was not finished with academy sports quite yet; he would finish the school year playing for West Point's tennis team. But both cadets probably shared the focus of their classmates as they counted down to their impending graduation on June 5, 1945. Once commissioned into the Army, would the new second lieutenants join the fight in Europe and the Far East? The answer to that question, in large part, rested in the hands of their former teammates and the soldiers they were leading in combat in last days of that cold winter overseas.

*****

As Hall and Kenna basked in the victory of their win over Navy and set their sights on new challenges, Hennessey's company and its fellow Trailblazers set their own sights—literally—on the murky tree lines across their muddy fields of fire. By now, they had realized that the Germans were unlikely to acquiesce to their gains in Forbach and beyond—and, once again, the lesson held true.

In the predawn darkness of March 6, the Germans counterattacked, skillfully infiltrating between the American companies and cutting off the 276th Regiment's F Company from the rest of the regiment. Supported by a pair of tanks, the enemy wasted no time in manning abandoned bunkers, setting up machine-gun nests, and calling in artillery and rocket fire. In response, B Company attacked from the west; G Company drove in from the east. Shortly after noon, the Americans had managed to restore the situation and resumed the attack northward into the high ground that separated Forbach from the Saar River.

In those wooded hills, G Company and its sister companies encountered their most formidable obstacle yet—a single-track railroad running along an embankment that stood 20 feet high. From embrasures under the tracks, German rifle and machine-gun fire flashed and winked evilly at any American soldier who risked showing himself. An antipersonnel ditch in front of the embankment protected the enemy position like a medieval moat; an antitank ditch foiled any effort to bring forward supporting armor. "To make a frontal assault without more supporting weapons would be suicide," the regiment's after action report noted.[5] It also reported that, off to the right of the railroad embankment, on the regiment's right flank, the 274th Regiment was encountering its own problems as it grappled with an obstinate enemy force that had turned the Simon mine complex into a German stronghold. G Company, on its regiment's right flank, also suffered from gunfire from the Simon mine.

For the moment, any farther advance seemed impossible. But looking across the antitank ditch to his front, Lieutenant Bieker recognized that G Company had to seize the high ground on the other side of the ditch if it had any hope of holding its gains so far. Bieker courageously led G Company across the ditch, even as German artillery shells rained down on their passage. Shrapnel and concussions from the blasts wounded Bieker and several of his men, but, undaunted, he pushed forward. Despite his wounds, Bieker remained on the battlefield and in command, organizing his position, caring for the wounded, directing artillery fire, and tying in his right flank as best he could with Companies I and L of the 274th Regiment. But enemy artillery continued to fall around him. Finally one exploded too close. This time, the blow was fatal. For his courage and leadership, Bieker would be posthumously awarded the Silver Star.[6]

With the company commander dead, Hennessey took command. As the unseen sun set on the gray horizon to the west, the Germans counterattacked. Supported by tanks, they blasted the woods occupied by G Company and tried to drive a wedge between the two regiments. But the late Lieutenant Bieker's skillfully positioned defenses withstood the challenge. As the Germans pushed forward, Hennessey called in a concentrated artillery barrage as the company's rifles, BARs, and light machine guns cracked and chattered in response. Confronted with such firepower, the enemy attack dissipated, leaving G Company to endure yet another uncertain night on the front lines.

The next two days, March 7 and 8, brought colder weather. Snow fell in the morning, turning to on-and-off rain showers. Muddy roads only became muddier as G Company and its sister units consolidated and improved their defensive positions during the daylight hours and kept up active patrolling during the night. Meanwhile, German artillery, rockets, and mortars continued to fall on hapless Forbach and among the American units. At one point, a prisoner of war warned that the Germans might use poison gas, prompting division supply officers to scramble to reissue to the Trailblazers their gas masks.[7]

Such a state of affairs continued for the next four days, although the skies cleared, the weather warmed, the roads dried, the mud hardened, and the fear of a gas attack evaporated. Orders arrived from battalion headquarters tabbing Hennessey as G Company's new commander, and he, like the other company commanders along the front line, pushed out patrols to keep the enemy at bay, even as German artillery, mortar, and rocket fire continued to torment the American lines. Nevertheless, between patrols and incoming artillery fire, the tired, dirty, bedraggled GIs of the 70th Infantry Division were able to take heart at the wisp of a rumor that, unlike so many others, was soon confirmed as true. One hundred miles to their north at Remagen in Germany, the 9th Armored Division had seized the Ludendorff Bridge over the Rhine River on March 7, opening an avenue of advance over that formidable barrier directly into the German heartland. The Rhine bridgehead was a devastating complement to Patton's Third Army's earlier push across the Saar and its capture of the ancient city of Trier, some 30 miles northwest and downriver of the 70th's positions. Patton's forcing of the Moselle River on March 13 and his resulting rampage eastward further exposed the German defenses in the Saarland to impending disaster.

The crumbling strategic situation to their rear must have contributed to the scene observed by American scouts outside of Forbach that same day: the Germans were withdrawing from their staunch defensive line along the railroad embankment and pulling out of the Simon mine complex.

Wasting no time, General Barnett hastily organized his regiments for a pursuit and unleashed them northward toward the Saar.

As Hennessey's company moved forward, the weight of his new responsibility as company commander lay heavily on his shoulders. But Hennessey rose to the challenge. "Time after time, when his company was subjected to heavy artillery and mortar fire, he led them forward and maneuvered them in such a manner that numerous casualties were avoided," his citation for another Bronze Star (this one for meritorious service) would read. "When one of his platoons encountered heavy enemy resistance, he would leave his Command Group to lend whatever assistance was needed or possible."

"At the completion of a mission, he personally assured himself that his men were properly cared for before looking after his own needs," the citation continued. "His courage and devotion to duty are in accordance with the highest military tradition." [8]

*****

By the afternoon of March 13, the 276th Regiment's GIs were slogging across the prewar French-German border on the outskirts of Petite-Rosselle, mindful of the thick minefields left behind by the enemy. The following day, they reached the southern banks of the Saar River, only to then turn to the deadly work of rooting out isolated bands of German defenders from positions on that side of the river. Meanwhile, on the northern side of the Saar, enemy pillboxes and emplacements rained fire on any GI who dared show himself as the Americans scouted for possible crossing points. This state of affairs continued for three days.

As the evening of March 16 drew near, the 276th Infantry Regiment's staff hatched plans to cross the river. Companies were directed to push patrols across the river at various points that evening and, should a beachhead be established, to follow such patrols in force. But such plans proved wistful thinking. Heavy German gunfire drove back each patrol's flotilla of paddled rafts.

For the next two days, the Americans had to be content with careful patrolling along the river's southern bank and, later, bringing up antiaircraft guns and tank destroyers to pummel the enemy pillboxes across the river with punishing direct fire. Even so, heavy barrages of German artillery shook the southern bank each night, underscoring the difficulty that a riverine assault would face. Nevertheless, under the cover of darkness on the night of March 19, the 70th Infantry Division tried to force the river once more.

For its part, the 276th Regiment slipped a patrol from Company C in a pair of boats across the Saar near Hostenbach, Germany, shortly before midnight. On the other side of the river, they found only an unoccupied pillbox but then stumbled into a minefield. Engineers were soon dispatched to clear it, while the remainder of the 1st Battalion, to be followed by the 3rd and 2nd Battalions, waited anxiously in the darkness along the southern riverbank for the word to cross.

By 3:00 the following morning, March 20, a narrow path through the minefield had been cleared and boats began ferrying the 1st Battalion across the river. As they arrived, the engineers turned their attention to assembling both a footbridge and a vehicular bridge. The footbridge was finished by 7:00 a.m., and the regiment's 2nd and 3rd Battalions quickly tramped across. The 8-ton vehicle bridge was completed by noon, and, with trucks, armored cars, and tank destroyers soon rumbling across it, the regiment could be confident that a bridgehead had been secured across the Saar.

Meanwhile, the 274th Regiment had mounted a similarly effective crossing at Ottenhausen, three miles to the east. Swinging to the right and east, the two regiments closed on Saarbrücken as their sister regiment, the 275th, crossed the river directly south of the city as night fell. No resistance was offered, and when March 21 dawned the German city awoke to find itself occupied by the soldiers of the Trailblazers. The 274th's soldiers had claimed the honors of first treading—warily—into Saarbrücken; the 276th had contented itself with occupying the city's western suburbs of Püttlingen and Altenkessel. Hennessey's G Company settled into the latter and, for the moment, awaited further orders.

CHAPTER 16

The Battle-Axe Strikes

Jack Hennessey had little way of fully appreciating the fact at the time, but the relative ease with which the Seventh Army and its subordinate units crossed the Saar River in the vicinity of Saarbrücken was in no small part due to the hard-charging tanks and soldiers of Patton's Third Army. At Saarbrücken, the Saar ran from east to west, and, with the Third Army punching relentlessly eastward across the rear of the southward-facing German defenders, the German commanders seemed to have realized that little would be gained by standing and fighting for the Saar. In this sector of the Reich, the proverbial game was over.

Hennessey was even less likely to know that bouncing along in a jeep in the olive-drab torrent of men and machinery that made up the Third Army was his old friend and teammate Ed Christl. Christl's 868th Field Artillery Battalion, along with its three sister battalions in the 65th Infantry Division, was helping Patton blast his way eastward across the Rhineland-Palatinate. "Never send an infantryman when you can send an artillery shell," a fellow American general had once said, and Christl, as a forward observer, was the death-dealing summoner of such shells.[1]

The 65th Infantry Division—the Battle-Axe—had spent slightly over a month at Camp Lucky Strike, preparing for deployment to the front lines. It was a luxury that the exigencies of the Western European campaign had denied the 70th Division, committed piecemeal to suffer the blows of Operation Nordwind in the Vosges Mountains at the turn of the new year. Still, one wonders how many men in the Battle-Axe's ranks felt any better prepared for combat when their own orders for deployment

Advance of 65th Infantry Division through France, Germany, and Austria, January 1945 to May 1945.

to the front lines came at the end of February. From February 25 to March 1, 1945, the division moved by train and truck eastward across France, rumbling and clicking through the cities of Beauvais, Compiègne, Soissons, and Metz, to finally reach an assembly area midway between Metz and Thionville. Maj. Gen. Stanley Reinhart set up his division command post in the village of Ennery.[2]

Reinhart's division was part of XX Corps, the famed "Ghost Corps" commanded by Maj. Gen. Walton Walker, which, in turn, was assigned to Patton's Third Army. Reinhart's orders directed him to relieve the 26th Infantry Division, which had been holding defensive positions along the Saar River at the fortress city of Saarlautern (today's Saarlouis). The handoff of positions soon began, and units of the 65th Infantry Division completed its relief of the 26th Infantry Division on March 9, 1945. At that point, the Battle-Axe was truly a frontline unit.

In the days that followed, the 65th Infantry Division conducted what a unit history described as an "aggressive holding action," complemented by intensive patrolling on both sides of the river and the extensive use of artillery fire against the enemy personnel and installations on the eastern bank of the river. Over the course of 10-day period, forward observers such as Christl called in approximately 1,275 missions, with almost 19,000 105-mm and 155-mm rounds dropped on the German positions.[3]

Meanwhile, Battle-Axe infantrymen such as Thomas J. Thompson— drafted into the army from his home in Richmond, Virginia, almost year ago to the day—held the line. Forty years later, he remembered those late winter days outside of Saarlautern.

> The winter of 1944–45 was bitterly cold; the wind blew, and it snowed a great deal. There was no way an infantryman could stay warm or keep his feet dry. The best you could do was keep your feet from freezing or from getting trench foot. Actually, we were better off than most, because for part of the time our position was in the French Maginot Line. The pillboxes were damp and cold, but at least we could keep out of the wind and snow.[4]

It would have been a rare man who would have volunteered to share such positions with GIs like Thompson when even a few hundred yards to the rear seemed to spell the difference between privilege and privation. But Christl was one such man. One evening shortly after his battalion's arrival on the outskirts of Saarlautern, the battalion commander gathered his officers in the dank cellar that served as his command post. As it came time for forward observation posts to be assigned—some at quiet overlooks in the hills along the Saar, others within mere blocks of the Germans amid the rubble and broken glass of Saarlautern—each lieutenant waited intently for his fateful card to be dealt. But then Christl cut the tension. With his usual quiet confidence, he asked for the most dangerous forward post.

"He knew no fear," an officer in the cellar that night later remembered. "All his enthusiasm shone forth and he was simply trying to say that it wouldn't be so tough after all."[5]

The days and nights that followed were, for the officers and soldiers of the 65th Infantry Division, plagued with unseen snipers, incessant machine-gun fire, and intense mortar and artillery shelling. In Saarlautern and across the river in the bridgehead in the Fraulautern neighborhood, certain streets were covered by sniper fire, and the GIs, as a matter of survival, learned to avoid those deadly streets as a matter of self-preservation. Meanwhile, patrols confirmed the grim warnings that the departing 26th Infantry Division has shared with its relief: every house, with its doubly reinforced walls, was in reality a potential pillbox, and tunnels connecting the urban strongpoints proved that the Germans had been preparing their defense for quite some time.[6] Christl's West Point classmate Frank Keifer earned one of his regiment's first Purple Hearts when a German tossed a potato-masher grenade at him during a night patrol. Later he earned a Bronze Star for personally blowing up an enemy bunker.[7]

For the Americans, the nightly race to the rear for rations, supplies, ammunition, and mail required running a deadly gauntlet, and, mortar shell by sniper bullet, the enemy began taking its toll of the GIs. So did ongoing efforts to keep field phone wires—blown apart each day by mortar blasts—connecting the frontline observation posts to their platoons and companies and connecting those same companies to their rear. Few nights were more unnerving for the men in a forward OP, placed within a few hundred yards—or feet—of the enemy lines and cut off from communication with their rear. The only thing worse was when the Germans discovered the location of the OPs and, calling in mortars, artillery, or *Nebelwerfer* rockets, blasted them to oblivion. The presence of an artillery forward observer team, identified by their radio antenna and binoculars, only added to the peril in the OPs. Knowing that the field artillerymen were tasked with calling and controlling fire missions, the Germans made any OP with a forward observer team a priority target.[8] Such was Christl's introduction to combat.

"We thought that we knew Ed well before we left the States, but we found we had a lot to learn in the awful test of battle," a fellow officer and classmate observed. "For it is in battle that men's Souls are tried. In the awful din of falling artillery and mortar shells or in the whine of machine gun bullets, or the fearsome sound of the 'Screaming Mimmie' a man becomes either a leader or one who is led."[9]

*****

March 13 dawned with the promise of an end to the stalemate along the Saar and Moselle Rivers. As XX Corps's 94th, 80th, and the 26th Infantry Divisions stormed across the Moselle River north of Saarlautern, the 65th Infantry Division's 260th Infantry Regiment launched its own limited attacked in the Saarlautern bridgehead in the hope of distracting the German command. Although the resulting two days of street fighting was both bitter and inconclusive, the attacks seemed to have sown the desired confusion. Two days later, on March 17, the 260th's sister regiment, the 261st, was able to put companies from two of its battalions across the river at Menningen. The reward for the 261st's success in that regard was, seemingly, an order for the 65th Infantry Division to join in the general assault.

The 65th Infantry Division executed that order at 4:30 a.m. on March 18. While the 261st seized the small town of Dillingen and the high ground east of Saarlautern, the other regiments, tasked with securing Saarlautern itself, could only measure their advance in the metrics of a few city blocks. The experience of Pfc. Frederick C. Murphy on that day of battle gives a vivid glimpse of what the Battle-Axe men faced on the streets of Saarlautern.

Murphy had graduated five years earlier from Massachusetts's prestigious Thayer Academy—coincidentally, a school founded in 1877 by the endowment of Col. Sylvanus Thayer, known at West Point as "the Father of West Point." Twice he had failed his physical examination as he tried to enlist. Finally, he succeeded on his third attempt and joined the 65th at Camp Shelby as a medic assigned to E Company, 259th Infantry Regiment. By March 18, 1945, he was crouching with the rest of E Company in the predawn darkness in Saarlautern, ready to launch their assault.

At dawn, the attack began—but the Germans were ready. Almost immediately, Murphy was wounded in the right arm. Nevertheless, he refused to withdraw for treatment. Instead, staying with his company, he continued forward, administering first aid to fellow soldiers under heavy machine-gun, mortar, and artillery fire.

The situation grew worse when E Company ran into a thickly sown antipersonnel minefield. Amid the exploding mines, more and more of Murphy's comrades fell dead and wounded. Still disregarding his own wound, the medic braved the danger of exploding mines, moving about through heavy fire and helping the injured—until he stepped on a mine himself. The explosion severed one of his feet. But in spite of his grievous wounds, he struggled on with his work, refusing to be evacuated and crawling from man to man, administering to them while in great pain himself and bleeding profusely. Finally, crawling toward another wounded GI, Murphy triggered another mine. The blast killed him. He would ultimately be awarded the Medal of Honor for his courage and self-sacrifice—but one suspects that such courage was not necessarily an isolated incident amid the chaos of Saarlautern's bloody streets that morning.[10]

Fortunately, the 261st's success at Dillingen gave the division an alternative approach, and so it shifted its attack in that direction. Leaving the 260th to secure Saarlautern, the Battle-Axe surged eastward. It covered 30 miles in two days, reaching the German city of Neunkirchen on March 21, and the pell-mell race east continued. A contemporary history of the division described those days:

> It was a continuous battle of transportation. The [G-4 and S-4, supply] sections were concerned about gasoline and C- and K-rations which were frequently as much as 100 miles to the rear of the Division. The [G-3 and S-3, operations] sections argued priorities on roads over which everyone wanted to move

simultaneously, and worried about getting personnel from one point to the next. For information on the enemy, the [G-2 and S-2, intelligence] sections relied less on foot patrols, and more on aerial and motor reconnaissance, and the hordes of prisoners which taxed the facilities of Prisoner of War Enclosures. For the 265th Engineers it was a battle of Bailey bridges. For the 565th Signal Company it was a battle of laying wire, of picking it up, and of laying it once more. Each unit had its own problem in the continuous battle of transportation, which can be the toughest fight of all.[11]

But as that same history noted, it was, at times, more than simply a battle of transportation. Sometimes, it was a very real fight—with very real consequences:

The battle of weapons was far from continuous. It was sporadic. One day it was a battalion which had some difficulty in taking a sizeable town. Another day it was a company or platoon savagely attacked by a determined band of SS troops left behind in the rapid advance. Or, on some dark night, on some lonely road, it might be a driver from the 65th Quartermaster Company ambushed by a sniper miles behind the frontline.... However small the skirmish on an operations map, the most important battle for any given GI in the Division is the one in which he participated.[12]

After capturing Neunkirchen, the division pushed on for another 80 miles and found itself, like other American units, queuing for a turn to cross the long pontoon bridge that Patton's engineers had thrown across the Rhine at Oppenheim. By April 1, 1945, Christl and the Battle-Axe were across the Rhine and hungrily eying what was, in many of their minds, the ultimate target—Berlin. The Nazi capital was 375 miles away, but in those heady spring days anything seemed possible.

*****

While Hennessey's G Company had been advancing on Altenkessel, his former teammate Christl and the 65th Infantry Division's tanks and trucks had surged past within five miles of their positions and across the division's front. As a regimental after action report told the tale, "the 3rd Army, moving north and east from our left flank, had advanced rapidly with armored columns across our frontal sector and had squeezed us out of the picture as a division."[13] With the Trailblazers left in the wake of the Third Army's advance, higher command shifted the 70th Infantry Division into the Seventh Army's reserve. General Barnett, in turn, directed the 276th Infantry Regiment to Reichenbach, some 20 miles northeast. For its part, Hennessey's battalion settled in the vicinity of Kottweiler, evicting German inhabitants from their homes and turning them into barracks and quarters. If the GIs felt any guilt at doing so, it was likely lessened when the weather turned once more and, on March 27, the spring rains began falling again.

While in Kottweiler, Hennessey's company and its sister units patrolled their sectors, mopped up pockets of enemy resistance, and continued their training of newly arrived replacements. They also faced the problem of controlling, interviewing, and classifying large numbers of Volksstrum troops and Russian, French, Slovak, and other displaced persons. Many of the DPs were former slave laborers of the Reich. Intelligence personnel interviewed all Volksstrum troops, and if it was decided that they were not dangerous, they were released to the custody of the *Bürgermeister* [mayor]. If they were considered a security threat, however, they were classed as prisoners of war and sent back to a POW stockade. All DPs were gathered together and, after screening, sent to higher headquarters for possible return to their homelands through the International Red Cross.

G Company's sojourn in Kottweiler ended on April 1 when the regiment decamped and moved 50 miles farther north, this time to the banks of the Rhine River. The regiment occupied a front along the Rhine from Bacharach south to Bingen and drew duty guarding the engineer-constructed bridges across the Rhine in this sector and the main supply route that ran from Bad Kreuznach and across the river. G Company, along with the other companies of the 2nd Battalion, encamped in the vicinity of Boppard.

Ten days later, the regimental command post shifted once more, this time 30 miles northeast from Reichenbach to Sankt Goar, directly on the Rhine River. An ever-widening area of responsibility pulled the regiment farther eastward as the month progressed, through Hanau and Frankfurt to Windecken, then southward to Gross Gerau, and then finally to Lohr, on the Main River. The 2nd Battalion occupied Würzburg, where its routine of guarding installations, patrolling, and generally maintaining law and order continued, and placed G Company in the vicinity of Kitzingen. German troops still surrendered, but, for the most part, Hennessey's war seemed to now be one of occupation rather than conquest. April turned to May with an unexpected mix of snow and rain that, despite what one might have augured from such omens, brought good news. Adolf Hitler, German radio announced on May 1, was dead.

In addition to such news, the first of May brought a DP of Russian nationality to Hennessey's company CP. The Russian warned Hennessey that he had seen approximately 50 German soldiers armed with pistols attempting to repair a wrecked jeep about 15 kilometers from Kitzingen. The location was beyond the Trailblazers' area of responsibility, but Hennessey forwarded the report to upper echelons nevertheless. Ultimately, the word came back from division headquarters to send out a patrol to investigate. Hennessey complied. With the Russian acting as a guide, G Company's patrol found no trace of the reported Germans. In such a manner, Hennessey's war in Europe quietly came to an end.[14]

CHAPTER 17

The Road to Eferding

For Jack Hennessey and the rest of the 70th Infantry Division, the month of April had been, for the most part, a time of inglorious relegation to rear-area guard duty. After they had endured bitter winter nights in the Vosges, the battle for Wingen-sur-Moder, and the struggle for Forbach, one suspects that the Trailblazer GIs offered few complaints.

But for Ed Christl and the 65th Infantry Division, attached to Patton's rampaging Third Army, April was a month of pell-mell advances, pivots, and more advances. After crossing the Rhine at Oppenheim at the end of March, the Battle-Axe sped through the Hessian metropolis of Frankfurt and slashed northward on an axis pointed at Berlin. In three days, the division covered 100 miles.

Christl's classmate and fellow artilleryman Jim Blandford, assigned to the division's 867th Field Artillery Battalion, raced along beside him. In the class's 50th anniversary history book, Blanford recalled those heady days of pursuit and destruction.

> When we began chasing behind our armor across Germany things became fluid, so a good share of the time was spent trying to find either my battery or the company or someone else I was assigned to support.... One of our most important functions was to keep ourselves and the infantry supplied with Esso road maps by going out ahead and raiding filling stations. The Army printers just couldn't keep up with the movement of our troops.[1]

Eventually, those road maps brought Christl's unit to the barrier of the Fulda River at Hattenbach. With reconnaissance across the river required and Christl riding with the lead infantrymen, the Minnesotan waded into the Fulda's frigid waters and swam to the other side. For the infantrymen with him, such a gesture was hardly surprising. Throughout the course of the advance from the urban battlefield of Saarlautern through the fields of the Rhineland and now into Germany's heartland, oft-repeated phrases such as "Call the tall LT—he'll get us artillery fire" or "Ask Lieut. Christl—he knows" had accompanied Christl wherever he went. And when he returned back across the river with the information necessary for a successful crossing, the GIs' faith in the artilleryman grew even larger.[2]

Once across the Fulda, the division pushed 75 miles onward to Mühlhausen, capturing the medieval fortress city without a fight. Nearby Langensalza, however, proved to be a harder nut to crack. It was a town with a bellicose history. Emperor Henry IV won a battle against rebelling Saxons and Thuringians there in 1075, troops plundered and burned it during the Thirty Years War in 1632, fighting singed it again in 1761 during the Seven Years War, and, in 1866, it hosted a battle between Prussia and Hanover during the Austro-Prussian War. As a battalion of the 65th's 261st Infantry Regiment, supported by armor and tank destroyers, pushed into the town, its remaining inhabitants witnessed yet another chapter of war. This particular fight was over in a day of sharp street fighting, punctuated by an artillery barrage that foiled German hopes of a successful counterattack.

In three weeks, the 65th had rolled 200 miles—and now Berlin was only 150 miles away. Looking at their maps, German commanders knew that the capture of towns such as Mühlhausen and Langensalza could not go unchecked. Under the cover of darkness on April 6, they dispatched a mixed force of some one thousand infantrymen, led by 16 armored vehicles – a collection of Panzers and self-propelled guns –to attack Struth, on the exposed left (northern) flank of the 65th Division. There the 3rd Battalion, 261st Infantry, had located its command post the previous day. If the Germans could take Struth, they could roll up the division's line and retake the formidable fortress that was Mühlhausen.

At 2:30 a.m., the fighting began as stealthy enemy soldiers crept up on American lines, drawing bursts of BAR fire and hurled grenades in reply. But numbers and determination were on the Germans' side. By dawn, Panzers were threatening the battalion's motor pool, while their comrades in the infantry attempted to infiltrate into the town from the north. In response, General Reinhart ordered the 261st to hold firm. The outnumbered infantrymen did just that, providing a hard core of resistance around which counterattacking battalions of GIs orbited to assault the Germans on their flanks. By the afternoon, the Germans, foiled in their effort to take Struth and threatened on both flanks, beat a surly retreat.[3]

But the Battle-Axe was not done with the enemy. After days of road-borne pursuit and advance, the division's four artillery battalions seemed to relish the opportunity to do what they did best. Bringing their 155-mm and 105-mm howitzers to bear under the direction of forward observers such as Christl, they rained explosive steel down on the fleeing Germans, even as American fighter-bombers swooped in to add to the carnage. By midafternoon, one could follow the route of the enemy's retreat by the black plumes of smoke rising on the northern horizon from wrecked Panzers and support vehicles.

The American infantrymen who fought to capture Langensalza and defend Struth were unlikely to know, of course, that the strokes of diplomats' pens at the Yalta Conference two months earlier had already proven to be far more decisive arbiters of such German towns' fates than the GIs' M1 rifles and their artillerymen's howitzers, no matter how skillfully or bravely wielded. At this point on the map, the 65th had already advanced far enough eastward to cross into lands promised at Yalta to Soviet occupation. Even though Berlin beckoned, the likely hundred thousand casualties that would be suffered to take the Nazi capital merely for the sake of prestige were, to say the least, daunting. It was, as Gen. Omar Bradley told his boss Eisenhower, "a pretty stiff price to pay … especially when we've got to fall back and let the other fellow take over."[4]

Besides, at this point in the campaign, rumors of a Nazi "Alpine Redoubt" in the mountainous reaches of southern Bavaria and in Austria were increasingly disturbing. In later years, historians would make sport by scoffing at the Allied concerns about a fanatical last stand by Hitler and his minions in the Alps, but in fairness to all parties concerned such hindsight was, like all hindsight, of 20/20 acuity. In such circumstances, a push southward into Bavaria, which would also have the benefit of liberating more POW and concentration camps, had a certain irrefutable appeal.

Accordingly, the 65th Infantry Division halted its push toward Berlin and, instead, relocated on April 9 to an assembly area in the vicinity of Berka, 12 miles southwest of Langensalza. For the next week, temporarily assigned as the reserve for VIII Corps, it mopped up bypassed pockets of enemy resistance and steadily shifted southward. For most Battle-Axe soldiers, the most memorable moment of this period was on April 13, when they awoke to the news that President Roosevelt had died in Warm Springs, Georgia. Roosevelt had been president for over 12 years; many of the division's young replacements could barely remember any other president.

*****

The 65th's divisional headquarters ultimately came to rest in Arnstadt where, on April 17, it reverted to XX Corps's control. In General Walker's XX Corps, the Battle-Axe added further heft to a fighting force that included the 71st Infantry Division, the 13th Armored Division, and, in reserve, the 80th Infantry Division. A task force comprising the 3rd Cavalry Group and the 5th Ranger Battalion added to the corps's lethality.[5]

Tasked with advancing on the Alpine Redoubt and linking with the Red Army forces advancing from Vienna, the Ghost Corps began driving southward and southeastward, with a line of advance that would dive into Bavaria, cross the Danube, and invade Austria. For the 65th's units, the road march took them through Coburg, Bamberg, past the outskirts of Nuremberg, and on to Altdorf, covering some 150 miles over the course of scarcely two days.

A road march of such speed would have been impossible if the infantrymen were on foot, but they piled atop each and every vehicle (organic, attached, or captured) in the division and in the armor formations accompanying it. It was neither pretty nor necessarily doctrinal but, in the spring of 1945, it worked. The Battle-Axe's four artillery battalions not only lent space on their own vehicles to the advance but, as the situation required, also "proved a speedy and inexpensive method of reducing … pockets of resistance to the proportions of tough, but local, skirmishes."[6]

But such was not always the case. Twelve miles outside of Altdorf, the division reached the town of Neumarkt on April 20. There the town's size, larger than other communities in the vicinity, offered the Germans better opportunities for a concerted defense against the mechanized juggernaut bearing down on them—as the division's 3rd Battalion, 259th Infantry, advancing with A Company, 748th Tank Battalion, and elements of the 808th Tank Destroyer Battalion attached, soon discovered. The Americans' advance was stopped short outside the town by an unexpected enemy arsenal of self-propelled guns, *Nebelwerfers*, and artillery. An unexpected cold front, which brought freezing rain and sleet, added to the misery. As the 3rd Battalion worked its way into town, Christl's classmate Blandford moved with the 259th's 1st Battalion in a bid to encircle the town.

Moving through the outlying woods, the infantry battalion was counterattacked by a German force—and realized, belatedly, that the cold temperatures and icy sleet had frozen most of the battalion's crew-served weapons. For a moment, it was a touch-and-go affair until Blandford was able to call in an artillery strike from his battery. "I … got on target before any any infantry mortars could be fired," Blanford recalled. "A proud day for us cannon cockers!"[7] Nevertheless, bitter fighting for Neumarkt continued for two days "until the town was burned over [the enemy's] heads and individual snipers were dug from their hiding places with bayonets and grenades.[8] On April 24, the town was declared cleared, and the 65th Infantry Division's advance rolled south.

By the end of the following day, the Battle-Axe's vanguard had already reached its next barrier: the Danube River. At this point along the advance, the Danube was guarded, as it had been for centuries, by the city of Regensburg. One day, the city, which boasted the best-preserved town center north of the Alps, would be declared a UNESCO World

Heritage Site. But in 1945, its medieval walls and solid buildings meant only meant one thing to the GIs—that it was a formidable obstacle that promised another tough fight.

To position his men to take Regensburg, General Reinhart quietly pushed two regiments by boat across the Danube downriver of Regensburg after midnight on the morning of April 25, near the towns of Matting and Kapfelberg. The German outposts in Matting awoke to find American bayonets at their throats. The outposts in Kapfelberg, however, were more alert, and there the Americans immediately encountered a wall of gunfire from entrenched troops. But the GIs pushed forward, even as the engineers began work on the construction of a bridge while simultaneously ferrying more troops and vehicles across the river.

The two landings had pinched the town of Abbach, and both landing forces turned to take the town. The fight was a bitter one, but once again firepower helped give the American infantrymen an edge over their adversaries. From positions back across the river, the division's artillery battalions, joined by the guns of the 808th Tank Destroyer Battalion and 546th Antiaircraft Artillery and even the mortars of the 94th Chemical Battalion, hammered the enemy holdouts. Christl's classmate and fellow forward observer Blandford recalled one such fire mission—and testified to the overwhelming firepower the Americans were willing to bring to bear to snuff out resistance.

> I could see what looked like about 50 German soldiers carrying stuff from the middle of a field to behind a hill in a steady stream through tall grass; I figured to at least scare them with a battalion time-on-target (TOT) concentration. I called in the mission and waited and waited, then fussed. I was told to WAIT! Then, "19 battalions, three salvos, TOT, on the way" over the radio; I was wishing I was a lot further away! Then, there was that flash and thunder right on target, a steady roar, then the sounds of the larger guns, from farther away, over several minutes. Surprisingly, afterwards, there were still a few enemy soldiers moving around, apparently checking on their buddies. War is hell.[9]

"To my knowledge that 19-battalion artillery concentration—it could have been 228 guns—was a record," Blandford added, "probably due to our ammo trucks being so overloaded they broke down frequently."[10]

By April 27, Abbach was secured, and the division moved northward and eastward on Regensburg, preparing for what could be the most difficult fight of the campaign—an assault on a densely packed, stoutly constructed medieval city.

Fortunately, fate intervened instead. The city's military commander had fled the scene the previous day, leaving his men to fight on. But a retired German army general stepped into the chaos, assumed command, and promptly negotiated a surrender to Brig. Gen. John Copeland, the 65th's assistant division commander. American lives, German lives, and a priceless cultural relic were spared.[11]

With the Danube breached and Regensburg secured, the 65th was placed in XX Corps's reserve for a 48-hour respite. But orders soon placed the division on the march once more. On May 1, it fell in behind the 13th Armored Division and followed the tankers and the Danube southward toward Austria. By midnight, they were across the Isar River at Plattling and then, passing through the 13th Armored, pressed on to the Enns River. "Here and there beautiful country estates stood untouched by the war," a supply officer riding with the 65th Infantry Division remembered. "Bavarian farmers coming from the fields would nod respectfully to GIs on the road. They knew the end was in sight."[12]

So did many of the GIs—or at least so it seemed. "Everyone, it seemed, wanted to take home a cherished dagger, Luger, or some other souvenir from Europe," that same supply officer recalled. "It got so bad at one point, I remember, the order went out to do 'more shooting and less looting.'"

*****

There was, in fact, more shooting to come. The division reached Passau and the Austrian border, on the Inns River, on May 2, enduring several skirmishes en route that failed to slow the advance. At Passau, the division found three hundred SS troops and a trio of tanks holding the town. The 2nd Battalion, 261st Infantry, moved into action, supported by gunfire of Christl's 868th Field Artillery, the 546th Antiaircraft Artillery Regiment, and the 808th Tank Destroyer Battalion. Shortly after midnight, they secured the town's surrender, but it would not be fully cleared of obstinate holdouts and snipers until later that day.

Eight miles south of Passau, the 1st Battalion, 261st Infantry Regiment, reached Neuhaus am Inn, on the Inns River opposite the Austrian town of Schärding, shortly before dawn on that same day. There a modern bridge spanned the river between Germany and Austria. But before the GIs could make it across, German defenders blew up the bridge in their face. The Battle-Axe's soldiers responded by calling for their bridge-building engineers—and their artillery.

Upon reaching the Inn's banks, those engineers joined with the 1st Battalion's infantrymen in trading machine-gun fire with the enemy positions across the river. Then they turned their attention to the construction work at hand. Any Germans with inclinations to challenge the engineers' handiwork were pulverized by a two-and-a-half-hour artillery and heavy weapons barrage.

Later that evening, the artillery unleased another barrage as the infantrymen took advantage of assault boats brought forward by the engineers and began to shuttle across the river. The GIs fanned out through Schärding; the shell-shocked German defenders, cornered in the town's cellars, offered little resistance. Over the course of the next day, more infantry battalions ferried across the river and were pushing southward. By 9:00 a.m. on May 4, the engineers' bridge was complete, and the remainder of the division was rolling across it. Now the division had the city of Linz—the second-largest city in Austria after Vienna—in their sights, 50 miles away.

Over the course of the morning, the division raced southeastward along an axis of advance that ran parallel to the Danube River 10 miles to its north. Here on the river's plain, a thick fog blanketed the countryside, limiting visibility to two hundred feet at times and denying the Americans the comforting presence of air support. Nevertheless, the Battle-Axe's columns kept a fast pace, rolling through Austrian towns with names such as Taufkirchen an der Pram, Sigharting, Sankt Willibad, Peuerbach, and Waizenkirchen, not even pausing to corral the hundreds of surrendering German streaming in the opposite direction. Those men were simply directed to the rear as the 65th Infantry Division's men kept its eyes on Linz, drawing closer with every mile.

About 30 miles into its journey, their division's vanguard reached the Linz suburb of Eferding as dusk approached on May 4. With its darkening skyline dominated by the Starhemberg Castle, with roots that reached back to the 11th century, Eferding offered an urbanized road hub that blocked the route from the west to Linz, approximately 10 miles beyond. Riding ahead of the rest of the division, a reconnaissance party of infantrymen from the 260th Infantry Regiment scouted ahead in six jeeps and drove cautiously into the town. Christl, volunteering as usual for frontline duty, rode with them to lend artillery support as needed. Word had been received that the Germans would offer no resistance; nevertheless, the men in the jeeps crept slowly along its seemingly deserted streets, with their eyes scanning the shadowy surrounding buildings, their ears pricked up, and their hands on their M1s.

Their caution proved justified. An Austrian woman stepped out and stopped the first jeep; there was a German antitank gun, manned by SS troops, just ahead. One of the squad leaders, Sgt. Dan Canak, of Reno, Nevada, joined with a private first class named Anderson and slipped forward to investigate.

They rounded a corner and, "to my surprise, I was looking down the muzzle of a German 88," Anderson recounted. "We got behind a fence and [Canak] knocked off a crew of four guys with that old trusty M1."[13] Canak's Silver Star citation, awarded for "aggressiveness and coolness under fire," would ultimately credit the Nevadan with not only those four crewmen but with shooting the crew's commanding officer as well. Then, when a German attempted to hurl a grenade at the Americans, Canak shot him as well.[14]

At that point, a general melee ensued. Recognizing the tactical importance of the intersection, the scouting party scrambled to secure it, even as four truckloads of German reinforcements roared up. The GIs dispatched the trucks in short order, and Canak's rifle claimed an enemy sniper firing from one of the nearby buildings. Then came a bitter fight to hold onto the intersection until the rest of the battalion could come forward. For three hours, it was a vicious street battle of exploding grenades, flashes of American M1 and German Karabiner 98k rifles, and ugly bursts of automatic fire.

During this close-quarters fight with the SS, Christl's usual fortitude seemed to have transcended into raw courage. "With utter disregard for his own safety, he exposed himself to intense hostile automatic weapons fire and led his men in the successful accomplishment of their mission," Third Army headquarters would ultimately declare.[15] But on Eferding's dark streets, where a hazy pall of gray gunsmoke blended noxiously with the black plumes rising from the burning trucks wrecked on the boulevard, Christl's winning streak game to an end. The US Army and US Army Air Forces suffered over 318,000 men killed in action (or dead from wounds) during World War II. West Point's Class of 1944 sacrificed nine classmates killed fighting the Germans or Japanese. And Ed Christl was among the last of them.[16]

As gunfire ceased in Eferding and quiet returned to the Austrian town, word of Christl's death made the rounds to the men he had served in the Battle-Axe. "I'd have killed a dozen of those S. S with my bare hands if I'd known they got that big LT," one little infantryman muttered to himself.[17]

The tragedy of Christl's death was only magnified by its timing. Division personnel reported him as killed on May 4, 1945. By the end of the following day, May 5, Linz was in American hands; by May 6, the division had drawn abreast of its ultimate objective, the Enns River, and effected the long-awaited linkup with the Red Army. Then, on the morning of May 7, three days after Christl's death, word arrived of Nazi Germany's unconditional surrender, to be effective at one minute past midnight on May 9. But General Reinhart, the Battle-Axe's commander, did not waste time in penning a letter to his men. Its subject line was simply "End of War."

"I have watched 'fillers' become combat infantrymen and untested officers become battle leaders," the general wrote. "I have seen our wounded and counted our dead. I feel with you your deep sorrow for your lost comrades, and I now rejoice with you that their sacrifice has brought peace and justice to the western world."

"But I realize, as you must too, that this is only a temporary respite," he continued. "Our job is not and cannot be done until Japan suffers the same punishment as was dealt Germany and Italy for the same crime."[18]

Fortunately for Christl's comrades, their war, like that of the 70th Infantry Division, would end in Europe. But men such as former teammate Bob Faas had yet to join the fray, and in May of 1945, as the battle for Okinawa spilled into its second bloody month, there was clearly still plenty of combat awaiting in the Pacific. And Faas, sporting the silver wings of an army aviator on his uniform blouse, was destined for it.

CHAPTER 18

Those G—D—West Pointers

In July of 1944, as Jack Hennessey and Ed Christl reported to Fort Benning and Fort Sill, respectively, Bob Faas's own set of orders directed him to Craig Army Air Field, in Selma, Alabama, one of the dozens of airfields hurriedly built by the US military in the frantic run-up to America's entry into World War II. Craig Field had opened in 1940. Although its mission included the training of B-26 Marauder medium bomber pilots, its focus was on single-engine training of aviation cadets still working toward their wings, of aviators transitioning into fighter aircraft, and even of a collection of British, French, and Dutch Allied airmen learning to fly.

Faas, along with 21 of his classmates from the Class of 1944, arrived at Craig to hone their skills in the P-40 Warkhawk. Their numbers included a trio of other Bobs—Missouri's Bob Algermissen, Texas's Bob Callan, and South Dakota's Bob Royem Jr.—as well as Washington, DC's Paul Bradshaw Jr., Florida's Jim Cowee, Oregon's Dean Crowell (destined to miss combat in World War II but to die on an air mission over North Korea in 1950), Illinois's Charlie Czapar and Bernie Sohn, army brats William Fairbrother and Ralph "Dusty" Rhodes, Pennsylvanian Stephen Farris (whose brother Robert was a B-24 pilot in Europe), Arkansan Dave Fitton, Mississippian Bill Fullilove, Texan Emmet Maxon Jr., Louisiana's Everett Mccoy, and, from Alabama, John T. Moore Jr.[1] The group of recent graduates also included John "Fat Jack" Combs, a Canadian-born New Yorker who, despite his genial exterior, carried a heavy weight on his husky shoulders that summer. His brother, Richard, an infantry officer, had lost his life fighting the Japanese on Bougainville in February; while he was on graduation leave in June, he had learned that his father had been killed in action while serving with Merrill's Marauders in Burma.

For the month of July, the classmates dodged thunderstorms across the Southeast, laced the hot, humid air at aerial gunnery ranges, and logged more hours in the P-40. Up to this point, Faas and his comrades at Craig has expected that they would fall into a relatively predictable chain of training and events: first, transition work and gunnery training in a fighter (as they had just completed with the P-40); second, assignment to a replacement training unit (RTU) for upgrade to a frontline fighter such as a P-38 Lightning, P-47 Thunderbolt, or P-51 Mustang; and, finally, assignment to a combat unit in a combat theater.[2]

For a time, events seemed to play out as they had planned and hoped. With their work at Craig completed, the cohort of West Point pilots traded the muddy Alabama River for Sarasota, Florida, and the blue-green waters of Tampa Bay. Here, at Sarasota Army Air Field, the pilots completed their next stage of training—and here the thread of future expectations became unraveled.

"The RTU graduated us, couldn't reassign us, and wouldn't run us through the program again," Emmett Maxon recalled. "That's when the CO began referring to us at 'those G—D—West Pointers.'"[3]

Looking to keep the young pilots gainfully occupied, orders shifted the men to DeRidder Army Air Base, in western Louisiana's Beauregard Parish, for further training in P-40s. Here, the instructor pilots were recently returned combat veterans, and the learning curve they imposed on the untested pilots was steep—and, at times, deadly. On October 19, 1944, Paul Bradshaw was returning to the field in a four-plane formation. While changing positions, he collided with his flight leader and spun into the Louisiana swamps below. His death marked the first that military operations claimed in the Class of 1944.[4]

By November, the pilots were east of the Mississippi River once more—this time attending the recently concocted Junior Officers' Course at the Army Air Forces School of Applied Tactics in Orlando, Florida. "The course was interesting, the area was quiet and pleasant, but there were no airplanes to fly," the class's 50-year history remembered. "It provided further weight of evidence that there was intent that the '44 pilots not be hurried overseas into combat."[5]

In January of 1945, as their training in Orlando ended, the small legion of West Pointers split up for yet more training. Some went to Mitchell Army Air Field in New York, others to Barksdale Army Air Field in Shreveport, Louisiana, some to bases in the San Francisco and Chico, California, areas, and still others to Randolph Army Air Field, in San Antonio, Texas, where they became instructor pilots. By now, each and every one of them was convinced that he would never make it out of the States and have an opportunity to fly in combat.[6]

Taking matters into their own hands, a group of the pilots tracked down Maj. Gen. Robert Harper, their old tactical officer from their plebe year at West Point. Now Harper was the Army Air Forces' assistant chief of staff for training, and the lieutenants pled their case to the general—or at least sought an explanation. They left the conversation with the impression that the pilots from the class of 1944 were to be held in the States until they had been commissioned a year. "The air war was essentially won and the final combat missions with experienced crews didn't need any more greenhorns."[7]

Of course, even flying in the States was dangerous enough, and, as the winter passed, mishaps claimed the lives of more of Faas's classmates. One of them was Arthur "Art" Bick, who, as a plebe, had shared the basketball court with Faas. Bick had been one of the air cadets slated for training in multiengine aircraft and, after ultimately qualifying in the B-24 Liberator, became an instructor pilot at Smyrna Army Air Field in Tennessee. On February 21, 1945, while on a cross-country flight, Bick's bomber fell out of the sky shortly after taking off from Dallas's Love Field and smashed into the flooded river bottoms of the Trinity River.

A local fisherman witnessed the disaster. "The plane was coming almost straight down with motors roaring," the man said. "I was two miles away in a boat, and the plane hit with such a crash that it jarred my boat."[8] Along with Bick, there were three other men aboard the B-24. None survived.

Faas likely read of Bick's death while he was en route back to West Point—but one wonders if he shared it with his fiancée awaiting him there. Probably not—what was to be gained by reminding a young bride about the perils her husband faced? At any rate, on February 25, 1945, Faas married Kathryne Frances Caylor at the academy's Catholic chapel.

At this point in his peregrinations, Faas was likely assigned to Mitchell Army Air Field, on Long Island, New York. By this point, the lieutenant, like most others, had probably clued in on the army's penchant for assigning lieutenants in alphabetical groupings, and so it came little surprise when Faas was joined by classmates Farris and Fairbrother at Mitchell Field to master the powerful P-47 Thunderbolt.

By the spring of 1945, the P-47—whose first prototype had first flown in 1941 and which had first entered combat in 1942—had earned a reputation nearly as impressive as its massive seven-ton metal bulk. Built by Republic Aviation, it was officially christened the Thunderbolt, but irreverent pilots, amused by the plane's similarity to the milk jugs of the day, were soon calling it "the Jug." Those same pilots, however, respected its turbosupercharged speed, performance at high altitudes, rugged durability, and powerful array of eight .50-caliber machine guns—four mounted in each wing. For Faas and his fellow pilots, the transition from their P-40 Warhawks to an aircraft that doubled up the Warhawk in terms of weight and horsepower must have been a daunting one. But one suspects that the observations of John Andrews, a veteran fighter pilot who transitioned from the P-40 to the P-47 in Italy, were probably shared by Faas:

> The P-47 was not a difficult aircraft to fly. It had plenty of power (2,000 horsepower), was stable (it had an elliptical wing, somewhat like the Spitfire), and had a wide-tread landing gear that made a smooth landing easy, especially for us who had been flying the narrow-geared P-40 for so long. The P-47 was much heavier than the P-40, and we brought it down the final approach at about 120 miles per hour, but we learned quickly and soon were very comfortable with this craft. With the P-40 we worried about engine failure (old engines and dust in the intake); the P-47 made us worry about running out of fuel.[9]

As the pilots' comfort with the P-47 grew, so did their confidence. On April 2, 1945, Farris even made news in his hometown of Swoyersville, in eastern Pennsylvania, when he buzzed his old high school.[10] Elsewhere, sadly, classmates continued to make news for other reasons. "Mid-Air Crash Kills 14 Fliers," the *Miami News* headlined on April 12, 1945, reporting on a collision shortly after midnight between two B-17s on a training mission north of Jackson, Mississippi. Two of Faas's classmates, lieutenants Charles Keathley and John Stevens, were among the dead.

Meanwhile, their training continued, even as the one-year anniversary of their graduation from West Point came and went. Their memories, memorialized in the Class of 1944's 50-year reminiscences, captured the general attitude at the time.

> To the '44 pilots, well-fed and safe to be sure, the near and longer-term future was a nagging concern. True, they were gaining experience, but looking at the Class of June '43 one year ahead, they saw men half-finished with combat tours, a few combat squadron commanders, career airmen seemingly drawing further ahead of them, leaving them in the dust. In the invincibility of youth, the heavy casualties, a nominal 25 percent among June '43's airmen, was ignored.[11]

Two days later, on June 8, the aviators received the long-anticipated orders directing them overseas—only two days after the anniversary of their graduation. It caused them to give credence to the rumor that they had all been held deliberately in the States for a year after their graduation. Regardless of such a rumor's authenticity, it seemed a moot point now. Bidding farewell to his wife Kathy, Faas, accompanied by Farris and Fairbrother, began the long journey to the island of Ie Shima, literally a third of a world away.

*****

Coincidentally, Faas's old coach, Ed Kelleher, was, at the time, bound for overseas duty as well. Nearly 30 years earlier, he had served in the US Army in France during World War I. Now, taking advantage of his off-season, he volunteered as a civilian athletic adviser with the army in Europe.

The need for such volunteers, while perhaps not immediately evident to today's casual reader of the history of the age, was, in 1945, compelling nevertheless. On V-E Day, General Eisenhower had sixty-one US divisions—1,622,000 personnel—in Germany and a total force in Europe numbering 3,077,000.[12]

With the collapse of the Third Reich, the divisions in Germany and Austria became occupation troops, charged with maintaining law and order. Their job, in those still uncertain days, was to imprint an Allied military presence on the land—and American commanders sometimes found themselves responsible for huge swaths of territory. The 70th Infantry Division, for example, was tasked with occupying some 2,500 square miles. Its soldiers, spread out in companies and platoons across the German countryside, manned border-control stations, maintained checkpoints at road junctions and bridges, patrolled for curfew violators, and guarded railroad bridges, army installations, refugee and DP camps, jails, telephone exchanges, factories, and banks.[13]

Such was not, of course, the mission for which those tankers, artillerymen, and infantrymen had trained. Nor was it permanent, and they knew it. Whether their next destination was to be home to the States or redeployment to the Far East, they were ready for the next stage. At best, morale suffered; at worst, discipline suffered. Eisenhower recognized this, and by July revised plans called for an occupation by a total of eight American divisions.[14]

In the meantime, American GIs and airmen with enough points on the Adjusted Service Rating were already streaming home. Calculated on individual bases for each enlisted personnel, it gave them one point for each month of service since September 1940, one point for each month of overseas service since September 1940, five points for each decoration or battle star, and twelve points for each child under 18 up to a maximum of three. Eighty-five was the magic number to gain top priority for a berth homeward.[15]

It was to those unfortunate souls with fewer than 85 points to whom the army turned for occupation duties—and, as the army readily recognized, the potential for a "monumental morale problem" was tremendous.[16] In response, the army decided to try to keep the occupation troops busy with training, education, and recreation programs. With respect to training, intended to prepare the low-score units for combat against the Japanese, it simply never started amid the reality of continuously reshuffling personnel, particularly as men moved through the redeployment pipeline.

The educational program, intended to both sustain morale and smooth the transition back to civilian life, was more successful, and American service men (and women) took advantage of the opportunities at such places as Shrivenham American University and Warton Army Technical School in England and Biarritz American University in France, to take two-month courses in fields including agriculture, commerce, education, engineering, fine arts, journalism, and liberal arts. In addition, some 32,000 soldier-students studied at 35 European civilian colleges. But the efforts did not stop there. Some three hundred so-called command schools were opened in the field, even down to the battalion level, with qualified military personnel and civilians, including English-speaking Germans, as instructors.[17]

"The command schools were a massive undertaking," one historian noted. "Seventh Army issued packs of 10,000 textbooks to each of its divisions and supplied hundreds of microscopes, transits, levels, phonographs, and other instructional items. In August, Seventh Army alone operated 134 schools, offering 133 courses to nearly 44,000 students."[18] Soldiers could also take free courses for high school or college credit through the US Armed Forces Institute, and, in the summer of 1945, 93,000 soldiers were enrolled in USAFI courses.[19]

The entertainment and recreation programs were equally important. By one count, 80 percent of the GIs could claim to be able to see at least three movies a week. Off-screen, stars such as Bob Hope and Jack Benny continued to perform with the USO, even after V-E Day, and smaller "jeep shows" made the rounds as well. Eventually, the larger "Soldier Show" productions were even able to hire civilian actresses (classified by the army as "civilian actress technicians") in a welcome improvement from the all-male casts of the war years.[20]

Middle-aged and stocky, Coach Kelleher could not hope to compete with civilian actress technicians, but he did know something about basketball. In addition to 100,000 dozen table tennis balls, nearly 350,000 decks of cards, over 16 million library books, and an undetermined number of footballs and softballs, the military had procured 21,000 basketballs for its occupation forces in Europe. Eventually, disparate units would field over three hundred basketball teams, and Kelleher, along with a number of other coaches, journeyed to Europe in the summer of 1945 to "tour Germany seeking adequate facilities for the anticipated widespread basketball program."[21] Additional duties included schooling athletic officers tasked with coaching their units' basketball teams.[22] Perhaps this would also be an opportunity for Kelleher to see his son, Sgt. Edward A. Kelleher Jr., who was stationed in Reims, France.[23]

By July 19, 1945, Kelleher was in Munich. It was then and there, amid the rubble of the capital of Bavaria, in the city that Hitler had christened the *Haupstadt der Bewegung* (the "capital of the [Nazi] movement"), that West Point's basketball coach suffered a fatal heart attack. It would take days for the news of his death to reach the States—and reach his widow—but, when it did, it made national news. "Death of the 50-year-old coach came at the height of his career, as the West Point lost only one game in his last two seasons under his fast-breaking system of play," the United Press eulogized, recognizing him as "one of the most colorful and successful cage mentors in the country."[24] At Fordham's Rose Hill campus, where Kelleher had coached for 19 years, a memorial mass held at University Church honored his life and passing.[25]

CHAPTER 19

The Fighting Furies

By the time word of his former coach's death reached the United States, Bob Faas had, by plane, train, ship, and/or some combination thereof, already reached Ie Shima. The small, oval-shaped island, a mere nine square miles in total area, lay three miles off the northwestern coast of Okinawa. It resembled, in the words of the army's official history, a "huge, immovable aircraft carrier," and, for that reason, as the larger Okinawa operations bled into their third week, the American army had dispatched its 77th Infantry Division to secure the island.[1] Landings against tough enemy opposition began on April 16. Six days of hard fighting followed before, late on the afternoon of April 21, 1945, the island was declared secured.

"Secured" proved to be a relative term. Unmarked minefields, unexploded ordnance, and diehard Japanese holdouts continued to claim casualties, even as the first US engineer units began arriving on the island to develop the captured Japanese airfields for American use. One of those casualties was Faas's classmate John P. Bradley, who had come to West Point by way of Texas A&M University and a stint as an enlisted man in the prewar regular army. Assigned to the 1903rd Engineer Aviation Battalion, he was killed in action on Ie Shima on May 4, 1945—the same day that Ed Christl was killed in action in distant Austria.[2]

Bradley's death, however, was not in vain. His fellow engineers not only quickly repaired the main enemy airfield but also began the construction of new strips, utilizing the island's coral foundation and the rubble of the town of Ie as runway building materials. They further benefited from the island's ample room for dispersal areas for aircraft and housing for personnel. Within a week after Bradley's death, the first fighter group was operating off of the island; by the middle of the month, all taxiways and runways were fully operational and radar and air warning facilities installed, even as construction continued. By the middle of June, three fighter groups and a night fighter squadron were operating from the airfield.[3]

One of those fighter groups was the 413th Fighter Group, commanded by legendary fighter pilot Harrison Thyng. It was to this group that Faas and his classmate William Fairbrother were assigned when they arrived on Ie Shima. More specifically, they found themselves assigned to the 1st Fighter Squadron, nicknamed "the Fighting Furies." Thyng's squadrons flew the P-47N Thunderbolt, one of the most impressive variants of the Army Air Forces' storied fighter. The pilot training manual for the Thunderbolt P-47N provided new pilots such as Faas and Fairbrother with a succinct discussion of the P-47N's role in the Pacific:

> This manual deals with the P-47N, a very long-range fighter-bomber developed to blast the Japs in the Pacific. Since its birth, U.S. bases have crept that much closer to the Japanese Islands, so the chances are that few 2,000-mile fighter missions will be required.
>
> Nevertheless, the strategic value of such an airplane is enormous. Wherever N's are based, the Japs are in danger of escorted bomber strikes or fighter sweeps over a radius of 1000 miles or more. This takes in quite a lot of territory, even in the broad reaches of the Pacific, and provides a constant headache for the diminishing Japanese air force. The airplane's value as a fighter bomber is enhanced by the large internal fuel capacity.[4]

That same manual described how Faas's new aircraft differed from the Thunderbolts he had flown in the States:

> At first glance, the N appears to be merely a P-47D with squared wing tips. With comparable loading, the flight characteristics are similar and much of the equipment is the same, but actually the P-47N is a different aircraft.
>
> The P-47N has a more powerful engine, internal wing tanks, electrification of many controls, an automatic pilot, homing radio, a tail warning radar, equipment designed to reduce pilot fatigue, and engineering changes demanded by the greater weight.
>
> The N is not difficult to fly, but study is required to get the most out of the plane. It was designed for missions requiring maximum performance. The pilot—you—must also be capable of that type of performance.[5]

On Ie Shima, the American fighter squadrons were blessed with double-strength staffing in fighter pilots, likely as a nod to the demanding requirements of the single-pilot, long-distance mission those pilots were required to fly. But even though he might be flying only half of the missions he might have otherwise garnered, each flight seemed to warrant some form of extra credit on an island that, until the very end of the war, was plagued with Japanese air attacks. Parker Tyler, an officer serving with the 413th, described the almost daily scene he witnessed on the airfield:

> A stirring drama was begun whenever our ships went on a mission. Heavy with a full load that varied with the mission, the 47's would hurtle themselves down the dusty runway, much as a broad or high jumper struggling to put forth his maximum effort at just the right moment to become airborne. Always, as the plane roared down the runway, we were conscious of the tragedy that was pent up and ready to be released by any error on the part of pilot or crew chief or materiel failure. Each take off was a lifetime that lasted 30 seconds. Each half minute a friend, his life, his family, his hopes, their hopes and ours flashed by. The moment the ship became airborne, we relaxed a bit and, as wheels began to retract and the boy gained altitude, we silently and unconsciously thanked God. Then turned to watch our next friend commit himself to the same cycle.[6]

Arriving late and to a unit well-staffed with pilots, Faas had only flown one combat mission with the 1st Fighter Squadron before taking to the air on his second—and last—combat mission on August 9, 1945. The day's orders dispatched his squadron, with rockets affixed to their fighter-bomber's wings, to attack the Matsuyama Air Field, on the northwestern coast of Shikoku. At Matsuyama, the Imperial Japanese Navy operated a fighter base that threatened the now almost daily B-29 Superfortress raids on Japan, and the Americans wanted to put an end to the harassment.

For the pilots of the 413th Fighter Group, the mission to neutralize Matsuyama Air Field would require a round trip of about a thousand miles, with a total of six hours alone in the cockpit. Practically all of that trip would be over the forbidding Pacific Ocean or hostile territory. At worst, mechanical difficulties or a stray Japanese fighter would present themselves en route. At best, there would merely be two or three hours of monotony, breathing oxygen through a rubber mask, fighting the urge for a cigarette, and studiously maintaining radio silence as the enemy target drew closer.

On this particular day, however, the tedium of the long-distance flight was shattered while the fighter group was still an hour south of Japan. A minute after 11:00 a.m., an unexpected glare lit up the northwestern horizon, following by an enormous, black, mushroom-shaped cloud that pushed skyward. For a moment, the discipline of radio silence broke, as the pilots chattered back and forth with one another about the unusual phenomenon they were witnessing. Although they had heard, two days earlier, President Harry Truman's announcement of the dropping of "a bomb on Hiroshima, Japan, … destroy[ing] its usefulness to the enemy," it was unlikely that any of the pilots imagined that they had just witnessed the second detonation of an atomic bomb or the destruction of Nagasaki.[7]

But even an event of such import was of little immediate relevance to Faas and his fellow aviators. Their attention was focused on the mission at hand, and, as they reached the Japanese shortly before noon, they found Shikoku socked in with thick, low-lying clouds. Nevertheless, trusting their weather reports, they dove down through the gray scud and were rewarded when they broke through into a narrow band of clearer, but still hazy, skies below. Almost immediately, they were met with the unwelcome sight of defiant black bursts of Japanese flak splotching the skies ahead of them. Undaunted, the squadron's Thunderbolts pushed forward and, within minutes, were racing across Matsuyama Air Field, lacing the sky with rockets that detonated amid the parked enemy aircraft and sandbagged gun positions below. But the Japanese gunners took their own toll as well.

First a burst of flak exploded just off the right wing of the P-47N piloted by John Heathcote, a native of Pennsylvania and a graduate of Fork Union Military Academy. With 55 combat hours already logged in his flight book, the 21-year-old had been with the 413th's initial deployment to the Pacific that spring. The blast of flak blew off the tip of Heathcote's right wing as he was racing across the enemy field at nearly five hundred miles per hour and barely five hundred feet off the ground.[8] The last time any of his comrades saw the young lieutenant, he was banking off to the right into the thick fog. His body was never recovered; the following March, the War Department declared him dead.[9]

Meanwhile, enemy gunfire wracked Faas's Thunderbolt as well, mortally wounding its engine. With oil covering his bullet-pocked fuselage and wings, Faas nursed his plane away from Shikoku.[10] Two of his fellow pilots, 1st Lt. William Kelly Jr. and 1st Lt. Walter Springer, flew alongside him, providing an escort and keeping an eye on him as he considered his options. By this point in the war, the American pilots were well aware of the likely fate that awaited them if they were captured by Japanese troops or fell into the hands of vengeful Japanese civilians. Accordingly, the overriding goal for a pilot in Faas's predicament was to get back over the ocean, where he could either bail out or ditch. Once in the water, he would hopefully be picked up by an Allied submarine on air/sea rescue duty or rescued by one of the navy's flying boats—the latter operations affectionately codenamed as "Dumbos." Accordingly, Faas fought for altitude and angled out over the ocean, likely breathing a sigh of relief as the Japanese coastline receded behind him.

Thirty miles off the southeastern coast of Kyushu, Faas radioed Kelly that he was going to bail out. He then lowered his seat, ducked low into the canopy, and, reaching forward with his right hand, grabbed and yanked the "T" handle on the upper right side of the canopy. With an ugly wrenching noise, the jettisoned canopy disappeared into his plane's slipstream, tumbling past his tail and into the unseen distance. Faas then quickly disconnected his shoulder harness, radio leads, oxygen tubing, and safety belt. For the moment, he kept his face mask on to protect his eyes from the cold wind and hot droplets of oil splattering back from the engine.

If he recalled the instructions of his flight instructors and his training manual, Faas pulled his P-47N up into a slow climb, banking gently to the left. Fighting the roaring wind that buffeted him outside the protection of his cockpit, he pulled himself out of his seat and climbed out onto his right wing. Then he hurled himself into space, forcing himself to wait a few nerve-wracking seconds before pulling his parachute's ripcord. He wanted to make sure that he was well clear of his now–pilotless aircraft before he deployed his parachute.

Fortunately, he was. For a few moments, Faas enjoyed the unexpected silence as he floated down toward the ocean. As he neared the waves, he loosened his parachute harness straps and then, seconds later, hit the gray Pacific with all the grace of a sack of potatoes hefted out of the back of a truck. Sputtering salt water, he disengaged from his harness and managed to deploy his life raft. He allowed half of it to inflate, pulled himself into it, and then inflated the rest of the raft as Kelly and Springer orbited overhead.

Once aboard his raft, Faas took stock of his modest collection of survival supplies: a desalination kit, a knife, a first aid kid, a fishing kit, a canteen, a poncho, smoke flares, a small can of oil, and a tin of fresh water. All in all, it was not a very impressive collection, and the downed pilot must have wondered how long they would last—or if the wind and current would eventually push him back to a hostile reception ashore on Kyushu.

Fortunately, if Faas was bothered with such questions, he did not have long to wait for an answer. A Dumbo was already in-bound to his position, and, within an hour, a US Navy PBM-5 Mariner piloted by Lt. (jg) Kenneth B. Lee landed nearby. Its crew soon hauled Faas on board and flew him to safety. By August 12, Faas was back with his unit—a mere three days before Japan's Emperor Hirohito announced his nation's unconditional surrender to the Allies and the world erupted in celebration of V-J Day.[11]

*****

In such a manner, the Class of 1944's role in World War II came to an end. By the final tally, the class would take pride in the fact that nearly three-quarters of its members had served in overseas combat theaters—and mourn the fact that 15 of them had died in military service during the war. The list of the fallen ranged, chronologically, from Paul Bradley Jr., killed in a training air crash in Louisiana, to Harlan "Speed" Holden, who lost his life flying a P-47 in Abilene, Texas, on July 24, 1945. Alphabetically, it ranged from Art Bick, another life lost to an air crash, to Andrew Woloszyn, a company commander killed when his jeep hit a mine near Piesport, Germany. Perhaps they, and their families, took some solace in the haunting stanzas of West Point's alma mater:

And when our work is done,
Our course on earth is run,
May it be said, "Well done. Be thou at peace."

Meanwhile, back at West Point, the years marched on. More new cadets endured Beast Barracks, more classes graduated, more lieutenants went off to war—and more basketball was played. Never again, however, would West Point's teams match that legendary run of 1944 and 1945.

Nevertheless, it does not take much for today's cadets—or at least the more astute ones—to recall the fated year when Ed Christl, with classmates Jack Hennessey and Bob Faas and teaming with Doug Kenna and Dale Hall, posted a perfect season.

Afterword

Edward C. Christl Jr.

The army posthumously awarded Ed Christl the Distinguished Service Cross—its second-highest decoration below the Medal of Honor—on October 1, 1945. "For extraordinary heroism in connection with military operations against an armed enemy in Austria," the citation read. "His dauntless heroism and supreme devotion to duty will live on as an inspiration to the men with whom he fought."[1] His memorial article in *Assembly*, the magazine of the West Point Association of Graduates, was more heartfelt: "Those who knew Ed will never forget his inspiring courage and devotion to duty and we who loved him so dearly will never forget his kind, considerate and generous nature and ready smile. It is with deep personal sorrow that we bid you farewell, Ed. Our loss is irreplaceable."[2]

On October 1, 1988, Christl's alma mater named its basketball facility (which had, by then, replaced the academy's field house—today's Gillis Field House—as West Point's home court) the Edward C. Christl Jr. Arena. West Point's intercollegiate basketball teams—today, represented by both men's and women's teams—play their home games at Christl Arena as part of the Patriot League. The arena's namesake is buried less than a mile north, at the West Point Cemetery.

Robert W. Faas

Bob Faas received the Distinguished Flying Cross for his service on Ie Shima. After completing his tour of duty in the Pacific, he returned to West Point in 1949 to join the Department of English after completing graduate studies in literature at Columbia University. He later served as air attaché in Belgium and Luxembourg, transitioned into jet fighters, and, after resigning his commission, moved to California to pursue a career as a stockbroker and realtor. Beset by declining health in the early 1970s, he moved to Mountain View, California, where he died of cancer on November 22, 1979. His ashes were scattered in the nearby Pacific Ocean.[3]

Dale Hall

After graduating from West Point with the Class of 1945 as a two-time All-American in basketball and as the *Sporting News* Men's College Basketball Player of the Year, Dale Hall became an armor officer. He was assigned to Germany (where, among other duties, he coached the 2nd Constabulary Regiment to the European Football Championship in 1947). Hall resigned his commission in 1949 and began a coaching career that would take him, initially, to Purdue University, New Hampshire, and Florida as an assistant football coach (and, at New Hampshire, as the head basketball coach). Then, in 1956, he became the backfield coach for the legendary Earl "Red" Blaik at West Point and, in 1958, succeeded Blaik as the academy's head coach.

After compiling a 16–11–2 record with Army, Hall left coaching and entered the business world with the Corning Glass Company. He later served as administrative director of the Butler Service Group; president of the Thunderbird Boat Company in Miami; president of Pool Boys Inc.; president of his own educational training company; president of James Fyffe Export/Import Company; and an associate of the Van Houten Real Estate Company. Hall died on August 26, 1996, the same summer that his grandson, Daniel Grieve, entered West Point and joined the Long Gray Line. In 2004, Hall was inducted into the Kansas Sports Hall of Fame; in 2018, West Point inducted him into the Army Sports Hall of Fame.

John Joseph Hennessey

Jack Hennessey remained in Europe after VE Day; his wife Mary was among the first military wives to travel by ship to Germany after the war ended. Their first son, John J., Jr., was born in Berlin in February 1947 – and would one day graduate from West Point himself. Later, as the Hennessey family returned Stateside, daughters Katie and Sally (and, still later, Hope and Jim) joined the family while Hennessey decided to make the military a career. Later assignments would include, among others, duty as the aide to the chairman of the Joint Chiefs of Staff and commander of the 3rd Battalion, 187th Infantry, 11th Air Assault Division, which was the test unit for the Army's airmobile concept at Fort Benning. On approval of air assault infantry operations in 1965, the 11th Air Assault Division converted to the 1st Cavalry Division and deployed to the Republic of Vietnam.

When the 1st Cavalry Division deployed to Vietnam, Hennessey commanded the Division Support Command and, later, its 1st Brigade. A string of promotions followed, culminating in him receiving his fourth star as a general officer in 1974 – only one of two officers in his class to reach that rank. He served as assistant division commander for the 82nd Airborne Division; assistant division commander (operations) and commander, 101st Airborne Division in Vietnam; commandant of the Command and General Staff College; chief of Reserve Components, U.S. Army; commanding general, Fifth U.S. Army; and, finally, Commander in Chief, U.S. Readiness Command (today's Central Command), MacDill Air Force Base, Tampa, Florida. He retired in 1979, bringing a military career of 35 years to an end.

After retirement, Hennessey served on the University of Tampa board of trustees and as executive director of the Tampa Bay area research and development authority under the University of South Florida. His beloved wife, Mary, died of cancer in 1983. In 1986, Jack married Donna C. Rood, whom he loved and lived with happily until his death in 2001.[4]

Edward A. Kelleher

The army ultimately buried West Point's former coach at what would become the Lorraine Military Cemetery, near the French town of Saint-Avold. There he was among the few—if not the only—civilians buried in one of the 10,489 gravesites that provided a final resting place to service members who gave their lives in the US military during World War II—service members from every state in the Union and the District of Columbia, as well as from Puerto Rico, Panama, Canada, the United Kingdom, and Mexico.[5]

Before 1945 was over, the committee running the NIT voted to name the trophy it presented to its annual winner the Edward A. Kelleher Memorial Trophy.[6] In 1972, Fordham University inducted Kelleher into the Fordham Athletics Hall of Fame.[7]

Edgar Douglas Kenna II

Doug Kenna graduated in 1945 honored as an All-American quarterback for leading Army football team to the 1944 National Championship. Later he would be inducted into the College Football Hall of Fame, the Mississippi Sports Hall of Fame, and, in 2005, West Point's Army Sports Hall of Fame. Commissioned into the Armored Infantry, Kenna served with the 4th Armored Division in Germany where, like his classmate, he drew additional duty coaching unit football teams and, from 1946 to 1952, was carried on the rolls as an assistant football coach back at West Point.

Later recognized by the *New York Times* as "a winner in football and business," Kenna resigned his commission in 1949 to embark upon a business career. He served as the president of the National Association of Manufacturers and held executive positions for several major companies, including the Avco Corporation, Mississippi Power and Light, Fuqua Industries, Robert B. Anderson Ltd., and the Carrier Corporation. Kenna died in Florida on January 28, 2013.[8]

Endnotes

Chapter 1

1 Douglas Stark, *Wartime Basketball: The Emergence of a National Sport during World War II* (Lincoln: University of Nebraska Press, 2016), 32.

2 Three decades later, in the wartime winter of 1944, the fame of "Vinegar Joe" Stilwell rested on other accomplishments. Now a three-star general, he was the deputy supreme Allied commander of the South East Asia Command, the senior adviser to Chinese leader Chiang Kai-shek, and commander of a polyglot collection of Allied forces in the China-Burma-India theater of operations.

3 "Fordham Mourns Death of Ed Kelleher—Ram Court Mentor," *Fordham Ram*, September 7, 1945.

4 "Fordham Mourns Loss of Atlantic 10 Legend Johnny Bach," Atlantic 10 Conference, January 19, 2016, http://www.atlantic10.com/ViewArticle. dbml?DB_OEM_ID=31600&ATCLID=210647788.

5 "Ed Kelleher, Basketball Mentor, Departs from Fordham Campus," *Fordham Ram*, September 10, 1943.

6 "Mr. KC Cites One Point: West!," *Democrat and Chronicle* (Rochester, NY), February 3, 1944.

Chapter 2

1 Stephen Ambrose, *Duty, Honor, County: A History of West Point* (Baltimore: Johns Hopkins University Press, 1966), 22.

2 Ibid., 140.

3 "Swarthmore College: A Brief History," Swarthmore College, accessed January 15, 2018, https://www.swarthmore.edu/a-brief-history#event-swarthmore-college-a-brief-history.

4 United States Military Academy, *The Howitzer (Class of 1944)* (West Point, NY: United States Military Academy, 1944), 317 (hereafter *Howitzer*).

5 "West Point Arena Named for St. Thomas Alumnus," *St. Thomas Alumni Notes*, Winter 1996.

6 United States Military Academy, Class of 1944, *Whom Shall We Send? The Half-Century History of the Class of 1944, U.S. Military Academy, the D-Day Class* (Fort Myer, VA: Class of 1944, US Military Academy, 1995), 28 (hereafter *Whom Shall We Send?*).

7 *Howitzer*, 130.

8 Don Carter, phone interview with author, February 2, 2018.

9 Wayne G. Sayles, *First to Fall: The William E. Cramsie Story* (Lodi, WI: Clio's Cabinet, 2008), 43.

10 Lars Anderson, *The All Americans* (New York: St. Martin's Griffin, 2005), 148.

11 *Whom Shall We Send?*, 42.

12 Ibid.

13 Ibid.

14 Anderson, *All Americans*, 149.

15 *Whom Shall We Send?*, 45.

16 *Howitzer*, 137.

17 "2000 West Point Cadets Learn How to Fight Axis," *Poughkeepsie (NY) Eagle-News*, August 12, 1942.

18 *Howitzer*, 137.

19 John S. D. Eisenhower, *Strictly Personal* (New York: Doubleday, 1974), 48.

20 Ibid., 49.

21 *Howitzer*, 149.

22 *Whom Shall We Send?*, 62.

23 *Howitzer*, 150.

24 Ibid., 162.

25 "Required Cadet Knowledge," United States Corps of Cadets Circular 351-2.

Chapter 3

1 "Army Sets New Record in Crushing Swarthmore," *Harrisburg (PA) Telegraph*, January 13, 1944.

2 "Army Give Routs Colgate, 69–44," *New York Times*, January 16, 1944; "Army Whips Colgate in 69–44 Clash," *Democrat and Chronicle* (Rochester, NY), January 16, 1944; "Five Faces Penn State Zone Defense Saturday," *Colgate Maroon*, January 19, 1944.

3 "Sports Shorts," *Brooklyn Daily Eagle*, January 18, 1944.

4 "Lack Ace Shot, St. John's Bow," *Brooklyn Daily Eagle*, January 19, 1944.

Chapter 4

1 "Lions Oppose Strong West Point Quintet," *Columbia Daily Spectator*, January 21, 1944.

2 "Army Quintet Tops Columbia, 55 to 37," *New York Times*, January 22, 1944.

3 "Army's Court Team Attracts Attention," *Evening Sun* (Baltimore), January 24, 1944.

4 Penn State University, *Penn State Men's Basketball*, 2011 media guide, 125.

5 *Howitzer*, 349.

6 "Army Coach Sees Tough Going," *Brooklyn Daily Eagle*, January 9, 1945.

7 *Howitzer*, 217.

8 Ibid., 163.

9 Robert Higham, ed., *Flying American Combat Aircraft of WWII* (Mechanicsburg, PA: Stackpole Books, 2004), 225.

10 "Aviation at West Point," *Flying*, (February 1944), 44.

11 *Whom Shall We Send?*, 68.

Chapter 5

1 Ibid., 14.

2 Katie Barbour, email correspondence with author, June 28, 2018.

3 Ibid., 28.

4 Jack Hennessey, letter to family, July 12, 1941.

5 *Howitzer*, 380.

6 John Hennessey, email correspondence with author, March 20, 2018.

7 "Undefeated Army Cagers Notch Sixth Straight in Beating Coast Guard," *Hartford (CT) Courant*, January 30, 1944.

8 "Midwesterners Dominate Cadets," *Democrat and Chronicle* (Rochester, NY), February 4, 1944.

9 "Overflow Throng to Watch Battle with Cadet Five," *Democrat and Chronicle* (Rochester, NY), February 5, 1944.

10 "Army Cage Power Blasts Varsity, 57–43," *Democrat and Chronicle* (Rochester, NY), February 6, 1944.

Chapter 6

1 "Cadets Whip Pitt, 63-32 – Some Army!," *Pittsburgh Press*, February 10, 1944; "Army Slaughters Pitt Panthers," *Philadelphia Inquirer*, February 10, 1944.

2 "Army Cage Five Goes Rolling Along under Ed Kelleher," *Ithaca (NY) Journal*, February 11, 1944.

3 "Army Five Takes 10th Game in a Row," *New York Times*, February 13, 1944.

4 "West Point Quintet Jars Penn, 55–38, for Eleventh in Row," *Philadelphia Inquirer*, February 17, 1944.

5 "West Point Quintet Jars Penn," *Philadelphia Inquirer*, February 17, 1944.

6 "Sports Slants: Ed Christl," *St. Cloud (MN) Times*, February 29, 1944.

7 "Undefeated West Point Quintet Routs Pennsylvania for Eleventh Victory," *Hartford Daily Courant*, February 17 1944.

8 "Hall's 23 Help Army Win 12th; Beats Villanova," *Philadelphia Inquirer*, February 20, 1944.
9 "Star of Unbeaten Army Out, Another Minneapolitan In," *Argus Leader* (Sioux Falls, SD), February 22, 1944.
10 James L. Noles and James L. Noles Jr., *Mighty by Sacrifice: The Destruction of an American Bomber Squadron, August 29, 1944* (Tuscaloosa: University of Alabama Press, 2009), 68.

Chapter 7

1 "Army Wallops NYU Five, 46–36," *Poughkeepsie (NY) Journal*, February 27, 1944.
2 "Shipley's Terp Cagers Green, Lack Stature," *Evening Sun* (Baltimore), December 3, 1944.
3 "Army Quintet Crushes Maryland Team, 85–22," *Morning News* (Wilmington, DE), March 2, 1944.
4 "Army Quintet Humbles Navy, 56–45," *Evening Sun* (Baltimore), March 7, 1943.
5 "Army Trims Navy, 47–40, to End Season Unbeaten," *Chicago Tribune*, March 5, 1944.
6 "Army Five Tops Navy by 47 to 40; Won All 15 Games," *New York Times*, March 5, 1944.
7 "Army Trims Navy, 47–40, to End Season Unbeaten," *Chicago Tribune*, March 5, 1944.
8 Ibid.
9 "Army Five Tops Navy by 47 to 40; Won All 15 Games," *New York Times*, March 5, 1944.
10 "Army Trims Navy, 47–40, to End Season Unbeaten," *Chicago Tribune*, March 5, 1944.
11 West Point Association of Graduates, *Assembly* (April 1944), 28.
12 *How Can We Win the Battle of Transportation?*," leaflet (Washington, DC: US Office of War Information, ca. October 1943).
13 "Army Five Tops Navy by 47 to 40; Won All 15 Games," *New York Times*, March 5, 1944.
14 Katie Barbour, email correspondence with author (June 28, 2018).
15 "Required Cadet Knowledge," United States Corps of Cadets Circular 351-2.

Chapter 8

1 *Whom Shall We Send?*, 75.
2 Ibid., 84.
3 Ibid., 75.
4 "Former Athlete at U. of Md. Destroys Two Nazi Planes," *Baltimore Sun*, April 26, 1944.
5 "117 Plane Review Set for Tomorrow," *Poughkeepsie (NY) Journal*, June 2, 1944.
6 *Whom Shall We Send?*, 77.

7 Ibid.

8 Ibid., 78.

9 "Mrs. Eisenhower Told of News at West Point," *Baltimore Sun*, June 7, 1944.

10 "Bush Counselor Visits Site of Father's Battle in 1944," *Tennessean* (Nashville), May 28, 2002.

11 West Point Association of Graduates, *Assembly* (June 1944), 6.

12 *Whom Shall We Send?*, 79.

13 *Assembly* (June 1944), 6.

14 *Whom Shall We Send?*, 78.

Chapter 9

1 "West Point Gives Diplomas to 474," *Wilkes-Barre (PA) Record*, June 7, 1944.

2 *Troy (NY) Record*, June 16, 1944; *Oakland Tribune*, June 23, 1944; *Los Angeles Times*, June 27, 1944; *Chicago Tribune*, June 17, 1944.

3 Eisenhower, *Strictly Personal,* 74.

4 *Whom Shall We Send?*, 84.

5 Ibid.

6 G-2 Section, 70th Infantry Division, *70th Division: Trail Blazers* (Camp Adair, OR: 70th Infantry Division, 1943), http://www.trailblazersww2.org/Docs/campadair.pdf.

7 *Whom Shall We Send?*, 89.

8 Hugh Foster, "The Infantry: Organization for Combat, World War II," April 26, 2000, http://www.trailblazersww2.org/history_infantrystructure.htm.

9 *Howitzer*, 1943.

10 Regimental Headquarters Company History (275th Infantry Regiment), accessed April 20, 2018, http://www.trailblazersww2.org/Docs/275tth_regHq.pdf.

11 Raymond Brubaker, "D-Day Plus 40 Years: G/276," oral history, July 1, 1980, http://www.trailblazersww2.org/Docs/g_276.pdf.

12 Frank H. Lowery, *Company A, 276th Infantry in WWII* (Modesto, CA: Frank H. Lowrey, 1995), http://www.trailblazersww2.org/Docs/CoA276Infantry.pdf.

13 Ibid., 22.

Chapter 10

1 Thomas W. McCaw, *History of the Field Artillery School, Vol. II: World War II* (Fort Sill, OK: US Army, 1946), 29.

2 John R. Walker, *Bracketing the Enemy: Forward Observers in World War II* (Norman: University of Oklahoma Press, 2013), 25–26.

3 Ibid.

4 Foster, "Infantry."

5 Ibid.

6 John B. Wilson, *Armies, Corps, Divisions, and Separate Brigades* (Washington, DC: Government Printing Office, 1999).

7 William R. Keast, Robert R. Palmer, and Bell I. Wiley, *The Procurement and Training of Ground Combat Forces* (Washington, DC: Government Printing Office, 1991), 482.

8 Ibid., 483.

9 Ibid.

10 Ibid.

11 Ibid.

12 Ibid., 484.

13 Ibid.

14 Ibid.

15 Ibid., 485.

16 Ibid., 479–80.

17 Ibid., 485.

18 *Whom Shall We Send?*, 85.

19 "Edward C. Christl, Jr., 1944," memorial article, West Point Association of Graduates, accessed November 12, 2017, https://www.westpointaog.org/memorial-article?id=0162ece9-ef97-42c6-9112-dff7935af11b.

20 *Whom Shall We Send?*, 486.

21 Ibid., 487.

22 Ibid.

23 Ibid., 488.

24 Ibid.

Chapter 11

1 Lowery, *Company A*, 32.

2 Ibid., 33.

3 "You Say We Have No Heroes?," *Tampa Tribune*, n.d.

4 Ibid., 41.

5 Lowery, *Company A*, 43.

6 Brubaker, "D-Day Plus 40 Years."

Chapter 12

1 "Presidential Unit Citation," July 19, 1945, 70th Infantry Division Association, http://www.trailblazersww2.org/history_puc.htm.

2 Jeffery J. Clarke and Robert Ross Smith, *Riviera to the Rhine* (Washington, DC: US Army Center of Military History, 1993), 509.

3 Lowery, *Company A*, 107.

4 Headquarters, 276th Infantry, "Narrative Report of 276th Infantry, Covering Period 19 November 1944 to 31 January 1945," February 16, 1945, http://www.trailblazersww2.org/pdf/276_AAR_Nov44_Jan45.pdf.

5 Headquarters, 70th Infantry Division, General Orders No. 68, http://www.trailblazersww2.org.

6 Lowery, *Company A*, 148.

7 Headquarters, 276th Infantry, "Narrative Report."

8 "Openers Won by Army and Navy," *Evening News* (Baltimore), January 12, 1945.

Chapter 13

1 Rick Atkinson, *The Guns at Last Light* (New York: Henry Holt, 2013), 524.

2 Lowery, *Company A*, 161.

3 United States Army, *They Have Seen the Elephant: Veterans Remembrances from WWII for the 40th Anniversary of D-Day* (Fort Lee, VA: US Army Logistics Center, 1985).

4 "Army Cagers Score 22nd Win," *Star Tribune* (Minneapolis), January 28, 1944.

5 "Unbeaten Army Stages Late Rally to Nose Yale Quintet by 44–43 Score," *Hartford (CT) Courant*, February 4, 1945.

6 Theodore Mataxis, "Oetingen Raid," 70th Infantry Division Association, accessed April 28, 2018, http://www.trailblazersww2.org/units_276_oetingraid.htm.

7 Brubaker, "D-Day Plus 40 Years,

8 Mataxis, "Oetingen Raid."

9 Lowery, *Company A*, 176.

10 Ibid., 193.

11 Ibid.

12 "276th Inf. Documents: Feb. 45 AAR," 70th Infantry Division Association, accessed May 10, 2018, http://www.trailblazersww2.org/units_276_documents_AARFeb45.htm.

13 Ibid.

14 Lowery, *Company A*, 195.

Chapter 14

1 "Army Cagers Beat Pitt for 25th Straight Win," *Harrisburg (PA) Telegraph,* February 8, 1945; "Army Still Unbeaten," *Star Tribune* (Minneapolis), February 8, 1945.

2 "Army Tramples UR for 10th Straight, 79–42," *Democrat and Chronicle* (Rochester, NY), February 11, 1945.

3 "Army Five Captures 26th Straight, 79–42," *Star Tribune* (Minneapolis), February 11, 1945.

4 "Cadet Coach Visions St. John's as Winner," *Brooklyn Daily Eagle*, February 13, 1945.

5 "Army Thrashes St. Johns, 56–39" *Des Moines (IA) Register*, February 15, 1945.

6 "Sportsletter for Overseas," *Philadelphia Inquirer*, February 25, 1945.

7 "Expect 11,000 Crowd at Twin-Bill Tonight," *Philadelphia Inquirer*, February 17, 1945.

8 "Temple Loses; Pitt Snaps Army's 27-Game Streak," *Philadelphia Inquirer*, February 18, 1945.

9 Ibid.

10 "Army Edges NYU in 54–51 Duel," *Democrat and Chronicle* (Rochester, NY), February 25, 1945.

11 Ibid.

12 "Army Basket Team Beats Maryland," *Baltimore Sun*, March 1, 1945.

13 "Army-Navy Basketball Game Will Be Heard Around World," *Central New Jersey Home News* (New Brunswick, NJ), March 3, 1945; "Army-Navy Basketball Game Will Be Heard Around World, *Brownsville (TX) Herald*, March 2, 1945.

14 "Sports Roundup," *Des Moines (IA) Tribune*, February 27, 1945.

Chapter 15

1 "276th Inf. Documents: March 1945 AAR," April 8, 1945, 70th Infantry Division Association, http://www.trailblazersww2.org/units_276_documents_AARMar45.htm.

2 "Army-Navy Basketball Game Will Heard around the World," *Muncie (IN) Evening Press*, March 2, 1945.

3 "Capacity Crowd Sees Soldiers Capture Title," *Cumberland (MD) Sunday Times*, March 4, 1945.

4 Ibid.

5 "276th Inf. Documents: March 1945 AAR."

6 Headquarters, 70th Infantry Division, General Orders No. 29.

7 "276th Inf. Documents: March 1945 AAR."

8 Headquarters, 78th Infantry Division, General Orders 571.

Chapter 16

1 Atkinson, *Guns at Last Light*, 538.

2 Sgt. Bill Jordy, *"Right to Be Proud": History of the 65th's Infantry Division's March across Germany* (1945), Lone Sentry, accessed May 21, 2018, http://www.lonesentry.com/65thbook/index.html.

3 Ibid.

4 United States Army, *They Have Seen the Elephant*.

5 "Edward C. Christl, Jr., 1944."

6 Nick Catania, *We Are Proud: History of Company 'C' 260th Inf.*, Shelby to Linz, Lone Sentry, accessed May 1, 2018, http://www.lonesentry.com/ccompany/index.html.

7 *Whom Shall We Send?*, 105.

8 Ibid., 180.

9 "Edward C. Christl, Jr., 1944."

10 "Frederick C. Murphy, Our Facility's Namesake," National Archives, accessed May 30, 2018, https://www.archives.gov/boston/exhibits/murphy. A few weeks after Murphy's death, his wife would give birth to his daughter.

11 Jordy, *"Right to Be Proud."*

12 Ibid.

13 "276th Inf. Documents: March 45 AAR," April 8, 1945, 70th Infantry Association, http://www.trailblazersww2.org/units_276_documents_AARMar45.htm).

14 Ibid.

Chapter 17

1 *Whom Shall We Send?*, 132.

2 "Edward C. Christl, Jr., 1944."

3 Catania, *We Are Proud.*

4 Stephen Ambrose, *Citizen Soldiers* (New York: Touchstone Books, 1997), 483.

5 XX Corps, *The Ghost Corps Thru Hell and High Water: A Short History of the XX Corps, U.S. Army* (n.d.).

6 Catania, *We Are Proud.*

7 *Whom Shall We Send?*, 132.

8 Catania, *We Are Proud.*

9 *Whom Shall We Send?*, 132.

10 Ibid.

11 Catania, *We Are Proud.*

12 United States Army, *They Have Seen the Elephant.*

13 "Last Battle Is Tough One for Reno Man," *Reno (NV) State Journal,* June 27, 1945.

14 "Renoite Kills Six at Once," *Nevada State Journal* (Reno), August 22, 1945.

15 Third United States Army, General Order Number 273, October 1, 1945

16 Admittedly, a discrepancy exists between the date of Christl's death (May 4, 1945) and that of the action cited in Dan Canak's citation (May 5, 1945). However, given the fact that the fighting for Eferding occurred during the night of May 4–5, such a discrepancy may not necessarily be unexpected. Newspaper reports indicate that Canak's patrol lost an officer in the fight, and Christl was seemingly the only officer in the division killed in Eferding. In this author's estimation, therefore, Christl was with Canak's patrol and was the officer killed in action with it.

17 "Edward C. Christl, Jr., 1944."

18 Maj. Gen. Stanley Reinhart, "End of War" (May 7, 1945).

Chapter 18

1 *Whom Shall We Send?*, 94–95.

2 Ibid., 95.

3 Ibid.

4 Ibid.
5 Ibid., 96.
6 Ibid.
7 Ibid., 97.
8 "Bomber Crashes Into High River; Recover 3 Bodies," *Abilene (TX) Reporter-News*, February 22, 1945.
9 Higham, *Flying American Combat Aircraft*, 13.
10 "Swoyerville School Notes," *Wilkes-Barre (PA) Record*, April 2, 1945.
11 Whom Shall We Send?, 96.
12 Earl F. Ziemke, *The U.S. Army in the Occupation of Germany, 1944–1946* (Washington, DC: Government Printing Office, 1976), 320.
13 Ibid.
14 Ibid., 321.
15 Ibid., 328–29.
16 Ibid., 330.
17 Ibid.
18 Ibid.
19 Ibid.
20 Ibid., 331–32.
21 Ibid., 332; "Kelleher Touring ETO," *Stars and Stripes*, July 14, 1945.
22 "Ed Kelleher Dies during ETO Tour," *Stars and Stripes*, August 5, 1945.
23 "Obituaries," *Asbury Park (NJ) Press*, August 5, 1945.
24 "Ed Kelleher Dies; Famous Coach," *Philadelphia Inquirer*, August 4, 1945; "Kelleher Dies of a Heart Attack," *Greenville News (SC)*, August 5, 1945.
25 "Plan Memorial Mass for Kelleher," *Brooklyn Daily Eagle*, September 18, 1945.

Chapter 19

1 Roy E. Appleman, *Okinawa: The Last Battle* (Washington, DC: Government Printing Office, 2000), 150.
2 "Memorial Article: John Pierre Bradley," *Assembly* (November 1994).
3 Appleman, *Okinawa*, 183.
4 Headquarters, Army Air Forces, *P-47: Pilot Training Manual for the Thunderbolt*, AAF Manual 51-127-4 (Washington, DC: Headquarters, Army Air Forces, 1945), 5, http://413thfightergroup.com/images/P-47_Pilot_s_Manual_1.pdf.
5 Ibid.
6 Parker R. Tyler Jr., *From Seattle to Ie Shima with the 413th Fighter Group (SE)* (New York: Patrick R. Tyler Jr., 1945), http://413thfightergroup.com/images/From_Seattle_to_Ie_Shima.pdf.
7 "Thunderbolts over Ie Shima" in *Air Combat* 2, no. 6 (1969).
8 "Lt. John Heathcote Missing since Aug. 9," *Evening News* (Baltimore), October 25, 1945; "City Flyer Missing since August Raid, Mother Informed," *Harrisburg (PA) Telegraph*, October 24, 1945.

9 "Lt. Heathcote Presumed Dead," *Evening News*, (Baltimore), March 22, 1946.

10 Thomas J. Mulvehill, *Those Darned Thyngs: A Historical Narrative of the 413th Fighter Group (SE) (16 June–15 August 1945)* (413th Fighter Group, 1945), http://413th-fightergroup.com/images/413th_Combat_History.pdf.

11 Fleet Air Wing One, "History of Air Sea Rescue, Ryukyus" (August 25, 1945).

Afterword

1 Third United States Army, General Order Number 273 (October 1, 1945).

2 "Edward C. Christl, Jr, 1944."

3 "Robert W. Faas 1944," memorial article, West Point Association of Graduates, accessed May 24, 2018, https://www.westpointaog.org/memorial-article?id=a3862b38-e3c4-45fc-a2c1-b41037cafe24.

4 "John J. Hennessey 1944," memorial article, West Point Association of Graduates, accessed May 24, 2018, https://www.westpointaog.org/memorial-article?id=1a722182-99fe-44a7-8647-bfdc34d2a932.

5 Lorraine American Cemetery and Memorial, accessed May 24, 2018, https://www.abmc.gov/node/398163#.W1CbOxJKhAY.

6 "Kelleher Trophy for N.Y. Tourney," *Philadelphia Inquirer*, December 28, 1945.

7 "Edward A. Kelleher," Fordham Sports, Hall of Fame, accessed May 24, 2018 https://fordhamsports.com/hof.aspx?hof=189.

8 "Doug Kenna II, a Winner in Football and Business, Dies at 88," *New York Times*, February 12, 2013.

Bibliography

Personal accounts

Brubaker, Raymond. *D-Day Plus 40 Years G/276* (1980). www.trailblazersww2.org.

Catania, Nick. *We Are Proud: History of Company C, 260th Infantry, Shelby to Linz* (n.d.). http://www.lonesentry.com/ccompany/index.html.

Lowery, Frank H. *Company A, 276th Infantry in WWII* (n.d.). www.trailblazersww2.org.

Tyler, Parker R., Jr. *From Seattle to Ie Shima with the 413th Fighter Group (SE)* (New York: Patrick R. Tyler Jr., 1945). http://413thfightergroup.com/images/From_Seattle_to_Ie_Shima.pdf.

Primary documents and contemporary sources

Fleet Air Wing One. "History of Air Sea Rescue, Ryukyus" (August 25, 1945). National Archives.

Headquarters, Army Air Forces. *P-47: Pilot Training Manual for the Thunderbolt*. AAF Manual 51-127-4 (Washington, DC: Headquarters, Army Air Forces, 1945). http://413thfightergroup.com/images/P-47_Pilot_s_Manual_1.pdf.

Headquarters, 70th Infantry Division. General Orders No. 29. www.trailblazersww2.org.

———. General Orders No. 68. www.trailblazersww2.org.

Headquarters, 78th Infantry Division. General Orders 571. www.trailblazersww2.org.

Headquarters, Third Army. General Orders Number 273. www.trailblazersww2.org.

Headquarters, 276th Infantry Regiment. "Narrative Report of 276th Infantry, Covering Period 19 November 1944 to 31 January 1945" (1945). www.trailblazersww2.org.

Headquarters, 276th Infantry Regiment. April 1945 After Action Report (1945). www.trailblazersww2.org.

———. February 1945 After Action Report (1945). www.trailblazersww2.org.

———. March 1945 After Action Report (1945). www.trailblazersww2.org.

———. May 1945 After Action Report (1945). www.trailblazersww2.org.

"How Can We Win the Battle of Transportation?" Leaflet. US Office of War Information, ca. October 1943. https://sos.oregon.gov/archives/exhibits/ww2/Documents/services-trans2.pdf.

Jordy, Sgt. Bill. "Right to Be Proud: History of the 65th's Infantry Division's March across Germany, 1945" (1945). http://www.lonesentry.com/65thbook/.

Missing Air Crew Report 44-87817. National Archives.

Mulvehill, 1st Lt. Thomas J. *Those Darned Thyngs: A Historical Narrative of the 413th Fighter Group (SE) (16 June–15 August 1945)* (413th Fighter Group, 1945). http://413thfightergroup.com/images/413th_Combat_History.pdf.

Reinhart, Maj. Gen. Stanley. "End of War" (May 7, 1945). http://www.lonesentry.com/65thbook/.

65th Infantry Division. *65th Infantry Division: Camp Shelby, Mississippi 1944* (Camp Shelby, MS: 1944). http://www.lonesentry.com/unithistory/65th_campshelby/.

XX Corps. *The Ghost Corps Thru Hell and High Water: A Short History of the XX Corps* (US Army, n.d). http://cgsc.cdmhost.com/cdm/ref/collection/p4013coll8/id/2971.

United States Military Academy. *The Howitzer (Class of 1945)* (West Point, NY: United States Military Academy: 1945). http://digital-library.usma.edu/.

———. *The Howitzer (Class of 1944)* (West Point, NY: United States Military Academy, 1944). http://digital-library.usma.edu/.

———. *The Howitzer (Class of 1943)* (West Point, NY: United States Military Academy, 1944). http://digital-library.usma.edu/.

West Point Association of Graduates. *Assembly* (April 1944). http://digital-library.usma.edu/.

———. *Assembly* (June 1944). http://digital-library.usma.edu/.

Secondary sources: Books

Ambrose, Stephen. *Citizen Soldiers* (New York: Touchstone Books, 1997).

Ambrose, Stephen. *Duty, Honor, County: A History of West Point* (Baltimore: Johns Hopkins University Press, 1966).

Anderson, Lars. *The All Americans* (New York: St. Martin's Griffin, 2005).

Appleman, Roy E. *Okinawa: The Last Battle* (Washington, DC: Government Printing Office, 2000).

Atkinson, Rick. *The Guns at Last Light* (New York: Henry Holt, 2013).

Clarke, Jeffrey J. *Riviera to the Rhine* (Washington, DC: US Army Center of Military History, 1993).

Cowley, Robert and Thomas Guinzburg, eds. *West Point: Two Centuries of Honor and Tradition* (New York: Warner Books, 2002).

Eisenhower, John S. D. *Strictly Personal* (New York: Doubleday, 1974).

Ekberg, William A. *Dress Gray: The Life and Times of a West Point Cadet* (Fargo, ND: Energy Center, 2010).

Hastings, Max. *Armageddon: The Battle for Germany, 1944–1945* (New York: Knopf, 2004).

Higham, Robert, ed. *Flying American Combat Aircraft of WWII* (Mechanicsburg, PA: Stackpole Books, 2004).

Keast, William R., Robert R. Palmer, and Bell I. Wiley. *The Procurement and Training of Ground Combat Forces* (Washington, DC: Government Printing Office, 1991).

MacDonald, Charles D. *The Last Offensive* (Washington, DC: Government Printing Office, 1993).

McCaw, Thomas W. *History of the Field Artillery School, Vol. II, World War II* (Fort Sill, OK: US Army, 1946).

Noles, James L. *Mighty by Sacrifice: The Destruction of an American Bomber Squadron, August 29, 1944* (Tuscaloosa: University of Alabama Press, 2009).

Sayles, Wayne G. *First to Fall: The William E. Cramsie Story* (Lodi, WI: Clio's Cabinet, 2008).

Stark, Douglas. *Wartime Basketball: The Emergence of a National Sport during World War II* (Lincoln: University of Nebraska Press, 2016).

United States Army. *They Have Seen the Elephant: Veterans' Remembrances from World War II for the 40th Anniversary of D-Day* (Fort Lee, VA: US Army Logistics Center, 1985).

United States Military Academy, Class of 1944. *Whom Shall We Send? The Half-Century History of the Class of 1944, U.S. Military Academy, the D-Day Class* (Fort Myer, Va.: Class of 1944, US Military Academy, 1995).

Walker, John. R. *Bracketing the Enemy: Forward Observers in World War II* (Norman: University of Oklahoma Press, 2013).

Wilson, John B. *Armies, Corps, Divisions, and Separate Brigades* (Washington, DC: Government Printing Office, 1999).

Ziemke, Earl F. *The U.S. Army in the Occupation of Germany, 1944–1946* (Washington, DC: Government Printing Office, 1976).

Secondary sources: Magazines and internet articles

"Aviation at West Point" in *Flying* (February 1944).

Foster, Hugh. "The Infantry: Organization for Combat, World War II" (April 26, 2000). http://www.trailblazersww2.org/history_infantrystructure.htm.

Mataxis, Theodore. "Oetingen Raid." (February 4, 1945). http://www.trailblazersww2.org/units_276_oetingraid.htm.

Tampa Tribune, "You Say We Have No Heroes?" (n.d.).

"Thunderbolts Over Ie Shima" in *Air Combat* 2, no. 6 (1969).

Websites

413th Fighter Group (SE). www.413thfightergroup.com.

70th Infantry Division Association. www.trailblazerswwii.org.

65th Infantry Division Association. www.65thdiv.com.

West Point Association of Graduates. www.westpointaog.org.

Index